Jacques Lacan

T0385645

Modern European Thinkers
Series Editors: Anne Beech and David Castle

Over the past few decades, Anglo-American social science and humanities have experienced an unprecedented interrogation, revision and strengthening of their methodologies and theoretical underpinnings through the influence of highly innovative scholarship from continental Europe. In the fields of philosophy, post-structuralism, psychoanalysis, critical theory and beyond, the works of a succession of pioneering writers have had revolutionary effects on Anglo-American academia. However, much of this work is extremely challenging, and some is hard or impossible to obtain in English translation. This series provides clear and concise introductions to the ideas and work of key European thinkers.

As well as being comprehensive, accessible introductory texts, the titles in the Modern European Thinkers series retain Pluto's characteristic radical political slant, and critically evaluate leading theorists in terms of their contribution to genuinely radical and progressive intellectual endeavour. And while the series does explore the leading lights, it also looks beyond the big names that have dominated theoretical debates to highlight the contribution of extremely important but less well-known figures.

Also available:

Hannah Arendt
Finn Bowring

Alain Badiou
Jason Barker

Georges Bataille
Benjamin Noys

Jean Baudrillard
Mike Gane

Walter Benjamin
Esther Leslie

Pierre Bourdieu
Jeremy F. Lane

Gilles Deleuze
John Marks

André Gorz
Conrad Lodziak and Jeremy Tatman

Félix Guattari
Gary Genosko

Jürgen Habermas
Luke Goode

Bruno Latour
Graham Harman

Herbert Marcuse
Malcolm Miles

Guy Hocquenghem
Bill Marshall

Slavoj Žižek
Ian Parker

Jacques Lacan

A Critical Introduction

Martin Murray

PLUTO PRESS

First published 2016 by Pluto Press
345 Archway Road, London N6 5AA

www.plutobooks.com

Copyright © Martin Murray 2016

The right of Martin Murray to be identified as the author of this work has been
asserted by him in accordance with the Copyright, Designs and Patents Act 1988.

British Library Cataloguing in Publication Data
A catalogue record for this book is available from the British Library

ISBN 978 0 7453 1595 9 Hardback
ISBN 978 0 7453 1590 4 Paperback
ISBN 978 1 7837 1723 1 PDF eBook
ISBN 978 1 7837 1725 5 Kindle eBook
ISBN 978 1 7837 1724 8 EPUB eBook

Typeset by Stanford DTP Services, Northampton, England
Text design by Melanie Patrick
Printed and bound by CPI Group (UK) Ltd, Croydon, CR0 4YY

Contents

I always speak the truth. Not the whole truth, because there's no way to say it all.

Lacan

I believe that truth has only one face: that of a violent contradiction.

Bataille

Acknowledgements

I would like to thank the following people who, in one way or another, have helped me write this text: Sara Barrett, Emma Bell, Geoffrey Bennington, Rachel Bowlby, Carolyn Burdett, Scott Davidson, Mark Dubois, John Dudley, Merl Fluin, Roddy Gallacher, Jim Grant, Claire Hodgson, Anne Hogan, Martin Jenkins, Angela Joyce, Valli Kohon, Vicky Lebeau, Michael Morris, Kathryn Murray, Sheila Murray, Sue Pike, Inge Pretorius, Rena Proud, Jacqueline Rose, Viqui Rosenberg, Kate Soper, Barry Stocker, Jenny Stoker, Gillian Tunstall, Will Viney, Wendy Wheeler, Peter Wilson, Andrew Wright, Jessica Yakeley and Marie Zaphirou-Woods. Special thanks are extended to five people who have been particularly generous with their time, advice, ideas and support, namely Anne Beech, Sira Dermen, Mary Fitzgerald, David Hansen-Miller and Bill Murray. Finally, this book is for the two people who have, during its writing, most engaged with me in the matter which psychoanalysis is primarily or significantly about, namely love. It is therefore dedicated to Teresa Fitzgerald and Miles Murray.

1

Stopping and Starting

About

This book is 'about' Jacques Lacan. Perhaps this is obvious or straightforward. Yet the fact that the word 'about' is included in the first sentence of this introduction in inverted commas (or 'scare quotes') indicates something else. It indicates that what Lacan was 'about' *isn't* obvious and that showing and addressing this might not be straightforward.

Thus the inverted commas indicate a problem. Yet they also indicate a solution to that problem. Both the problem and the solution are outlined below.

Here is the problem: it *is* difficult to say (because it is difficult to know) what Lacan was 'about'. This is most obviously true of his pronouncements: his essays, papers, talks, seminars and books. He spoke or wrote in riddles. Quite often, he contradicted himself. It's a challenge to write about him clearly, simply and accurately because it's difficult to understand what he meant. To make things worse, he didn't want to be understood – at least some of the time. For various reasons, it is hard to know what he was 'about' *intellectually*.

Lacan was also *personally* difficult. He sometimes seemed mad or even pernicious and he often seemed obscure. Yet this didn't seem to bother him. Indeed, his eccentric behaviour seemed willed. It's thus hard to discern what his intentions were. Why did he act as he did? These questions indicate another reason for the inverted commas around the word 'about' above. The question 'what was Lacan 'about?' doesn't just mean 'what did his ideas mean?' It also means: 'what was he up to?'

Thus in trying to discern what Lacan was 'about' one has to grapple both with what he said and meant and with what he did and why he did it. How might one begin to do this? There is a way; in fact there is more than one way.

A first (and obvious) way is to try to comprehend what Lacan *meant to say*. As indicated above, this is easier said than done. Yet it's not impossible. Lacan's pronouncements were opaque, but if one knows what was beneath them, one can decipher them. What was beneath them (often) was ideas. These ideas usually partook of theories and philosophies. Some of these were Lacan's and some of them were taken by him from others and adapted to his own purposes. All of the theories and philosophies that Lacan used can be understood (although some are more readily comprehensible than others). This book is firstly an attempt to convey and explain all of this. It is an attempt to show what the ideas that Lacan produced or borrowed meant. It is also an attempt to do this accurately and clearly.

Yet Lacan's ideas, apart from sometimes being difficult to understand in themselves, are made more complex by his use of them. The theories that he borrowed or adapted are either obscured by his language, or altered from their source form, or mixed up with each other. This is even true about Lacan's 'original' ideas.

Furthermore, understanding Lacan's use of his own and other peoples' ideas not only involves understanding them, but also understanding him. He was complex just as his ideas were and there are links between these two 'facts', or types of complexity. All of this means that it is difficult – even impossible – to come at Lacan 'head on'. One has to come at him and his ideas another way, or more exactly in other *ways*.

Mountain

What is called 'Lacan' is quite massive and strange. Inverted commas are being used this time to stress as much. When people use the terms 'Lacan' or 'Lacanian' or 'Lacanianism' they are sometimes referring to him and sometimes referring to other things, including his ideas, his theories, his personal life, his professional involvements, his (or a) psychoanalytic orientation, his (or a) philosophical orientation, his aesthetic influences, his institutional involvements (and battles), his intellectual legacy, his professional legacy, his followers, his empire, his (or a set of) ethics and his (or a) clinical approach. There are a very large number of phenomena and an even larger number of issues covered by the word 'Lacan'. They are great in their number, complexity, constitution and degree of crossover. Once again, they are not well explained by Lacan (or, often, Lacanians). In some ways this is understandable. It's because the phenomena and issues that attend Lacan are multiple and entangled and often so obscure that they *can't* just be approached straightforwardly. They're best approached slowly and carefully and variously.

In a sense Lacan (or Lacanianism) is like a mountain. A mountain is a sort of edifice. When one first approaches it (especially 'on foot' or 'from the bottom') one can't see it, or one can only see part of it. It's even possible that one doesn't see it at all, because one can be too close to something to see it and/or because one hasn't seen it before and doesn't recognise it. It's even arguable that a mountain *can't* be seen fully (even from the air, because some of it will always be concealed, at least by shadow). Thus if one is going to get a sense of the mountain at all (and certainly if one is going to try to 'conquer' it), one has to find a way of approaching it, which includes finding a way of 'looking at it' so that one can *see* it properly. Furthermore, if one is going to try to understand it more fully (and 'conquer it' more fully) one should also approach it in other and different ways. After all, mountains are very different from different angles and there is often more than one way 'up' them.

In this book, Lacan (and Lacanianism) *is* approached and considered in a number of ways. One can put this differently by saying that the book looks at many different facets of Lacan. In fact, it deals with all of the facets of him implied in the listing of the phenomena related to him above. It deals with Lacan's personal life, his professional life, his artistic interests, his institutional involvements, his ideas (and so on). It often deals with these separately, although periodically and in the end, it considers them together. In doing this, of course, the book is attempting to get a sense of 'the mountain' *gradually* and from one perspective at a time (or sometimes two or even three at at a time). Importantly, it is not attempting to see or show Lacan 'all at once'. It nevertheless engages with a hope that by the end, much of him might have become 'visible' after all.

Here again is another sense in which this book is 'about' Lacan. It is arguably the most important sense. This book considers Lacan partially, gradually, variously and (sometimes) indirectly. It considers what is *about* him; it moves *about* him. The reader's patience is humbly requested in this respect. It might sometimes seem as if this book is off-topic; it isn't. *Everything being considered here has to do with Lacan*, even if it isn't obviously 'essential' to him or 'derivative' of him. 'Lacan' is best considered in all of his manifestations: biographical, psychoanalytic, psycho-biographical, historical, artistic, theoretical, philosophical, institutional, political, personal and so on. He can and should be looked at in many ways; he can and should be looked at in *other* ways.

Art

This last point can be sharpened with reference to another analogy, that of modern or contemporary art. Lacan was certainly influenced by such art and in many respects, he was like it. He could be seen to resemble an abstract painting or sculpture. Examples might include any of Jackson Pollock's 'drip' paintings of the late 1940s, or Carl Andre's 'Equivalents' series of the 1960s, many of which comprised touching rows of bricks stacked two-high. In both cases, some people are drawn to these artworks and some people are repelled by them. Some find them beautiful and profound and some find them ugly and senseless. Yet in either case people don't necessarily know what they mean.

Responses to Lacan, like responses to these particular examples of modern art, are mixed and/or polarised. He is loved and hated, accepted and dismissed. Like them, he is difficult, sometimes impossible, to understand *at least at first sight.*

If one were trying to understand Lacan, one might sometimes have to refer to writing *about* one's object, just as one might have to in an attempt to understand modern art. Such writing attempts to *explain* its object. It might note, for instance, that Pollock's painting is a sort of record of the action he undertook when he made it (which is why it is called 'action painting'). In the case of Andre, it might point out that the 'Equivalents' are made out of stuff that doesn't normally appear in art galleries (but on building sites) and that they therefore suggest that art is not *confined* to galleries. Now the point about such writing in these cases is that it is *something other than the art itself.* In order to understand modern art, one has to look *elsewhere.* It doesn't speak – or rather speak clearly – *for itself.* In more or less exactly the same way, one can't really understand Lacan very well *by just looking at him* (or his work), just as one cannot always understand modern art by doing so.

Reiteration

The point here is that understanding Lacan requires looking at something *different.* It means, once again, looking *about* him – not *at* him, at something *about* him – not him. Thus an important sense in which this book is 'about' Lacan is the sense in which it (necessarily) refers to something *other* than him.

Yet again, the reader's acceptance, or indulgence, of this strategy is requested in advance. What follows will often refer to subjects, theories, philosophies, thinkers, people, institutions and practices that are *not* Lacan and that are *not* – in themselves – Lacanian. Examples include Descartes, dialectics, Freud, phenomenology, the International Psychoanalytic Association, Breton, Structuralism and Hegel. It's actually not possible to understand Lacan wholly or thoroughly without referring to these people and things. Much of this book will do that. May the reader forgive it for its apparent digressions and trust that they're really not digressions at all. All of the different ways of looking at Lacan adopted in this book lead back to him because they are all 'about' him in the end. One has to get out of Lacan, to get back in to him. It now only remains now to show that this is true.

Beginning

Beginnings are a problem. They're difficult to locate; they're hard to decide on. How does one start? Where does one start?

These questions imply other, more particular ones. Is this beginning right? Should it be starting in a different way? Should it, for example, be getting straight to the point by stating who and what Lacan was, where and when he was born, how he lived and what he said and did? Is *this* the appropriate start? It seems factual after all. Yet this doesn't necessarily make it *true*.

Does Lacan's story truly begin with his life and work? Might it not have begun before he was born, in the stories of the lives of his forbears? Equally, might it have begun *after* his death but *before now*, in assessments of him by his peers, family, critics and biographers? In both cases things would have already begun and *this* beginning might be too late. It might, alternatively, have come too soon. Maybe Lacan's story hasn't really been told yet. Perhaps too little is known or too little has been shown about the detail of his character and the quality of his work to make a sound judgement about him *now*.

Does the subject of Lacan properly start, or has it already started, or will it start, *somewhere else*? Do any of these possibilities make *this* start a false one? What's the specific problem here?

Specific problems correspond with general ones. The problem with *any* beginning is that it always *could* be different: it might not be the best one; it might not be what it seems; it might be elsewhere; it might not be a beginning at all (this problem even persists *after* one has begun – the beginning could always *have been* different too).

Beginning is complex. Yet it's both possible and necessary; here's how.

Resumption

Psychoanalytic practice comes up against the problem of beginning just mentioned – or at least a problem that is very similar. A patient – or analysand – comes to the consulting room with an issue that is difficult for him to articulate. It is complex and obscure and painful. What's more, it both implies and obscures other issues, ones to do with the past. It sometimes seems as if *prior* issues need to be dealt with before the current one can be addressed. Yet the current issue is both the barrier and the key to understanding what has gone before. Where to begin?

Perhaps surprisingly, the psychoanalyst's answer to this question is: anywhere. Psychoanalysts start with something arbitrary. They first of all ask their patients – or 'analysands' – to say the first thing that comes to mind. Being unpremeditated, and hence uncontrolled, this first thing might be something unexpected. Yet it might also imply *something else.*[1] This something else might give way to *other* associations that are related with each other and indeed with the problem that the patient bought into the consulting room in the first place. All might form part of a network of associations or *relations* that could begin to outline – and illustrate and perhaps even explain – 'the subject' at hand (where this subject is both the problem – the crux of it – and/or the patient 'himself').

This description of clinical psychoanalytic methodology is pertinent to the 'problem' or 'subject' of Lacan that the chapter began with. Perhaps one might 'begin' by approaching Lacan in a loosely psychoanalytic way.

One might then start with something *associated with Lacan* (rather than something determinative of him or declarative about him). It wouldn't matter if the association in question were loose, but it would have to lead somewhere else. This in turn, might set off the sort of relational matrix described above, which, with luck, might trace what 'analysis' bears a general hope of attaining: truth, in this case truth about 'Lacan' (including why he did and said what he did and what he meant by it).

To start this process off, of course, one would have to say something random, that is say the first thing that comes to mind. Just as much as anything else, this might be *vinegar.*

2

Sweet and Sour

Transformation

Vinegar is often fermented from wine, which is itself fermented out of fruit. Fermentation is a process of transformation by agitation of specific elements of a given substance. It transforms the taste of what is fermented. For example, it turns saccharine grape juice into tangy wine. Yet this alteration of taste is not unidirectional and does not always eliminate sweetness and tend towards the sour. Wine can, for instance, retain the fruitiness of its source as well as being acidic. Its flavour can involve contrasts, between honeyed and nutty or creamy and tart. The secondary fermentation by oxidisation of the alcoholic content of wine into vinegar can also have unpredictable effects. It will often acetify the liquid, make it taste sharp rather than fruity and turn smooth wine into harsh vinegar. Yet it can also produce tastes that multiply, vary or contrast with prior ones, producing vinegar that is, for example, saccharine and astringent or smooth and dry.

Now all of this is interesting enough, but how is it relevant? How does it relate to the subject of this book, the subject at hand?

Entrance

By the time of his death in 1981, Jacques Lacan was a well-known, controversial and influential French psychoanalyst and intellectual. Yet what was he at the time of his birth? Perhaps this seems like an odd question. At birth he hadn't become what he was yet. Perhaps questions about birth are beside the point here.

Yet Lacan came into the world in certain circumstances (just as everyone else did) and these will have had some influence on him. Even if his circumstances didn't *determine* his fate, they were relevant to what happened – or what could have happened – to him. Even if he overcame and/

or ignored them, they indirectly shaped who he was (because he would
then have become who he was *despite* them). Thus the circumstances that
attended Lacan's birth might have had some *indirect* – one might say *opposite*
or *negative* – influence on him (he might have repudiated them) and/or
may have influenced him positively by shaping what he was. He might
have been effected, influenced or changed by his circumstances, *even if he
thought that he wasn't.*

In general the formation – one might say fermentation – of Lacan's
character was subject to a play of forces, some of which aligned with his
will and some of which didn't. From the outset, this play influenced what
he *might have been.* The types of being that fall into this category, – that is the
list of 'things' that Lacan *might have been* – is strikingly long and revealing, as
what follows will show. It ranges from merchant to politician (he avoided
becoming the former and dreamt about becoming the latter) from general
practitioner to philosopher (ditto) and from failure to achiever (his school
reports were critical; his career was an apparent success).

So what was the subject of this book born into and what was he inclined
or disinclined to be?

Lacan was born in Paris in 1901 into a family that could legitimately
claim membership of the bourgeoisie. His grandfather had married into
this class in the mid-late nineteenth century when he wed a woman whose
forebears had long been makers of a popular brand of vinegar.

Jacques' paternal grandfather Emile Lacan was a merchant whose wife
Marie Julie was the daughter of Paul Dessaux, owner of *Dessaux Fils*, manu-
facturers of wine vinegar based in Orléans. Paul had inherited the business
from *his* father Charles-Prosper. Around the beginning of the nineteenth
century Charles-Prosper was an enterprising employee of the Greffier-
Hazon vinegar making company. He left this firm, competed with it and
eventually took it over. When he passed *Dessaux Fils* on to Paul it was
in good shape but threatened by competition with other firms including
ones that manufactured spirit vinegar.[1] Paul's daughter Marie Julie married
Emile Lacan in 1866. Shortly afterwards Paul died and the family firm
was taken over by his brother Ludovic. The young heir modernised and
expanded the business to include manufacture and distribution of a wide
range of condiments. He fought off his competitors. His in-law Emile
assisted him in the construction of a business empire. Emile was a smart
and effective salesman – his own father had been a grocer and draper
from Château-Thierry. At the end of the nineteenth century after years
of successful commercial travel Emile settled in Paris. His son Alfred –
Jacques' father – followed in his father's footsteps but without travelling.

He became Dessaux's chief Paris agent. By the time that he had attained this position the actual and commercial family that his in-laws had built up and that he had become an important member of was established and successful. It remains so today. The Dessaux-Lacan clan had used labour, guile and thrift to build a legacy that ensured their heirs became and stayed solid members of the French bourgeoisie. Jacques' forebears – his father's fathers – had come up in the world.

Jacques' maternal line charted a similar trajectory. His mother Emilie was the daughter of Charles Baudry, a goldbeater who bought property. Jacques' grandfather on his mother's side thus rose from the position of labourer to that of craftsman to that of investor. He was able to retire in old age and provide both Emilie and her sister Marie with respectable dowries. (Roudinesco, 1990, pp. 3–6) It might be an exaggeration to say that life was sweet for all of Charles-Prosper and Charles' descendants. Yet neither was their destiny a sour one. By the twentieth century most were privileged and well-off if not happy. They and their antecedents had invested their money and energies into their work and had profited from this investment. The story of the Dessaux-Lacans is therefore one of hardship overcome, work done and rewards granted. By the time Jacques was born his ancestors had been striving since at least 1800 to grant themselves, their families and their descendants respectability, wealth and *la bonne vie*. They had succeeded, although not without cost.

Autonomy

Jacques would also succeed and would also pay a price for his success. Yet he didn't compare his own experience with that of his forebears. At least he never did so publicly or in any of his much read writings or listened-to addresses. When he published an essay about the people he considered to be *his* antecedents, he didn't mention his family or its history.[2] (EC, pp. 51–7) Neither, apparently, did he do so privately. Why is this so? In her biography of Jacques Lacan, Elisabeth Roudinesco proffers a few facts that might suggest an answer to this question. She does this while recounting something of the history and mythology of vinegar-making. Roudinesco says that, as well as being a condiment and preservative, vinegar was originally a cheap and vulgar wine, a short cut to oblivion for the long-suffering peasant. She adds an even more striking fact reported by some historians. At first, the fermentation of vinegar was quickened in a base and secret manner, through the addition of human excrement. (Roudinesco, 1990, p. 3) What does this suggest? The means that gave Jacques and his family the good life had its origins in commonality and shit. Did he reflect on this fact and make anything of it? He didn't seem to.

This might seem surprising. Jacques wasn't one to suppress a good or revealing idea if it occurred to him. He also knew the importance of what happens to one, of what shapes one, of the force and significance of one's individual and family history. He was, after all, a psychoanalyst. Yet he was keen to leave his past behind. This involved not acknowledging the influence of history, upbringing or experience on *him*. This is only the first of many paradoxes about Lacan that will be noted in what follows. He was a psychoanalyst who doesn't appear to have psychoanalysed himself.

Elisabeth Roudinesco provides material that amplifies this paradox. She stresses Lacan's acute sense of his own autonomy. He was 'by temperament a free man' who considered himself 'self-made'. This meant that he repudiated any influence on or shaping of him by his family, especially where this might have involved curtailment of what he wanted, how he wanted to see himself, or what he wanted to be. 'Lacan would acknowledge no outside authority whatsoever over his person or the managing of his desires.' Roudinesco doesn't explore the implications of this point much, but she does make her subject seem *very* paradoxical by making it. Lacan theorised and stressed the relevance of individual history to the formation of 'personality', but ignored its effect on his own.[3] He took the idea of authority seriously in his work but didn't take the fact of it seriously in his life.[4]

Indeed, Lacan didn't just repudiate authority and family. He disavowed society and history: he was keen to escape his class. This was despite the fact that his forebears had stopped being peasants long ago. Although he did have class identifications, these didn't correspond with his parents'. They placed him at least at the level of the 'haute-bourgeoisie', one step up the social ladder from his mother and father, who hadn't transcended 'petit-bourgeois' status. Lacan saw himself as unique, as someone whose fate hadn't been determined by his social or familial origins. He emphatically didn't see himself as the son of a vinegar merchant.

Repetition

Despite – or perhaps because of – his repudiation of his family's influence on him, Lacan's fate does look like theirs. He did work hard and he was successful – at least superficially. Yet the qualifications made to this claim are important ones. To say that he may have succeeded *superficially* and that he might have only done so *because* his family also did so implies that he might not have *truly* succeeded in the way that he wished and that his success might not have been of his own doing. Of course, all of this may have also been true of his family (*they* may not have entirely succeeded in the way they wished and on their own terms). Yet whether Lacan's success was really success, or his own, or not, he may have been repeating his family's fate – or aspects of it – without knowing it.

Unconscious repetition of the fortunes and misfortunes of a previous generation is a commonplace of psychoanalytic theory and practice. Psychoanalysts frequently have to point out to their patients that they may not be of their own making and that this might have something to do with their parents. The same observation can clearly be made in Lacan's case.

Yet to say this is to put Lacan in a particular position that he always resisted being in: that of the patient. Still, a peculiarity of becoming a psychoanalyst is that it *requires* one to *be* a patient that is to undergo a 'training analysis'. Lacan underwent such an analysis with great reluctance (about the process) and disdain (for his training analyst). He didn't finish the analysis – and hence his training. Yet he became, by his own account, a hugely influential psychoanalyst.

Paradox

This last point shows – once again – how *paradoxical* Lacan was. His paradoxes abound. They concern his history, class, identifications and 'personality'. What's more they pertain to 'events' that took place before and during, but also after his life. They relate to and qualify his 'origins'.

Still, explanation will have to wait, at least for the moment. There's something else this book should be continuing with now: Lacan's story. This story has already begun. The rest of it needs to be told.[5] Yet how does one do this when the main character in the story is paradoxical? How does one get on with Lacan's story when it is continually interrupted by the contradictions in his character?

There is a short answer to this question: one doesn't just concentrate on the paradoxes. More exactly, one tells the story simply, or one does so as far as one can. This sort of strategy might look as if it avoids paradoxes, but it doesn't, necessarily. It might acknowledge them, but put them aside until they can be dealt with later. This could happen when relevant material – including narrative and theoretical material – comes to light. This material might then be brought into the story and brought to bear on the paradoxes in question. The story and its meaning and thus the character(s) that it contains might then be made clearer. This is the general approach that will be taken in this book.

It will be pursued now, and in relation to an aspect of Lacan's story that is well-known, namely the one that has to do with his success. Lacan *was* successful. Not even his detractors doubted this success was real. He was a well-known, influential and important figure. Yet Lacan's success was also mixed and ambiguous. It represented a sort of paradox and this will have to be shown and dealt with too.

Success

Lacan became a psychiatrist and then a psychoanalyst. The institutions that trained him to do what he did (his school, training hospital and psychoanalytic institute) were prestigious. He had a rewarding career. In keeping with his ambitions, he became well-known in Paris and made and spent quite a lot of money. He mixed with people of financial, cultural, social and intellectual status: lawyers, artists, businessmen, politicians, clerics, civil servants, academics and medics. He became a renowned and influential member of the Parisian intelligentsia. He partly achieved this by being a lecturing and training analyst in a series of psychoanalytic institutes that increasingly bore the public stamp of his teaching and name. In other words the institutions he taught in became known as 'Lacanian' ones.

Lacan's profile was compounded through lectures to and friendships with non-psychoanalytic intellectuals. He gave lectures – as opposed to training seminars – at élite institutions like the Sorbonne. These were published alongside some of his influential papers in his Écrits in 1966.

The Écrits were nominally concerned with psychoanalysis, but also engaged (in apparently complex and informed ways) with science, philosophy, the arts, politics and culture. The relatively large and attentive audience and readership of these lectures/writings included not only psychoanalysts (practitioners as well as trainees) but also scientists, journalists, university students and professors. Lacan addressed them in a convoluted, allusive and abstruse manner. It was as if he was testing their intellectual ability against his. If they understood him they were his peers, if they didn't they were his inferiors. Some promising students found him inspiring; some renowned academics found him incomprehensible.[6] This was either a testament to his genius or to his intellectual vanity.

Equivocation

Lacan's success has been manifest but has also always been questionable. It's arguable that his renown as an analyst masked a lack of self-insight. He believed that humans were flawed, but acted as if he wasn't himself. Throughout, he played an ambiguous or ironic role: the hubristic psychoanalyst, the egotistical dissector of the ego. This would matter less if his ideas were universally revered, or at least if everyone took them seriously. Yet while some call him a genius, others dismiss him as sham. Complications like these seem too great to ignore, or at least to put off for too long. They seem as if they threaten the ability to tell Lacan's story *at all*. How should one deal with them?

One should balance the need to tell Lacan's story simply with the necessity of registering its paradoxes. One should explain him in a way that is clear, but that accommodates what is complex about him. In all cases, one should employ a *double* strategy.

It might seem that this is *already* being done. Isn't the strategy of alternation advocated earlier a double one (in so far as it involves *first* telling the story simply, *then* dealing with its complexities)? Yet the double strategy advocated here aims to do a bit *more* than this. Although it will put off complexities, it won't *just* do so (because it *can't*, because they *are* so persistent and insistent). As well as dealing with Lacan in an *alternately* complex and a simple way, it will also attempt to deal with him in a complex and simple way *at the same time*. How will it do *this*?

In fact, this book will deal with Lacan complexly *and* simply in *various* ways. Yet there is one way that it will do this that should be highlighted here. It amounts to a sort of *paradigm*, in terms of which one can not only register Lacan's complexity, but also his whole being in all of its various modes. It involves saying the following: Lacan was split.

Splitting

To say that Lacan was split is to say something complicated in a simple way. Splitting *is* complex. Schizophrenia – in which more than one 'personality' exists in 'one' person – is an example. What could be more complicated than one person being more than one? Yet the idea of this can be expressed simply – as 'schizophrenia'.

The term 'schizophrenia' can act as a good, initial summing up of a patient's condition. It can also be a 'starting point' and even a 'guiding thread' for the analysis of the condition (or a patient who has the condition) itself. All in all, it can both symbolise the condition *and* imply and accommodate its complexity and can also do so while allowing a description and an explanation of it that is clear.

Thus saying that Lacan was split – like diagnosing and (properly) treating someone as schizophrenic – not only allows one to treat one's subject in terms of both his continuities and his paradoxes, but to consider both *at the same time*. This approach deals with 'schizophrenia' *as well as* its symptoms and 'splitting' as well as what it splits. It thus registers, represents and comprehends complication – the complication of a symptomatic condition – *even as it is simplifying it*. It remains clear *even as it is complex*.

If one wants more justification for this 'split' approach to Lacan, one need only compare it with other approaches to 'him'. Its efficacy *contrasts* with the *in*adequacy of other analyses. Many 'Lacanian analyses' *aren't* good. They don't provide an account of him that is sophisticated *and* clear.[7] They are either too complex (or obscure) or too simple (or simplistic). Each class of account (complex or simple) concentrates on one aspect of Lacan or Lacanianism (complexity or simplicity) at the expense of the other. Such accounts end up providing weak or inadequate evaluations of 'Lacan'. It's better – at least more efficacious – to treat 'him' as split. This means not treating him as one thing or another, but as more than one thing. It means treating him in terms of a process, model or figure that is simple, but also registers complexity. To treat Lacan as split (as indicated in the penultimate section) is thus to treat him as simple and complex *at the same time*.

A further point is worth making here, one that relates the current approach to another one that was elicited earlier. Because the current approach treats its subject as split (*and* complex) it regards him *variously*, or *as various*. If Lacan is split this means that there is more than one of him, or that he should be regarded in more than one way.

Lacan is not best understood as a single, coherent and summarisable individual or 'person' (he's too secretive and contradictory for that). Neither is he entirely comprehensible through his work (it's part-incomprehensible and contradictory too). *Many* aspects of Lacan: his behaviour, his writing, his influence, his legacy, his reputation – don't make sense *in themselves*. Yet they *do* make sense when they're considered *together*, when they're *related to each other*.

This notion that there are a *variety* of dimensions of Lacan complements the sense of Lacan as split being put forward *here*. He didn't use his own experience to expound his own theories (as Freud did) and didn't apply his theories to himself. His life and his work were split off from each other and he was split 'in himself'. Yet it's precisely in this that one sees his 'variety'. To say that Lacan's life and work – his 'intellectual' and 'personal' selves or 'public' and 'private' selves – are *split* and to say that they are *multiple* amounts to saying the same thing. The *various* and the split dimensions of Lacan are *the same*.

It's important to have made this link between the 'split' and the 'dimensional' or 'various' arguments that have been introduced in this book so far, as this link will be active in what follows. Right now, however it's equally important to continue to deal with the subject of those arguments: Lacan, more particularly to continue to tell his story. So far, this story has been told in a rather general and slightly fragmentary way (it's dealt with Lacan's origins, his rough position in the history of ideas and his eventual status, (and 'success'). It now needs to deal with him in more detail, both on a personal and an intellectual level.

A good way to begin to do this is go back to the beginning. More exactly, it's to return to *a* beginning: the beginning of Jacques.

Restarting

Jacques Marie Emile Lacan was born in the Boulevard Beaumarchais in a *quartier bourgeois* in the centre of Paris on 13 April 1901. His early years were spent in an apartment that was owned by his grandfather, Emile. Jacques' father Alfred and his mother Emilie were living in this apartment at the time of his birth.

Jacques was the couple's first child. His mother subsequently bore a girl, Madeleine, and two more boys, Raymond (who died young of hepatitis) and Marc-François. Jacques' sibling relations were relatively happy ones. This wasn't true about his paternal relations. More exactly, his *grand-paternal* relations were troublesome.

By many accounts, Jacques' grandfather was a tyrant. Emile dominated, controlled or directed much of the lives of his wife, children and grand-children.

Emile's son Alfred didn't openly oppose this domination; yet neither did he continue it in his dealings with his own family. He treated his wife and children with love. Alfred adopted a kindly attitude towards his immediate family and a passive one towards his father. It's arguable, of course, that this stance wasn't *simply* passive and that it may have been passive/aggressive. Alfred's demonstrated love for his family may have represented a latent rebellion by him against his father. Yet he didn't openly challenge Emile, at least at first.

Yet where Alfred's feelings about paternity were implicitly ambivalent, Jacques' were explicitly so. They were also qualitatively different. All this was apparent in Jacques' manifest feelings and attitudes towards his 'fathers'. He loved his father and hated his grandfather. Emile was seen as 'frightful and 'horrible' while Alfred was 'loved and loving'.

The contrast between Alfred's behaviour towards father figures and Jacques' is telling. Alfred responded to his father's domineering nature by capitulating to it and by adopting an opposite but non-oppositional (that is non-contentious, but possibly passive/aggressive) attitude. He was intimidated by Emile and didn't have the confidence to confront him. Jacques, however, *didn't* have a father who was undermining his confidence. He was loved uncritically by Alfred (as he was by Emilie). This didn't just make him self-assured, it made him egotistical and defiant. Jacques' antagonism towards his grandfather was palpable and extreme.

According to his brother, Marc-François, Jacques met all Emile's punishment of him with a 'curse' which was even 'a curse on all fathers'. (Roudinesco, 1997, p. 8) Throughout his youth – and throughout his life – he was contemptuous of his grandfather and everything he represented. Unlike his own father, Jacques assumed a position of superiority and/or authority in relation to Emile. From what other position could he have presumed to 'curse' him?

Jacques thus dealt with Emile's authoritarianism by assuming *greater* authority himself. It's worth noting that he didn't just do this as a child and in relation to family members, but also as an adult and in relation to his colleagues. In his youth, Jacques' authority was mostly imaginary: it was the assumed authority of a child over an adult. In later life it would be real. Jacques became the head of a school, the leader of a movement, the guru of a cult. Once he had assumed these positions and his followers had accepted them, none of them told him what to do.

Fractures

Lacanians mostly ignore the *issue* of Lacan's authority. More exactly, they *accept* their master's authority and ignore or disavow his authoritarianism. They don't ordinarily refer to instances of the latter, although there are many. When they are confronted with the *fact* of Lacan's authoritarianism, they qualify it. They point out that he was both ironic and philosophical about it. Yet however conscious – and even self-conscious – Lacan was of the anomalies of authority, he *didn't* renounce it. Rather he assumed it repeatedly (and both consciously and unconsciously) throughout his life. He was sure of his position in the family: he demanded privileges as the eldest child; he assumed a certain *social* position: he looked down on his family for being 'petit-bourgeois'. In his teaching, he claimed the moral and intellectual high ground: he criticised, revised or dismissed the work of others. When he became the leader of his own psychoanalytic school he wrote all its rules (including the rules for the training of psychoanalysts) single-handedly. The fact that he *did* do this self-consciously didn't significantly mitigate the authority with which he did it (by then all Lacanians knew that Lacan was The Master). Instead, his self-consciousness amounted to a *disavowal* of this authority, one that belied the split in his relation to it.[8]

Hence Jacques was authoritarian and his followers avoid or excuse this fact rather than straightforwardly acknowledge it. This is a sort of supplementary disavowal or splitting, one that mirrors the one that Lacan enacted in relation to (his own) authority himself. Yet to be fair to the Lacanians, their attitude isn't entirely unrelated to the truth. In not being straightforward, it inadvertently refracts a certain truth, a truth about what Lacan was, or more precisely, what he wasn't. *He* wasn't straightforward. To be sure, he was both *manifestly* and *effectively* authoritarian (he liked being in charge and in many cases he *was*). Yet beyond appearances and aside from his displays of power he was *ambivalent* about authority. This is not only evident in his 'adult' behaviour in the psychoanalytic community and its institutions, but also in his 'childhood' attitude towards paternity as embodied by Alfred and Emile. Both represented *the father* for him but one was good and one was bad. For Jacques, both paternity and paternal authority were *split*. This splitting operated on the side of the subject as well as that of the object. Jacques' attitude was split *in itself*. In condemning his grandfather, he conducted an anti-authoritarian rebellion against him, but also acted like him in being authoritarian.

Jacques thus had authoritarian tendencies *and* a split in his attitude towards authority.[9] It would be better to say *splits* here, as splitting was evident in his image of authority, his identification with it *and* his identity *per se*. His position wasn't *just* authoritarian and split; it was *hyper-ambivalent* and *multiply* split.

Technically, Lacanians *disavow* both their master's authoritarianism and his splitting. Yet the image and the effect of both extend beyond him to them and the institutions they belong to. Lacan's autocracy, contrariness and ambivalence undoubtedly contributed to the splitting and/or

re-formation of four major psychoanalytic associations he was a member
or leader of in France. One of these continues to be affiliated to the International Psychoanalytic Association (IPA) but only because Lacan and his
followers no longer belong to it. Two others became 'Lacanian' before
dissolving or imploding as a consequence of internal conflict. A fourth
continues as a bastion of Lacanian orthodoxy but has been repeatedly
split *from*.

Indeed *repeated* splitting has characterised Lacanianism. Yet neither
Lacan nor his followers have ever accepted responsibility for the international, national and local rifts that characterise them. In all cases, they
have blamed or held responsible *the other*, whether this other has been the
IPA, individuals and groups who have remained affiliated with it, other
institutions, Lacan's enemies, non-Lacanian groups, Lacanian groups who
have not kept faith with Lacan and/or Lacanian groups who have not
been Lacanian enough.

Interestingly, Lacanians' blaming of *the other* for the marginalisation
of Lacanianism has sometimes involved *a condemnation of authority from
a position of authority*. Such condemnation has often been *written into* the
statutes and edicts of Lacanian institutional law (as well as having been
passed on in Lacanian cultural lore).[10] Lacanians and Lacanianism are thus
as split in their attitudes towards authority as Lacan 'himself'.

Rifts

Splitting on the part of Lacan and Lacanians has thus meant continued
and current conflict between them. Some of the history of Lacanian
splitting will be recounted more specifically and in more detail later on.
What mention of it here helps to accentuate is the *prior* splitting that the
young Jacques was subject to – the splitting that the splitting of his legacy
part-derives from. The depth and quantity of the splits that have beset
Lacanianism retroactively reinforce a sense that the young Lacan had *very*
mixed feelings about authority.

Jacques' childhood rebellion against *and* identification with authority
may even have been catalytic in effecting conflict in his immediate family.
More precisely, it may have prompted a sort of rebellion in his father. If
Alfred's passivity hid aggression it didn't do so indefinitely: his resentment
of Emile built up. He eventually showed it and the two men fell out. The
rift became trans-familial. Jacques' mother Emilie disliked Alfred's mother
(her mother-in-law) Marie Julie *and* her daughters Marie and Eugénie
(Emilie's sisters in law). A split opened between the Lacans and Alfred's

immediate family. When he retired Emile returned to Orléans to live and he took his family with him. Alfred's family moved from the boulevard Beaumarchais apartment to one in the rue de Montparnasse. All of this happened between Jacques' birth and the advent of The First World War. (Roudinesco, 1997, pp. 7–9)

Theory

What, overall, do Lacan's childhood and its legacy reveal? They show that Lacan and Lacanianism are complex, but that their connected stories involve clear and recurrent themes. These include *ambivalence* about and *disavowal* and *repetition* of *splits* around certain conflicts – notably ones to do with authority.

This all indicates, obviously enough, that the 'Lacanian story' is a psychoanalytic story. Yet it is not *simply* this: it's a psychoanalytic story in more than one sense. It's both a story about psychoanalysis and one that can be psychoanalysed. Astute readers – or even just attentive ones – will have noticed that the story is already being engaged with in *both* of these senses in this text.

The story will be expanded on now in the latter – that is the analytic – sense, albeit briefly. A quick and provisional theorisation and analysis of Lacan's youth follows. The simple *narrative* of that youth will be picked up subsequently and with reference to Jacques' adolescence.

Oedipus

Given Lacan's professional, pedagogic and theoretical preoccupations, it's hard not to bring Freudian ideas to bear on his story, especially the early parts of it. More exactly, it is hard not to identify Oedipal issues in his youth. One there sees an implacable authority that invites ambivalence, attachments to and 'splits' from parents, conflicts between and over women and a family rift or splintering. Anyone who is familiar with the basic tenets of psychoanalytic theory will recognise Oedipal (and even pre-Oedipal) themes here.

The theory of the Oedipus Complex is a cornerstone of what both Lacan and Freud had to say. In a way that will be explained later, it takes general relations and conflicts between parents and children to be basic to human life and development. All such relations, conflicts and developments are played out in the family. Now conversely (and rather obviously) the family is made up of figures (mother, father, son, daughter) that these relations and conflicts take place *between*. Because (less obviously, but as later chapters will explain) relations between figures always comprise a *structure*, the family *is* a structure. It is in this structure that the child finds himself or herself placed at birth.

The son, for instance, is conditioned (that is influenced and limited but not determined) by the family structure and his relations and position in it. Such relations and position are not neutral – they are emotionally invested. For example, the mother is an object of love for her son (he is also *her* love object). This not only implies the certainty of a structural (and emotional) relation but also the possibility of a structural (and emotional) *conflict*. This could happen, for example, where love is not reciprocated, where the mother does not love the son (or vice versa), which could cause despair. Alternatively (or additionally) conflict could be caused if love were directed elsewhere and if the mother (unsurprisingly) loved someone other than the son (most obviously the father), which could prompt jealousy. This last example indicates that maternal/filial relations are not only restricted to or played out in a smaller structure – the one that holds between mother and son – but also within a greater structure – the one that holds in the family (and even beyond the family). The family structure has multiple points of intersection and is thus made up of multiple relations. These can hold – or not hold – between any and all family members. Family dramas (or family romances as Freud liked to call them) can get played out between any and all of these points, or people.

Here's a more detailed account of the effect of family structure described above. The mother is an object of love for the father as well as for the son. If she reciprocates the father's love, she may not return the son's (love is not infinite, after all). Conversely, if she reciprocates the son's love, she may not return the father's. This *complex* situation puts the father and the son in competition with each other for the mother's love. It might lead the son to fantasise about doing away with (that is killing) the father and having (that is having sex with) the mother. This is of course what Oedipus did.[11] *That* Oedipus did this, that he did it unconsciously and that this resonates with the situation of modern 'humanity', led Freud to declare that the latter is in, or suffers from, the same condition as the former. In other words, 'modern man' is bedevilled by 'The Oedipus Complex'.

This is a simple and general description of the Oedipal matrix, including a description of a particular and classic (or Classical) way in which the drama implicit in it unfolds. The description includes reference to 'structural' aspects of the modern family and the Oedipal situation because Lacan's description of both of these phenomena does too. Lacan would claim that his description – including its structural orientation – derives from Freud's (others would disagree and claim that Lacan's argument is an adaption, alteration, misappropriation or perversion of Freud's).[12]

In any case, the Freudian and Lacanian descriptions of the Oedipal situation will be laid out and differentiated progressively as this text proceeds. The purpose of the reference to the Oedipus Complex *here* is to highlight its relevance to Lacan's story. There is clearly enough similarity between the gloss of the Oedipal situation provided above and what has been revealed about Lacan's life to note some significant correspondences between them. Doesn't the Oedipal familial structure part-mirror Jacques' and the Lacans' situation? Aren't there fathers and sons at odds here? Doesn't their conflict involve possession, authority and love? Isn't the conflict partly over women? Didn't the Lacan family split? Furthermore, isn't there a parental, even *a paternal* relationship between Lacan and his followers (and between psychoanalytic 'authorities' and Lacan)? Aren't *these* relations Oedipal? Don't all of the relationships mentioned above involve types of repetition, idealisation, disappointment, incest, patricide and betrayal?

Simplicity

The Oedipus Complex and its attendant dramas are clearly traceable in the various situations and history of Lacan and Lacanianism. They are identifiable in the vicissitudes of Lacan's family life and in the arrangement and dissolution of the institutions he committed his fate to (not to mention in the pretext and the subtext of his writing).

All this will be shown gradually and throughout the course of this book. Full and *complex* Oedipal aspects of Lacan's history and situation will take a while to unpack and explain. The complex can be and already is being borne in mind in provisional terms, and with reference to a simple term: splitting (which is why the penultimate paragraph described the Oedipal aspect of Lacan's situation as a series of splits). The splits concerned were between parents and children and family and institutional groups. Yet they weren't and aren't only evident in Lacan's youthful personality and domestic and institutional engagements. They were apparent in his teenage and school experience too. It's to this aspect of Lacan's story that this text will now return, by resuming the *narrative* of Lacan's life, especially around the time of his adolescence.

School

Lacanians sometimes represent Jacques' performance as a pupil as 'brilliant'.[13] This is only half-true. His schoolwork was inconsistent. He gained high marks in some subjects and average ones in others. This wasn't so much a result of his intellectual limitations as of his emotional ambivalence about his background and adolescent experience.

Jacques parents were French, bourgeois and Catholic. They sent him to a school that was all of these things too. Yet he wouldn't be made in their image. They always behaved respectably; he didn't. His school reports described him as bright but lazy and funny but conceited. He was sure of himself, but often sick or truanting. This combination of melancholic and precocious traits made him like the young Nietzsche, who was one of his youthful idols. The identification was both aspirational and subversive. It allowed him to adopt the stance of 'aristocratic radicalism' attributed to his hero.[14] Lacan never entirely relinquished this stance; he always saw himself as both superior and a rebel. In adolescence, the stance was complemented by an flirtation with extreme right-wing nationalism, as expounded by Charles Maurras. Like all forms of extremism, it had its violent aspect. Jacques became both more sophisticated and less civil than his parents. This made him a greater *and* a lesser bourgeois than them.[15]

Culture

As adulthood loomed, this tension was heightened. Jacques assumed the dress of a dandy and a savage wit. He dressed and spoke like Oscar Wilde and developed an affection for clothes and ideas from England. Yet his aesthetic interests remained Continental. His was keen on the modern avant-garde that was at its most radical and influential in France and Germany. Its proponents were both élite and subversive. Jacques met André Breton and Philippe Soupault around about the time of their experiments in automatic writing.[16] They had both been very involved in Dada and would officially found Surrealism a few years later. The former movement was anarchistic; the latter was Marxist and Freudian. Both movements were practised by cliques whose arbiters (especially Breton) were exclusive and authoritarian. They appealed to Jacques' snobbishness as well as his disposition to sedition.

The violent atheism and anti-clericalism practised by the Dadaists and Surrealists eroded Jacques' Catholic beliefs. Yet even these weren't relinquished without ambivalence, as they too could be agents of both obedience and insubordination. A few years before his renunciation of God, Jacques had been a successful student of his religion, influenced by of one of his teachers, Jean Baruzi. The academic, rationalistic Catholicism that Baruzi taught him contrasted sharply with both the mystical, urbane sort practised by his mother's family and the pietistic, provincial sort practiced by his father's. Jacques attained very high marks in theology by espousing a faith that his family didn't understand. He was thus able to both please and irritate them at the same time. (Roudinesco, 1997, pp. 9–14; 1990, 104–5)

It is worth pausing briefly to comment on the nature and range of the contradictory philosophical, ideological and aesthetic *positions* taken up by the young Jacques. He was both radical and conservative. His radicalism was both left wing and right wing. He was religious and secular. The English won his loyalty and love, but so did their historical arch-enemies, the French. Is any of this surprising? Jacques had been 'good and bad' at school, behaviourally and intellectually. His parents must have had high hopes for him, but despaired of him too. The child clearly 'had an ego' in both the clinical and the common senses in which this phrase might be used. He both had a sense of self and one that was 'egotistical'. What this all says about him reinforces much that has been said so far, namely that he was singly and multiply 'split'. This splitting was clearly personal and would also become professional.

Career

Jacques' struggle with what he should think and feel extended to what he should be. This was most obvious in his adolescent deliberations about his future. His flirtations with extreme art, politics, philosophy and religion were partly experiments intended to help him discover what he wanted to devote his life to, what *career* he wanted to pursue. Did he want to be an artist or a priest or a philosopher or a politician? He wrestled with the idea of each of these practices/professions, engaging with them in their most radical and hence most testing forms. Perhaps he failed the tests set – or they failed him. He didn't become an artist or a politician or a philosopher or – like his brother – a priest.

Yet Lacan didn't relinquish these roles either. Later, when he was older, better known and had an attentive audience, he played them all.

This was evident when, for example, he held forth on the modern world. He didn't just pass judgement on modern psychoanalysis, but also artistic modernism, US modernity, modern philosophy and the modern place of God.[17] These judgements were delivered with authority, *as if* Lacan *was* an artist, politician, philosopher or priest. He never quite gave up his options; he wanted (to be) everything. Whether he succeeded in this aim or not is a matter for debate.[18]

Whichever was the case, Jacques' career-ambivalence persisted. The contrast between his youthful attitude and his brother's is instructive in this regard. Unlike Jacques, Marc-François *did* commit himself to becoming something. At the age of twenty-one, he took orders as a monk at the Abbaye de Hautecombe. This was (and is) located over 400 kilometres from Paris on Lake Bourget, not far from the French borders with Switzerland and Italy. Marc-François kept up this vocation until his death aged 84. Following Christ meant forgoing all other paths; being a monk meant not being anything else. Jacques' ambivalence about his interests, by contrast, *didn't* end decisively. His dilemma may have been existential but his choice – at least in the Sartrean sense – wasn't. In other words he *didn't* make a choice, or at least not a real one. If he had done it would have meant being one thing rather than another (e.g. being a philosopher rather than a psychoanalyst, or vice versa). It would have involved *losing* as well as choosing something.[19] Jacques didn't want to do this and he acted as if he didn't have to. This meant *holding on* to all of his phantasies. It also meant *continuing* to be ambivalent about them.

Poly-mathematics

Controversy about his eclecticism never put Lacan off. In many senses, he relished it. Not only did he not relinquish his researches in unfamiliar fields, he extended them. As his career progressed, he engaged *less* with psychoanalytic theories and *more* with other ones. This is ironic, given that he increasingly claimed to be isolating what was 'fundamental' to psychoanalysis and to be doing so by 'formulating' what is *essential* to it.

The irony is well exemplified by Lacan's late and quite notorious logical, mathematical and topological speculations. He claimed that these offered an overall, accurate, rigorous and definitive formulation of psychoanalytic principles.[20] He even claimed that they offered an effective critique of philosophy and science *per se*.[21] They don't. In fact, there's a debate about whether they achieve anything *at all*. In any case they confirm a contention that's been held to in this book so far. Lacan's speculations, researches and theorisations, although sometimes 'brilliant' were idiosyncratic. They were looking to discover or establish something that is *essential* to psychoanalysis *outside of* psychoanalysis (for example in logic, topology and mathematics). In other words Lacan's method was split, just as he was. Lacan wanted to be an acclaimed para-logician, a supra-formulator and a scientific (as well as philosophical) polymath (a sort of *poly-mathematician*). Yet he *only* convinced *his followers* that he was any such thing.[22]

The division – between what Lacan would like to have been and what he was – corresponded with the conflict between the various and particular roles that he played but couldn't decide between or give up (psychoanalyst, philosopher, healer, teacher, priest, genius, rebel etc.). *All* of these conflicts were probably symptomatic of a fear of and ambivalence about loss. In other words they were borne of a terror that success as one thing means failure as another, that gaining something means giving something else up, or that sacrificing one thing means losing everything.

Loss

There is, as it happens, an appropriately psychoanalytic way of understanding ambivalence of this sort, which pays particular regard to its origination in fear of loss, more exactly loss of something *valuable*. In psychoanalytic terms, this fear can be described as fear of real or symbolic 'castration', that is fear of the loss of what is literally or symbolically 'phallic'. Importantly, it is set off in the context of the Oedipus Complex. Wouldn't it be appropriate, to return – albeit briefly – to a consideration of this complex? Wouldn't it then also be appropriate to again speculate about its effects on Lacan?

Of course, one could point out that Lacan knew full well about the Oedipus Complex (just as he knew full well about authoritarianism). It might then seem illegitimate to analyse him in terms of it. Yet as he would be the first to admit, the complex is *unconscious*. That is, it acts on one without one's knowledge. Knowing about it is no guarantee that it doesn't affect one. Understanding it doesn't mean that it doesn't shape one's wishes, fears and behaviour. Thus Lacan's knowledge of the complex (and even his sophisticated theorisation of it) wouldn't absolve him from being subject to it. With all this in mind, it seems correct to return in a general way to the complex in question and in a particular way to Lacan's subjection to it. More exactly it seems right to consider a certain *castrating* aspect of it.

Triangulation

According to Freud and as suggested earlier, important aspects of the Oedipal drama involve the father and the son. Others involve the mother. In one especially important regard, all three are involved. In *this* case *conflict* arises between the father and the son as a consequence of their competition *for* the mother. This conflict involves desire, threat and fear. It is played out in the following way.

The son sexually desires the mother. His father directly or indirectly prohibits this desire (he takes his wife to be *his* exclusively). The son fears the harm that the father might do him if he disobeys his father's prohibition. More particularly, he feels a threat to that with which he desires his mother. He thinks his father will punish him by cutting off his penis; he fears he will *lose* it; he becomes anxious about his own literal or symbolic 'castration'.

According to Freud, the 'normal' way for the boy to resolve the Oedipus Complex is for him to acknowledge this threat of castration, to accept his father's prohibition and to give up his phantasy of 'having' his mother. He can then turn his attention to other females beside her and direct his desire towards them. The promise of having these others is what facilitates and smoothens the transferral of his desire from one object to another. The father will usually approve of this development, which conforms with psychological as well as social norms (which is precisely why it's 'normal') and which ends or at least lessens the conflict between him and his son. (Freud, [1924] 1984, pp. 315–20)

There are obviously also advantages for the boy in accepting this 'development'. He gains the possibility of the acquisition of another love, one that might adequately substitute for his original one. However, this acquisition might never be realised or it might not equal what he originally had (or thought he had). In short, the girl might not be as attainable, lovable or desirable for the boy as the mother is. Oedipal development, even if it involves the substitution of one love object for another, might always involve a loss. For the boy, the potential or actual loss of his mother might feel devastating; it might feel like the loss of a primary and irreplaceable object. It might also feel to him like a *subjective* loss, more precisely a loss to his ego – to his sense of self, self-confidence and self-esteem – much of which he might have *got* from his mother. (Freud, [1927] 1984, pp. 345–57)

What does this all mean? Principally, it means that the boy might 'refuse' the prohibition presented to him in the 'castration threat' and also might 'decline' the offer of an adequate substitute for his mother made alongside it. This would mean that he would *not develop*. The boy would then have decided that the sacrifice of his mother – or even the idea of it – isn't worth it. He would also have chosen to ignore and/or defy the real or imagined threat being issued by his father. Doing this in an assertive and unequivocal way would amount to refusing loss – and even the possibility of it (the possibility of the loss of the mother and/or the possibility of loss in general). Conversely, it would allow maintenance of a certain self- image. The boy who refuses the possibility of the loss of his mother can go on believing the image of himself that he receives from her: as exclusively loved, as legitimately self-loving and as more important than anyone else. Such a boy can – at least in phantasy – retain his self-conscious self-evaluation that is his *narcissism*.

This way of being (which involves this refusal of the possibility of castrated being) might be very gratifying for the son. Yet it would also come at a cost. This would be the cost of the difficult and painful denial of various truths: that there is a father, that he is a rival, that he therefore represents a threat, that the mother may both be loved by and love him, that she may have to be given up (even if only in death) and that her narcissism-feeding love might have to be given up too. There are obviously conflicts between all of these truths and the scenario that the castration-refusing boy might choose to believe in and act out. In *that* scenario he would have his mother to himself and – because he would have her love – would have confidence *in* himself. Yet of course that scenario is phantasmatic. Its cost is the repression, containment and disavowal of the losses its maintenance denies.

Return

There are clearly correspondences between the Oedipal scenarios described above and aspects of Lacan's early life. He had a father who indulged him in his desires and a (grand)father who didn't. This means he experienced two fathers or, one might say, two aspects of 'the father'. Just as significantly, he was his mother's favourite. (Roudinesco, 1997, p. 7) It was a difficult situation. He was and wasn't prohibited from seeking love. He did and didn't receive it. This must have felt conflicting. What did Lacan do with his conflict? It's arguable that he hid it and that he did so increasingly as he was growing up. This hiding was also a sort of mastering. It minimised conflict and shut off the possibility of loss that such conflict promised.

It's arguable that Lacan's childhood Oedipal strategies carried over into his youth and young manhood. When it came to choosing different careers, he mitigated the conflict between conflicting choices by making *all* choices (that is by making no choices). He denied the possibility of the loss of *given* futures by promising himself all futures. In fact, he denied loss in general by thinking himself capable of anything and everything.

Lacan played this role throughout his adult life. As an expert, a teacher and a man he came across as supremely confident. He thought of and presented himself as exceptionally experienced, knowledgeable and insightful. Yet how much of Lacan's confidence was authentic? How much of it was based in the secure knowledge that he was right and that he had the experience and credentials to back his claims and his self-presentation up? Conversely – how much was a denial? How much was Lacan refusing to believe in the possibility of a loss: of his position, of his status, of his ability to seduce others, of the love and admiration that others felt for him? How much was his whole being the denial of the possibility of his 'castration'?

Ending

Yet to ask such questions too insistently – and certainly to answer them too soon – would be to get ahead of oneself. Not enough has been established about Lacan at this point to judge him, or at least to judge him fairly and comprehensively. Before Lacan can be judged, a lot more needs to be said about him.

Up until now Lacan's youth has been considered. The next chapter will mostly deal with his young adulthood and early professional life. This will involve a closer engagement than has so far been undertaken with his *ideas*.

3

Sense and Nonsense

Ambivalence

Thus Lacan's 'progress' through the first three decades of the last century was unsteady, partial and wayward. As the last chapter showed, he was torn between art and science and theology and philosophy, between the transcendent and the immanent and God and man. He couldn't decide whether he wanted to be a politician or a doctor, a priest or a philosopher.[1] In the end he settled for medicine. Yet it wasn't the end and he didn't settle: he became a doctor then a psychiatrist then a psychoanalyst. Although he increasingly relinquished the first two of these roles, he never gave either of them up completely. He used his doctoral title to remind everyone he was a psychiatrist and he continued to practise medicine in a sporadic, selective and status-conscious way (for example he was Picasso's personal physician).[2] Eventually he became – or became known as – a psychoanalyst.

Lacan's personal aspirations and affections were as divergent as his professional ones. He indulged his parents (he wanted their love and pride) but also defied them (he thought that he was better than them). Elsewhere, he craved affection and admiration (for example, from women) but indulged in and invited hostility (for example, from men).[3] The young Lacan's professional life *and* his personal life were rent with contradictory impulses, opposite identifications and mixed motives. In becoming himself, he became divided from himself.

Division

All this shows that Lacan's division is important. Yet what's also important – indeed crucial – is that it isn't just attributable to 'him'. 'Lacanian division' affects more than just Lacan 'himself'. It is *various*. This was suggested in the last chapter; it is spelt out in this one. Lacan's work is *marked* by division. It is fragmented, ambiguous and contradictory. It is also informed, insightful and brilliant. As a consequence of all this, opinion of the work is divided too.

Lacanian division is also 'thematic'. It is most obviously and significantly so *in* Lacan's work. Division is a *theme* of that work. In other words Lacan *theorised* division as well as being subject to it. He frequently invoked a 'divided subject', one that is riven by 'the law of the signifier'. For Lacan, division was a precondition of psychical and human life; his ideas presumed and stressed it.

As if that wasn't enough, the institutions that Lacan founded are 'divided' too. *This* division is a decidedly complex one: it is historical, theoretical and symptomatic. Lacanians hold division as an article of faith. Following their master, they describe language, humanity, and even 'the world' as riven by conflict and ambivalent desire.[4] They understand contemporary culture in terms of these things, see them in all forms of human life and seek to effect tolerance if not mitigation of them through psychoanalysis. In short, they diagnose and treat the world as divided. Yet they are divided too, to the extent (and it is a large extent) that they are dissident, sectarian, and fractious. Lacanians were forced to split from the IPA, who they treat as an enemy; they also fight among themselves – over which of them is more Lacanian. Thus division is not just a tenet, but also a characteristic, even a symptom of Lacanianism.[5] Lacanians not only view the world as split, but are split themselves.

Many 'Lacanian' divisions are mentioned above. Yet there is a particular sort of *link* that appears to hold between some or all divisions mentioned that requires immediate consideration. This link is a powerful one. It is worth both making *and* questioning; this will be done now.

Anticipation

There is a link between Lacan's personal division and the division of all he thought, created and instituted. It has been at least suggested in this book so far. The link is a real one (even if it is also a 'broken' one). Lacan's division from himself prefigured his theorisation of man as divided from himself – his *personal division* informed his *theories of division*. Furthermore, this personal division fore-tended the intellectual and political division of the institutions that have taken their world-view *from* Lacan. What does all this suggest? Lacan's division *anticipated* Lacanian division.

This notion of anticipatory division presumes a series of divisive events and phenomena in Lacan's life that can be seen as not only having affected him, but also his theories and institutional activities. Lacan's divided life seems to have instructed his divided work and legacy.

To the extent that it is claiming as much, this book looks biographical in orientation. It seems to be working on the basis of an idea that Lacan was divided and that Lacanianism *issues* from him but also *reflects* him and is thus divided too. This sort of – biographically oriented – account would suggest that Lacanianism is primarily the (brilliant but) flawed *product* of a (brilliant but) flawed man.

This book might even more precisely appear to be *psycho*biographical. After all, it has already part-*psychoanalysed* Lacan. It has taken aspects of his psyche to explain *him*. It has also suggested that the split character of his ideas *and* of the tradition he founded stem from his own split psyche. All this indicates that Lacan's pronouncements about human division were expressions of troubles in *his own life*. It also suggests that his complex theories, his arcane political wranglings and his fractured legacy reflect and/or *repeat* that life. They are *marked* by the muddle that Lacan's life was and they *act out* the conflicts he had. From this point of view Lacanianism in general – and its preoccupation with division in particular – not only seems like a psychobiographical, but also like a *psychopathological* effect of Lacan.

Separation

Yet this psychopathological effect is not only what this book is concerned with. It's not *just* a biography or psychobiography. In other words it won't *only* treat Lacan's actual or psychical life as primary. Neither will it just regard his work and/or his critical and institutional legacy as a secondary effect of that life. Lacanian theories, for example, will be focussed on individually and not just as pathological products; they'll be granted at least as much prominence and attention as Lacan will.

In order to register the onset and the significance of the non-psychobiographical dimensions of this book, it might be useful to give an example of how its periodic concentration on Lacan's *theories* (rather than Lacan) and their divisions (rather than divisions in him) will take place. Here is one.

Logic

Later, what Lacan called 'the logic of the signifier' will be examined. According to him, this 'logic' instructs the formation and use of human language, which encompasses thought (although the 'speaking being' might not be thinking while he's speaking) and intention (although intention may not always be conscious). Lacan had quite particular things to say about 'the logic of the signifier'. For example, he said that it doesn't need to 'justify its existence in terms of any signification whatsoever'. (EC, p. 416) This means that linguistic utterances need not be – and often aren't – meaningful or true. What one says may not make sense, or be what one intended, or be coherent, or be consistent, or be truthful. This most obviously happens when one is hysterical, or over-anxious, or half-asleep, or semi-conscious, or in any situation in which one is speaking and in which the significance of what one says is obscure, lacking, or absent. Lacan thought that such situations were common enough to represent something fundamental about human speech. Thus in some cases – and to some extent in all cases – language functions autonomously and independently of any generally accepted signification(s) or any particular purpose or intent on the part of the person speaking. One might say that it functions according to 'another logic' ('the logic of the signifier') which is not straightforwardly or apparently one of meaning or truth.

This strange 'logic' will be explained more fully later on. Yet it will also be questioned. How can it be possible for language not to answer to 'any signification whatsoever'? More exactly, how can this be 'logical'? Lacan takes the term 'signifier' from Saussure. He also takes the idea that meaning is constituted in language from him.[6] Yet if meaning is constituted in language, how *can* language be meaningless?

One can put this even more logically (and why wouldn't one, since what one is supposed to be dealing with is 'logic' here)? What Lacan says about the 'logic of the signifier' indicates that 'language is meaningless'. This statement (like all statements) has to make sense to be true. Yet if it does make sense, it *isn't* true (that 'language is meaningless').[7] The statement implicitly depends upon something that it explicitly denies: meaning. To put it another way: the statement refutes what it proposes. It thus can't logically be the case that language yields 'no signification whatsoever'. The 'logic of the signifier' is not logical.

Non-sense

Lacan's theory of the 'logic of the signifier does make a *sort of* sense. It does describe a certain sort of language or linguistic utterance that is not apparently meaningful and that isn't instructed by any clear or conscious intent ('madness' – of all sorts – is the exemplar of this sort of language).

Yet the theory manifestly doesn't describe or explain *other* sorts of language (for example 'logic', or 'critical language' or even 'common sense'). More importantly, it doesn't describe language in general (at least with any consistency or accuracy). Still, Lacan frequently and universally reduced the functioning of language to that of 'the signifier' and to the supposed 'logic' that drives and structures its organisation and use.

Thus in a particular and limited way the theory of the logic of the signifier makes sense, yet in many important respects it doesn't. Because it both does and doesn't make sense, the theory is 'split'.

To sum up: psychobiographical and psychoanalytic approaches will be used in this text, but they will not dominate other ones. A number of legitimate approaches, including theoretical ones, will be employed. They will vary, but will also agree in uncovering 'splits' in the subject of their analyses. For this reason (and despite differences in their orientation or exact object) they can and will be used consistently.

Others

There is yet another approach that will be employed in this book that is worth mentioning before going on. This is a sort of 'comparative' and 'originary' approach. It involves relating Lacan's ideas to the ideas of *others*, specifically others that have influenced him. Taking account of such influence is not only helpful but also necessary if Lacan's ideas are to be properly understood and assessed. Why is this so?

Accuracy

All of Lacan's important ideas can be seen as having had their origin in the work of other thinkers. Sometimes Lacan declared this – and did so very loudly. It's well known, for instance, that he considered himself a Freudian. He went so far as to say that 'It is up to you to be Lacanians if you so wish. As far as I am concerned, I am a Freudian.' (Lacan (1981) As well as identifying Freud as his primary influence, Lacan cited *other* theorists as the originators of some of the key 'discoveries' that have been associated with him. For example, he frequently named Saussure as the thinker responsible for having identified the 'logic of the signifier'. He asserted that the 'algorithm' of the sign that this logic presumes 'should be attributed to Ferdinand de Saussure'. (EC, pp. 414–5)

Now this attribution by Lacan of some of the origins of his own thought to other thinkers is important, not least because it is questionable.

For instance, Saussure never used the phrase 'logic of the signifier'. Neither did he foreground the signifier (as opposed to the signified) in language (nor yet did he declare its 'autonomy', as Lacan did). Furthermore, he didn't treat language 'algorithmically' (at least not literally, self-consciously or in a manner that corresponds with the way in which a mathematician would use the term). All in all, Saussure didn't quite say what Lacan said he said.[8] Lacan's claim that Saussure's ideas form the basis of his own thought is as dubious as it is tantalising.

Indeed Lacan's representations of the ideas of a *number* of thinkers – and/or his claims that these ideas properly informed his own – are both intriguing *and* questionable. This is not only so for reasons of *accuracy* but also for other reasons.

A further significant issue related to the matter of the derivation of Lacan's ideas from others' is that of *originality*. The question of whether Lacan's ideas were *his own* is a relevant one, particularly where Lacan's influences were undeclared.

Sometimes Lacan avowed the origins of his ideas, yet *sometimes he didn't*. Henri Wallon, for example, discovered and named both 'The Mirror Stage' and 'The Imaginary'. Lacan consistently presented both of these notions as his own and didn't directly cite Wallon as the source of them. They're among the best-known and most studied 'Lacanian' concepts.

This omission not only raises the question of originality, but also of authenticity and even of *plagiarism*. These questions are very real and important ones and will be addressed as this text proceeds.[9]

Status

This is because, however much it is analysed, the status of Lacan's 'borrowing' is never resolved. For example, one can say that Lacan's use of Saussure was inaccurate, or one could say that it was *altered*. Lacan clearly used Saussure's ideas *differently* than Saussure did. What's not clear is whether he did this because he didn't understand the ideas (in other words he misrepresented them) or because he decided to change them (in other words he 'developed' them). It's also possible (because understanding and alteration are not alternatives) that Lacan *did* understand the ideas but changed them in any case.

One can see this matter of Lacan's borrowing as one of *influence* as well as, or instead of, one of *accuracy*. One can treat them as matters of opinion or debate. Yet there's a cost to suspending judgement on these matters, because doing so allows the belief that in the end the theories that Lacan produced as a consequence of his 'borrowings' are more or less consistent and that there's therefore no real problem with them. This is the position that expositors of Lacan's work (of whom there are many) effectively take when they explain his ideas, inferring and expounding a coherent logic in them in the process. Yet the argument about Lacan's consistency is not addressed and resolved by such active or passive imputation of sense to him.

Partum

What *is* arguable is that Lacan's borrowing, like Lacan, was split 'at source'. Thus every aspect of that borrowing was suffused by an opposite character. Lacan's work was innovative but not original, derivative but not faithful, taken but not acknowledged, attributed but not accurate, informed but incorrect and unique but not authentic. In short, his borrowings were multiply and fundamentally *split*.

4

Man and Window

Story

Doing everything promised in the last chapter means resuming Lacan's story but not just, of course, his 'life story'. It also means recounting his intellectual biography, recovering the intellectual history he was part of, explaining and assessing his theories, comparing these with those of his influences and antecedents, putting him in the historical and intellectual context of his peers, analysing his personal motivation and behaviour, registering his institutional and intellectual influence and gauging and judging the overall cultural reception and influence that he and his ideas, practices and institutional initiatives have had.

All of these elements are part of the 'story' of Lacan. Obviously, it isn't a 'short story'.[1] It is resumed now and with reference to other characters apart from Lacan and other scenes than that of his childhood and domestic life.

As shown, the young Lacan prevaricated about what sort of a professional to be. Eventually, he elected to become a medic. Almost immediately after having done so, he chose psychiatry as his medical specialism. This allowed him an option to become a psychoanalyst. After a few years, he took up this option.[2]

Training

The details of all of Lacan's early training are as follows. He undertook the specialised study of 'mental and cephalic disorders' in 1927. This marked the beginning of his psychiatric training, his general medical training having begun the year before. He concentrated on his specialty until 1932, the year after he acquired the title of 'Doctor' via a defence of a thesis on paranoid psychosis. (Lacan, [1932] 1975)

Lacan's specifically psychiatric training began at one of the top mental hospitals in France: the Hôpital Saint-Anne. In 1930 he spent two months at the Burghölzi clinic in Zurich, at which pioneering psychiatric work had been done by Carl Jung and Eugen Bleuler. He then returned briefly to Saint-Anne's as an intern before moving on to the Paris Préfecture de Police. This was a headquarters, but served other functions than police management. Among these was the assessment and preliminary treatment of the city's 'insane' prior to their release or removal to asylums. The 'consultant' psychiatrist whose dominion was the 'special infirmary' in which such cases were undertaken was the visionary and maverick Gaëtan Gatian de Clérambault. Lacan spent a year at the Préfecture before moving on to complete his psychiatric training at the Henri Rouselle hospital. After having completed his medical (and psychiatric) training he began to train as a psychoanalyst. In order to do this he had to join the relevant (and at that time only) French psychoanalytic society: The Société psychanalytique de Paris (SPP). He also had to undergo a 'training analysis', which he began in 1933.

Suffusion

Although it's obvious from the above that Lacan's training wasn't only psychoanalytic, he was nevertheless engaged with psychoanalysis *from early on* and *before* he was specifically trained in it. Psychoanalysis was devised by Freud at the turn of the nineteenth century into the twentieth, the period in which Lacan was born. Lacan grew up in a time and place (and a corresponding *milieu*) in which psychoanalysis was beginning to be understood and taken seriously. This was happening in both the French medical profession and French culture per se. More exactly, it was happening in certain Parisian medical and academic (specifically psychiatric and psychological) circles and certain Parisian artistic groupings. During his youth and into his twenties and early thirties (that is both before and during his medical and psychiatric training) Lacan moved in such circles and groups.

It's thus well worth evoking and investigating the mediated and/or indirect influence that psychoanalysis had on Lacan in his youth and young manhood. Doing this will involve taking account of both *medical* scenes and *cultural* ones. Two scenes in particular are worth recounting. One scene took place in a specific culture in which psychoanalysis was appreciated and nurtured: surrealism. The other was the scene of the discovery of psychoanalysis.

Surrealism

Many people are familiar with the term 'Surrealism'. For most, it represents a style of visual art. The style is figurative, that is it mostly depicts individual objects in a verisimilar way ('as they appear') yet it also involves strange juxtapositions or metamorphoses of such objects. Well-known examples of Surrealism include Méret Oppenheim's *Fur Cup* (1936) and Salvador Dalí's *Lobster Telephone* (1936) or his 'soft watches' (in *The Persistence of Memory,* 1931). In general such art is meant to disorientate or shock its viewers with the intention of prompting them to think – or to see the world – differently, specifically in a more creative and critical way.

Surrealism is nearly a century old. Its figures, devices and techniques have been identifiable in many visual arts, formats and media – including popular ones like film and video – for more than half a century.[3] Yet painting is the art form with which Surrealism is most associated, at least from a historical point of view. It was Surrealist painters like Dalí, René Magritte, Paul Delvaux and Max Ernst who first popularised Surrealism and who developed the visual style that it later became recognisable as. It was this style that was copied and/or extended into other popular formats (as well as films and videos, these have included album covers and advertisements).[4] Dalí, significantly, knew and collaborated with Lacan. Yet he and his painter-contemporaries did not 'invent' surrealism. That was done by others who were mostly *not* painters and whose practice and influence predated Dalí's.[5] It's worth considering these others, as their more original (and more philosophical and political) ideas not only inspired Dalí, but also Lacan.

Surrealism was a radical artistic, cultural and political movement. Its precursor in the arts was Dada, which was conceived by Hans Arp, Richard Huelsenbeck and Tristan Tzara in Zurich in 1916. (Nadeau, p. 59) Dada was an anti-art (as well as an art) movement. Its founders abhorred all artistic conventions. Discerning and reviling an alliance between classical or traditional art and bourgeois culture, they visited symbolic and literal destruction on both through inept or offensive 'exhibitions' or outrageous and iconoclastic 'displays'. (Richter pp. 220–2) This led, for example, to the showing of profane objects like Marcel Duchamp's (in)famous *Urinal,* which was first exhibited in the New York Independents' exhibition in 1917. Other Dadaists practiced a kind of performance art that mocked both art and performance. Examples include Arthur Cravan's onstage undressing while belching and Huelsenbeck's unlistenable 'sound-poems'.

(Nadeau, pp. 58, 60) Thus the Dadaists made themselves into art objects, but did so in a way that was verbally and visually disorienting. They aimed not only to challenge their spectators' expectations, but even to question the very practices they were engaged in: art, performance, communication. It will be shown that Lacan did the same, by (increasingly) turning his lectures into intense, odd performances, by playing the eccentric genius that was 'Lacan'. His purpose was not only to disrupt expectations but also to interrupt an apprehension of him and his words that depended on a *conscious* understanding of them.

Early surrealistic activity took place a few years after 1916, not in Zurich, but in Paris. It was significantly (though not exclusively) *literary*. Tzara moved to Paris in 1919. His cause – and Dada's – was taken up by the editors of the journal *Littérature*: Breton, Louis Aragon and Phillipe Soupault. The obviously political and revolutionary aspect of Tzara's thought and action, which had been anarchistic for the Zurich Dadaists, resonated with the Parisians' Marxism. The literary interests declared by the title of their journal were no less modern or provocative. They enthused about the daring verbal experiments carried out by French symbolist poets like Arthur Rimbaud and the Comte de Lautréamont. (Balakian, pp. 69–76 and 77–89)

The Surrealists' philosophical interests were equally cutting-edge. They preferred German (for example Hegelian) ideas to French (for example Cartesian) ones. The Surrealists' Germanic preferences set them firmly against the French academic and educational establishment, who were chauvinistically pro-French in all matters of philosophy and art.

The movement started by Tzara's group and continued in different ways by *Littérature* was arguably more subversive than any other modernist form. (Roudinesco, 1990, pp. 135–8) It began as a type of performance, continued as a type of literature and eventually comprised a poetic, dialectical, revolutionary, artistic, cultural and political practice that appealed to radicals of all sorts, not just in Paris but elsewhere. This practice had superseded the name Dada by 1922 and adopted the name Surrealism by 1924. By this date, Surrealism was centred on Breton. Even before 1924, he was Surrealism's leading figure and main spokesperson. He catalysed the movement by organising its activities and writing its manifestoes. (Breton, 1972) As mentioned in the last chapter, he met the young Lacan. The writing, ideas and activities of the former had a significant and radical effect on the latter.

Force

It's widely acknowledged that psychoanalysis was among the cultural currents on which Surrealism was borne. A number of the early Surrealists were former medics and had come across psychoanalytic ideas during their medical studies or researches. Aragon and Breton had met as medical auxiliaries at the beginning of the First World War. (Breton, 1972, p. 5) By 1916 Breton had begun to read Freud as part of his training as a psychiatrist. He would shortly abandon his medical career but would continue to absorb psychoanalytic ideas that would show up markedly in his surrealistic pronouncements and practices. He both met and corresponded with Freud and referred to him favourably in Surrealist manifestoes. (Breton, 1972, pp. 10–12, 21–4) The Surrealist group as a whole frequently employed psychoanalytic means to achieve their ends. Most obviously, they invoked unconscious forces in the creation of surreal phenomena and opposed such forces to the oppressive and repressive ones they discerned in conventional society, key amongst which were the forces of *reason*. Yet how exactly did the (unconventional) marriage of psychoanalysis and Surrealism come about? In order to understand this – and to clarify Surrealism's link with Lacan as well as Freud – it's necessary to recover a fragment of *Breton's* story.

Automatism

In the first manifesto of Surrealism, written in 1924, Breton described how he had chanced upon the technique that was to become his primary means of composition and a common practice among his collaborators in the Surrealist movement. He recalled that one day in 1919, just as he was falling asleep, a strange phrase occurred to him: 'I cannot remember it exactly, but it was something like: "There is a man cut in two by the window"'. (Breton, 2972, p. 21) Just as his pleasure in this phrase was causing him to reflect on its poeticity, others, which were equally bizarre, followed. He let these phrases take the shape that they would, allowing himself only to 'write' them down, giving little thought to their origin and less to their sense or value. The technique allowed him to compose some bizarre and beautiful verses like 'Monsieur V':

Instead of a star

L'Arc de Triomphe
which resembles a magnet by its shape only

            shall I besilver
            the hanging gardens...
While growing
he looks at himself in a pearly shell
            the iris of his eye is the star
of which I spoke...
  In art one can hardly describe
  The device for catching the blue fox

(Breton, 2006)

(Quoted by kind permission of Black Widow Press from André Breton, *Poems of André Breton: A Bilingual Anthology*. Edited and translated Jean Pierre Cauvin and Mary Ann Caws.)

Breton's method involved indulgence of an intuition that 'the speed of thought is not greater than the speed of speech' and a concomitant presumption that the processes of language might not be directed by ideas, or even by sense. This presumption, which was confirmed by the obscurity of his poetic products, led Breton to question whether linguistic processes were primarily directed by conscious intent or even by meaning in general. As shown above, similar questions were later to preoccupy Lacan and to instruct *his* theoretical speculations about 'the logic of the signifier'. For his part Breton began to wonder whether linguistic processes might be self-activating or, to use another word that means the same thing, *automatic*.

As noted, Breton was a psychiatrist as well as a writer. He employed the term 'automatic' in the same way that other psychiatrists and neurologists of his time did to describe the spontaneous and apparently incomprehensible speech of their patients. Lacan would be trained to use the same word in the same way. The relevant psychiatric presumption was that certain psychotic patients spoke 'automatically' and without self-conscious thought about what they were saying. They were the vehicles of an autonomous outpouring of language, machines for the production and expressions of an argument whose logic escaped them (and everybody else). In his role as surrealist-in-chief Breton encouraged his literary and artistic collaborators to indulge their own dynamic and automatic outpourings. These would draw on the creative and destructive powers of the unconscious and pull up or chop down bourgeois – and rationalist – presumptions at their roots. The first 1920s products of the surrealists' endeavours which, like Breton's, were verbal and written (later ones would be drawn or painted) were accordingly referred to as 'automatic writing'. (Nadeau, pp. 87–8)

Marcelle

Lacan's medical and psychiatric training (mostly) took place in the second half of the 1920s, the decade in which the first surrealist manifesto was written and in which the most seminal and radical (that is the most *avant-garde*) surrealist writing, action and art was produced. Like Breton (who he had of course met) Lacan was a medic who had a keen interest in literary and artistic experiments as well as Freudian theory. More specifically, like Breton, he was paying close attention to a dimension of language that exists and functions independently of meaning. He would later refer to this dimension of language as the order of the signifier (and hold that it functions, as indicated earlier, according to the '*logic* of the signifier'). By the time his medical and psychiatric training was almost over, automatic writing – and drawing – had become a common surrealist device.[6] Lacan was even instrumental in the production of some automatic writing himself. More exactly, and not least because one cannot entirely own automatic products, he was encouraging and analysing the automatic writings of another.

This other was 'Marcelle', a twenty-four-year-old schoolteacher, who Lacan treated in 1931 in the course of completing his medical internship. Marcelle had a delusional condition. She claimed that she was Joan of Arc and also that the state owed her twenty million francs compensation for sexual and intellectual deprivation. She believed that she was not only saving France but also 'renewing the language'. This compelled her to produce writing in which words and phrases were combined in a highly random, unconventional and creative manner. An example is her letter 'To the President of the Republic, Monsieur P. Doumer, at present on vacationing in gingerbread and mintstrel land'. In this letter, she informed the president that she 'should like to know everything so as to give you the but mouse so of a coward and of a test cannon' but that because she could not ('know everything') she had to guess 'from the unkind things done to other people...that my five Vals geese are chickwee and you are the bowler hat of the Virgin Mary and test pardon.'[7]

Lacan used a term that implies psychical and literary conflict – "schizographie" – to describe Marcelle's writing. It's notable that one of the ways in which he identified this conflict was in a *textual tension* between the *random* and the *formal*. Later in his career – and very influentially –

he would make much of a concomitant tension in language between something arbitrary (the sign) and something structured (language *per se*). The tension is apparent in Marcelle's texts in associations between images (for examples nouns and names like 'bowler hat' and 'Virgin Mary') which appear arbitrary, and the syntactic and grammatical devices that link them (for example prepositions and articles like 'of the') which are conventional. Lacan noted that 'syntactic structure is nearly always respected' in Marcelle's writing yet that it is also accompanied by 'manic assonant association'. This discordance between grammatical form and symbolic liberty produced texts of 'remarkable poetic value'.[8]

Of course, Marcelle's 'poetry' would very much have appealed to Breton, not least because it resembled his own. Witness, for example, 'The schedule of hollow flowers' or the 'ear of fishes' or that 'what remains of the blood-stained engine is overgrown with Hawthorn: at this time the first deep-sea divers fall from the sky'. (Breton, 2006, pp. 16–17, 22–3)

Origin

Lacan and Breton shared more than an appreciation of the way in which language is both contingent and organised, determinative and autonomous. Lacan's comparison of Marcelle's writings with 'a mode of writing that calls itself sur-realist' was direct. (Lacan, [1931b] in Lacan, [1932]1975 p. 379) Just as importantly, it was accompanied by a judgement that Marcelle's linguistic activity was 'staged elsewhere'. This judgement accorded with Breton's claim that the automatic phrases that had occurred to him 'became perceptible to the mind without its being possible to discover in them (without a rather elaborate analysis) a previous determination'. (Nadeau, p. 87) Lacan and Breton's views both imply that 'automatic' phenomena, be they artistic or pathological, derive from something (or come from somewhere) that is not perceptible or comprehensible to conscious-ness. Both views stress the linguistic constitution of such phenomena, which makes them irreducible to something organic or conceptual. Thus automatic phenomena aren't primarily of the body or of the conscious mind; they are originally linguistic and unconscious. More exactly, they derive from the unconscious *as it was discovered and described by Freud*.

Hysteria

Lacan and Breton's general appreciation of the richness and interpret-ability of automatism and their specific association of it with both unconscious and linguistic phenomena can be traced back directly to the discoveries that led Freud to establish the first principles and practices of psychoanalysis. The scene of this discovery is the *other* one (apart from the scene of surrealism) that was mentioned above as having been both co-terminous with Lacan's youth and as having facilitated his involvement in psychoanalysis. The scene will be recounted now.

In 1885, having begun practising neurology in Vienna, Freud travelled to Paris to work with Jean Martin Charcot, one of the most influential neurologists of his own or indeed any age. Charcot had been treating and studying hysteria. His work would end up discrediting accepted conceptions of the condition, which took it to be sex-specific and crudely organic. Before Charcot, hysteria was commonly thought to be a female malady. The organ said to precipitate it was the womb, whose misalignment was often taken to be its cause (the root hyster is from the Greek *hustera* meaning 'womb').

Charcot challenged hysteria's sex-specificity. In other words he questioned the prejudice that it *is* a 'women's disease'. Freud later extended Charcot's questioning of sexual difference – as Lacan did – into an investigation of the boundaries of sex and gender differentiations *per se*. In other words he – and later Lacan – asked whether distinctions between 'male' and 'female' are biological and/or psychological and even whether they are absolute distinctions *at all*. (Freud, [1905a] 1984 and Lacan, [1972–3] 1998)

On the substantial point, however, Charcot didn't only overturn the idea that hysteria was sex-specific but also the presumption that it was *biological*. He reasoned that hysteria might not be 'of the womb'. It followed that it might not only not be 'female', but also not *organic*.

As indicated, such suggestions contradicted received medical opinion, which noted that hysterical symptoms beset their sufferers' bodies or bodily organs. Manifestations of hysteria included paralyses, often of limbs, extremities and the face. These same organs and others would often also be subject to contractions, convulsions and tremens. Yet although such symptoms, in their dramatic physicality, invited the imputation of an organic cause, others were more enigmatic. Some hysterics were periodically struck with anaesthesia, a condition of general insensitivity and unawareness. Others went into trances or they daydreamed or sleepwalked. All of *these* symptoms involved similar states – of insensibility, incomprehension, detachment or forgetfulness – that *weren't* just physical. They were *mental* disturbances – as well as physical ones. Charcot noticed an affinity between these and another disturbance of mentality: hypnosis. He began practising it on his patients. He then discovered that hypnosis of hysterical patients could both induce and relieve their symptoms including, remarkably, physical ones. So, for example, it could not only cause paralyses, but also alleviate or even eliminate them. Hypnosis, which is most obviously a mental alteration, could effect hysterics' mental *and* physical life.

Charcot reasoned that although hysteria is part-physical, it is sympathetic and similar to hypnosis, and thus might be not only mentally influenced but even mentally caused. Rather than residing in bodily matter (or substances or process) the cause of hysteria might be in *ideas*. In other words: hysteria might be *ideogenic*.

Bombshell

Around half a century later, Lacan took on a medical case that resembled some of those treated by Charcot. It took the form of a female patient who had suffered the trauma of a shell destroying her house while she was in it in June 1915. Lacan did not treat her until 1928 at which time he described her condition to the Société neurologique and wrote his presentation up in a medical journal. (Lacan, 1928, pp. 233–7) The patient had been trapped in her collapsed house after the bomb blast. She subsequently appeared paralysed, her upper body bent forward in a frozen pose that seemingly obliged her to sway from side to side when walking. It was because of this feature of her ailments that she was deemed to be suffering from abasia, a condition in which muscle control is lost during perambulation. Lacan's presentations were mostly restricted to a description of the patient's symptoms. These included behavioural disturbances as well as paralysis. This might have prompted him to diagnose hysteria. It didn't, or at least it didn't *then*. A few years later he reviewed the case again and revised his diagnosis. His revision took account of some of the discoveries made by Charcot. However, Lacan's revision was not prompted by him having just become exposed to Charcot's ideas, with which he had been familiar for some time, or to any increase in his estimation of these ideas. It was prompted by his growing appreciation of the work of the person who would make revolutionary use of Charcot's discovery: Freud. In order to show this, it's best to resume the story of the latter's development of the work of the former.

Application

Charcot's discoveries reminded Freud of ones made by a friend and colleague of his from Vienna, Joseph Breuer, who had also experimented with hypnotic treatment of hysterics. On his return from Paris Freud began to collaborate with Breuer in the development of analyses and treatments of hysteria. Between 1893 and 1895 the pair published a set of case histories and a theoretical paper that were not only to revolution-ise the treatment of hysteria and eventually neuroses in general, but also mark the birth of the new science and practice that was to facilitate this revolution: psychoanalysis.

Breuer's first involvement with the phenomena that were to lead to the development of psychoanalysis was in his treatment of a young woman named Bertha Pappenheim, who was pseudonymously referred to as Anna O in Breuer's account of her case. When Breuer first met Anna she had been nursing her seriously ill father and had developed an illness herself while doing so, the most marked early symptom of which was a severe cough. About four months after she had begun attending her father other symptoms developed including headaches, a squint and mild contractures. By the time of the period immediately following her father's death another four months or so later her illness worsened such that she was also suffering anaesthesias, paralyses and serious dysfunctions of sight and speech. She also fell into hypnotic states that Breuer noted with special interest. During these states Anna first of all told stories and then, as her condition intensified, had hallucinations, which she described as she was having them. Breuer observed that Anna's physical symptoms (her paralyses, paraesthesias, squints, etc.) as well as her 'mental' ones (dissociation, somnambulism, agitation etc.) were calmed or disappeared after these episodes. Anna was also aware of the therapeutic effect of verbalising her thoughts which she called the 'talking cure'. (Freud and Breuer, 1983 [1895], p. 83) Lacan was later to point out that Anna's monologues, which were many and complex, prefigured the standard psychoanalytic practice of ameliorating psychical conflicts by 'working through' difficult material. (Sem. 1, p. 20) He was also to repeatedly stress what Anna had implied about psychoanalysis: that its element is one of speech[9] and that deviations from this principle risk loss of its insights and therapeutic effectiveness.[10]

Not all of these theoretical and clinical implications were understood by Breuer (Lacan made a habit of retrospectively explaining and clarifying early psychoanalysts' ideas for them).[11] Yet many were *facilitated* by him.

Because he recognised the benefits that hypnotic states produced in Anna, Breuer began inducing as well as observing them in her. By doing so, and by continuing to encourage Anna to speak, he achieved some remarkable therapeutic improvements, which became all the more marked as Anna's speech began to reveal the origins of her illness. These became apparent as she began to relate earlier appearances of the manifestations of that illness. In doing so, her monologues became less preoccupied with the description of hallucinations or the production of fictions than with the detailed recollection of the appearance of her symptoms. These were generally traced backwards as Anna recalled earlier circumstances in which each symptom had occurred, arriving finally at the first one, the account of which often served to alleviate or remove its current occurrence. For example, Anna became repulsed by, and unable to drink, water. She traced her hydrophobia back through a recollection of a woman acquaintance in whose presence she had once felt dislike. This memory activated an earlier one, of the woman's dog being allowed to drink water from its mistress's glass. Once the origin of Anna's disgust of water had been identified, her hydrophobia disappeared. In a more dramatic and significant case, Anna traced the paralysis of her right arm to a disturbing incident that took place while she was nursing her father. One night, while doing so, she had fallen exhausted on a chair. Her right arm, which she had slung over the back of the chair, had 'gone to sleep'. Anna had done so too, but in the sense in which the term is conventionally meant, and lightly. In this half-asleep, half-awake state she hallucinated a black snake coming towards the wall to bite her father. She tried to fight the snake off but found her arm paralysed and, on inspection, transformed. More exactly, she saw her fingers as little snakes and the nails on them as tiny death's-heads. This memory, which would have delighted the surrealists, referred back to another that involved sight of a snake-shaped object, a bent branch, which seemed to have first occasioned paralysis of Anna's arm. The verbal recollection of this apparent first instance of paralysis and the telling or re-telling of its subsequent occurrences, contributed to the symptom's eventual disappearance. (Freud and Breuer, 1983[1895], pp. 83–94)

Diagnosis

In many respects, the condition of the war-traumatised patient treated by Lacan bore a striking resemblance to Anna's. The bombing of Lacan's patient's house had left her bent from the waist and swaying transversally but stiff-backed, in an attitude of 'pseudo-contracture'. This symptom was effectively a sort of paralysis, like the ones that troubled Anna's extremities. Indeed, the bomb-traumatised patient had a frozen right arm and walked on tiptoes, as if _her_ extremities were paralysed. She was also tortured, as Anna was, by voices, visions, 'auditory hallucinations' and 'waking dreams'. When Lacan first reported on her state as a young intern in 1928, he could have taken it to be a case of hysteria as identified by Freud. He also might have recommended that it be treated psychoanalytically and in a way that had by then been prescribed by Freud, whose 'science of the mind' was being practised in a small-scale but influential way in Western Europe. Yet in 1928 Lacan was training – and identified himself – as a psychiatrist rather than as a psychoanalyst. The psychiatric institutions he worked and learned in were respectable but conservative and chauvinistic. They treated psychoanalysis as a fashionable, foreign and questionable pseudo-medical practice that was experimental, far from proven and antipathetic to the French sensibility and psyche. (Roudinesco, 1997, p. 21–2) It's thus not surprising that Lacan first saw his war-damaged patient's condition as _physical_ rather than as psychical and thus not as hysterical in the Freudian sense. In this regard he followed early twentieth-century psychiatric (rather than psychoanalytic) protocols that took the origin and aetiology of 'mental' disturbance to be organic. It's true that Lacan specifically saw his patient's condition as being neurological and that this corresponded with Freud's _general_ orientation (Freud was a neurologist by training and profession). Yet in 1928 Lacan mostly accepted the opinion of his teachers, who were members of the French medical establishment. They saw the kind of dysfunction at issue not only as neurological but also as _fundamentally_ organic and _probably_ hereditary, since this was what 'nervous illness' was taken by them to be. Unlike Freud, whose 'Germanic' innovations they mistrusted, they didn't accept that neurological (and hence psychological) functions could be significantly influenced by non-organic phenomena like psychical trauma which was seen by them as a symptom of mental illness rather than a cause of it. For both cultural and career reasons, Lacan respected and accepted this establishment view. It's thus no surprise that he first diagnosed his patient's ailments as abasiatic, that is as consequent on a loss of muscle control itself resultant from neurological deterioration that was organic in origin. Any psychical deterioration accompanying the condition was deemed to be secondary and to have had neuro-organic determinants too. (Lacan, 1928)

Yet Lacan's last word on the case wasn't spoken in 1928. He returned to it in 1933 as part of a general review of his work to date. By this time, his intellectual and institutional influences and affiliations had altered significantly. He had read Freud, begun to train as a psychoanalyst and begun to undergo psychoanalysis himself. His primary profession – which was still psychiatry in 1933 – had also begun to yield to more 'dynamic' and psychically-inflected theories of mental illness. Lacan had not only begun to accept such theories, but even to extend them and to regard Freud as a pioneer.

Thus when he reviewed his war-traumatised patient's case in 1933, he came to a very different conclusion about it than he had in 1928. He noted that her injuries weren't organically caused – at least not primarily or exclusively. The *physical* damage done to her by the bomb-blast was superficial. Her trauma had thus been of the sort explained by Freud and Breuer. It had been primarily *psychical* and had 'presented no neurological sign of organic origin'. In other words, it presented a 'problem of hysteria' in the sense that the term was understood in psychoanalytic theory. (Lacan, 1933c)

Birth

The mention of theory as well as practice above is apposite with reference to Freud's development as well as Lacan's. By 1895 Freud had provided a powerful explanation for and an effective treatment of hysteria. Yet he didn't just treat and give a clinical account of 'nervous illnesses' by discovering and showing that hysterical symptoms had ideogenic 'causes' (specifically – traumatic memories). He also inferred that such 'causes' were *hidden* by hysteria (and *in* hysteria). Crucially, he did this by way of speculation as well as observation and with reference to his own conceptualisations of mental functioning, for instance 'repression'. In other words, he provided a *theory* of hysteria as well as an explanation for it.

Furthermore, Freud didn't just seek to theorise the specifically pathological mechanisms of mental functioning. He sought to demonstrate the relation of such mechanisms to mental functioning in general. That he thought such relations exist and are worth investigating shows something significant about his approach to the mind. For him, psychopathological and normal mental states are not entirely distinct. The former are a sort of extension or perversion of the latter. Yet precisely because of this, both pathological and normal states are discernible in and basic to the mind and mental functioning.

One could put this more prosaically by saying that we are all 'a bit mad'. For example, we can all worry to the point of being 'a bit neurotic'. Types and signs of mental disturbance are apparent in all of us. This continuity between pathological and normal states means that psychopathological functioning bears something of normal mental functioning and vice versa. Thus Freud's theory of hysteria corresponded with and was developed alongside a general theory of the mind.[12] The conditions that Freud's patients presented with were various (neuroses, hypochondrias, hysterias, obsessions, perversions etc.) but all said something about normal as well as aberrant mental functioning and so all contributed to Freudian theory *in toto*. This theory identified crucial as well as general aspects of the mind. Two such crucial aspects are *repression* and the *unconscious*.

It's worth spending some time understanding these concepts and the relations between them, because they structure not only Freudian theory, but Lacanian theory too. According to Freud, the notions of the unconscious and repression are fundamental to the explanation of psychical functioning in particular and human life in general. Lacan repeatedly insisted on the importance of both concepts and he often cited Freud when he did so. For example, he acknowledged that the 'unconscious' is a strange word, but that 'Freud didn't find a better one, and there's no need to go back on it', not least because it's 'a very precise thing'. (Lacan, [1973] 1990, p. 5) So what is the unconscious according to Freud? How did he discover it and what does it have to do with repression? Understanding all of this, as well as understanding Lacan's repeated insistence on the importance of these notions means going back, as Lacan preferred, to Freud.

Theory

Although he had treated Anna between 1880 and 1882, Breuer's case history of her illness was not made available until 1895 when it was published in a book alongside other case histories written singly by himself or Freud. The book, *Studies in Hysteria,* also included two theoretical sections, one written by Breuer and one the republication of an earlier paper by Breuer and Freud. The dual-authored section has a long title which is usually referred to in an abbreviated form as 'The Preliminary Communication'.[13] It is a distillation of Freud and Breuer's discoveries about, insights into and theorisations of hysteria and related conditions. It draws on cases that they had treated since the early 1880s. Freud and Breuer describe hysteria in terms of a number of essential psychical phenomena and functions that subsist in pathological and normal mental states alike. As indicated above, the conceptualisations employed to explain these phenomena and functions include *the unconscious* and *repression*. Both became fundamental premises of Freudian – and by extension psychoanalytic – theory from 1895 on.

Before expounding Freud and Breuer's theory of hysteria *per se*, it's worth re-emphasising the influence of both this theory and Freud's *general* theory of the mind on Lacan. This influence was increasing and long-term. As noted, Lacan first took Freud seriously in the late 1920s, before and during his revised analysis of his abasiatic war-traumatised patient. He engaged with the Freudian theorisation of hysteria again in the first two years of his 'Seminar' (1953–4 and 1954–5) which examined Freud's technical writing and his notion of the ego respectively.[14] He did the same in an even fuller and subtler way in the 1970s in the context of his consideration of female sexuality. (Lacan, [1972–3] 1999, esp. ch.6) *Between* the 1920s and the 1970s he raised the question of hysteria in other contexts, usually recalling what Freud had said about it and assessing what this meant for psychoanalytic theory. His comments often invoked specifically Freudian conceptualisations of the unconscious and repression. In fact, Lacan nearly always cross-referenced his own psychoanalytic investigations, discoveries and explications with Freudian theory (and of course practice).

This all signals *Lacan's Freudianism* ably enough. It also warrants the exposition of the Freudian theorisation of hysteria that follows immediately here.

In 'The Preliminary Communication' Freud and Breuer asserted that hysteria is 'caused' – or more accurately precipitated – by trauma. Though many of the manifestations of hysteria are physical, this precipitation is not organically endogenous; it does not originate in the body of the individual beset by it.[15] In other words it has its origin in something *external* to (or at least other than) the body of the traumatised subject. This something is hence not *biologically* determinative of the disturbance that it effects. The example of one of Anna's symptoms having been set off by the sight of a dog drinking from her acquaintance's glass demonstrates this. The event was 'external' to Anna, yet it activated her hysteria.

Thus what precipitates hysteria is traumatic but does not come from within the body of the hysteric as organic illness does. It is not caused virally, or by heredity, or gynecologically. Neither is it exactly something that is *visited upon* the body, as physical accidents are. In fact, what is *decisive* in hysteria is not really physical at all. Freud and Breuer cited the *precise* origin of hysteria as *mnemic*. According to them, it is not just trauma, but the *memory* of trauma that activates hysteria. This is once again apparent in the example given above. Anna's hydrophobia was not exactly 'caused' by seeing her acquaintance's dog drink from her glass so much as set off by a *memory* having been formed of this event and by this memory continuing to have an effect. *Memory* of trauma both activates hysteria and sustains it. To sum up: hysteria depends upon both *the formation* and *the persistence of a memory of trauma*. This memory can be *associated* with a physical event but is not physical *in itself*.

Once one knows that hysteria is not only precipitated but also maintained by traumatic memory, one can infer something significant about its mechanics. In order to be able to sustain it, the reminiscence that underlies and 'drives' hysteria has to be charged with energy that 'fuels' its symptoms. In other words it has to be 'cathected'. This is what keeps the symptoms that are activated by traumatic memory alive.

Practice

Now this account of the aetiology of hysteria is rather abstract and although it accords with the theoretical account of it provided by Freud, it doesn't say much about the hysteric's experience of the condition, or the (normal and abnormal) phenomena that Freud observed in his consulting room that led him to be able to theorise it. Freud made some general clinical observations about hysteria in 'The Preliminary Communication' too. He observed that when someone has a traumatic experience they form an image of it that will be emotionally charged (this charge is the 'cathexis' mentioned above). The charge can be expelled by way of an emotional response, for example by weeping or becoming aggressive. The technical term for this is 'abreaction'. Clear examples of it can be seen in rage-fuelled public altercations (such as arguments over accidents like 'road rage') or in unmediated mournful responses to the death of a loved one ('weeping and wailing', 'breaking down' etc.). Now for all sorts of real-world and/or psychical reasons, such abreactions might not happen. The emotion associated with the trauma may be too painful to experience 'in the raw' (not everyone is willing and able fully and immediately to vent their feelings). In such cases, the traumatic memory is likely to remain cathected, or 'charged'.

Roughly speaking, a cathected traumatic memory can have two sorts of fates. If it remains un-abreacted, it will start to cause and fuel hysterical symptoms in the person whose memory it is in. Alternatively, this person might begin to talk about (or around) the memory in question. In that case the memory might be abreacted (however slowly) and might not cause, or continue to cause, symptoms. (Freud and Breuer, [1895] (1984), p. 83)

In any case talking about a traumatic memory will tend to de-cathect it, deplete the energy active in it that fuels symptoms and lead to those symptoms' diminution or disappearance. Not talking about a traumatic memory will often leave it free to continue to feed symptoms, which will thereby persist. It almost goes without saying that it was these clinical discoveries that led Freud to begin to develop psychoanalytic *practice*. He (and Breuer) encouraged their patients to *speak*, to track their own associations with such speech, to speak about these too and to repeat this process in a way that might lead back to and uncover the roots of symptoms in traumatic memories (as Breuer did with Anna O). As well as uncovering such memories, such speech would de-cathect them, that is flush out the emotional energy that sustained both them and symptoms.

Thus Freud and Breuer's discoveries in relation to hysteria had theoretical *and* clinical implications and the latter as well as the former had significant effects on Lacan. It was Freud and Breuer's remarks about the therapeutic effect of talking that would lead Lacan to stress the distinctly psychoanalytic point that it is in *speech* that the hysteric bears her suffering. Her recourse to the ameliorative function of 'language' permits her to 'sustain' her condition in an articulated form rather than an unsustainable symptomatic one. (Lacan, [1964a] 1987, p. 12) This is of course similar to saying that the hysteric's best way of dealing with her symptoms is to talk them out. Although Lacan's formulation of the hysteric's condition is not identical with Freud's here (this particular issue will be addressed shortly) it does significantly concur with it in making language the sole and primary means of the symbolisation and effective therapy of hysteria. Furthermore, Lacan stressed that it was through careful attention to the hysteric's 'language' that Freud 'discovered the mechanisms of the unconscious'. (Lacan, [1964a] 1987, p. 12) This discovery was a gradual and complex one and it had a profound effect on Lacan's thinking.

Occlusion

At first, Freud and Breuer thought of hysteria as a sort of 'schizoid' state. Their patients' conditions alternated between states of relative normality and states in which hysterical symptoms were more dramatically apparent. For example, some of Anna's symptoms (like her paralyses or her coughing) were continuous but in a passive or low-level way during the daytime, while others (hallucinations, convulsions, 'absences', 'speaking in tongues', somnambulism or phantasies) would appear or worsen during the evening or at night. (Freud and Breuer, [1895] 1984, pp. 73–83) This led Freud and Breuer to think that hysterics periodically get into a distinctly hysterical state (in which all or more of their symptoms were manifest and intense) and that this state alternated in them with another one of relative normality (in which fewer of their symptoms were apparent but less dramatic). Unsurprisingly, the two doctors became preoccupied with the more 'hysterical' state. They reasoned that if a hysterical state was caused by a traumatic memory, then the memory must be active in that state. Yet their problem was that it was not to be seen there. More exactly traumatic memories are *invisible* or *hidden* or *occluded* in hysteria. For instance, Anna's hydrophobia was a symptom of a disgusting memory. Yet it didn't *reveal* that memory, at least not directly.[16] Now if we allow that Anna was conscious (or at least mostly or partly conscious) in her hysterical states (as well as her less hysterical ones) then it's clear that the causes of those states – specifically the traumatic memories that set them off – *weren't* conscious, that is they weren't immediately apparent to Anna (or for that matter her doctors). Yet they *were* in and active in Anna's state and mind (or state of mind). In other words, the traumatic memories that were at the root of Anna's illness and symptoms were *unconscious*.

Specificity

It was only a short step from this for Freud and Breuer to speculate that there is an 'unconscious' area of the mind in which traumatic memories reside. This 'topographic' description of the unconscious allowed it to be designated not just adjectivally but as a noun, that is as *the* unconscious. Thus unconscious phenomena are present and active in the unconscious. This claim might seem unremarkable (even tautological). After all, philosophers and psychologists recognised the existence of an unconscious mind long before Freud did. Yet it's important to note that the Freudian unconscious is not the same as the unconscious as it has been (and is) largely understood by non-psychoanalytic experts (and by non-experts too). When such people refer to the unconscious, they often mean that region of the mind which contains phenomena which might currently not be conscious, but that might be accessible with ease or with a slight effort of concentration. One might not currently recall what one had for breakfast, or the name of a holiday location one visited a few years ago. Yet these facts are retrievable because they are in one's mind even though they are currently absent from one's consciousness. They are 'unconscious' in the normal sense. By contrast, what is in the Freudian unconscious is largely *in*accessible. The hysteric is not aware that her symptoms are the consequence of a traumatic memory. She is not even aware of the *existence* of such a memory. If she seeks to retrieve it (or any trace of the real cause of her condition) she will probably not find it, or at least not recognise it for what it is. This is because it is actively kept away from her consciousness. This not only means it is 'unconscious' in the Freudian sense, it also means that it is 'repressed'.

Dynamism

Thus observation of the effects of and speculation about unconscious phenomena led Breuer and Freud to uncover another key psychical phenomenon: 'repression'. They had discovered both a force and a concept. Freud continued to expound both as he formalised his clinical discoveries and conclusions as metapsychology in the early twentieth century.

Traumatic memories – or indeed any uncomfortable and psychically charged phenomena – are inimical to consciousness for all sorts of reasons. For example they disturb one (as memories of an accident or death might) or one doesn't like to think of oneself as having experienced them (for example when they are sexual and thus uncomfortable – as most sexual or sexualised experiences would have been for Freud's turn-of-the-century Viennese bourgeois female patients). Thus such phenomena are *unconsciously repressed*, that is *actively and dynamically* kept away from consciousness by a force that is *not* conscious.[17] The Freudian unconscious and repression are thus fundamentally linked, or as Freud put it they are 'correlated' to a 'very great degree'. (Freud, [1915a] 1984, p. 147)

Lacan eventually and completely accepted this link. For him – increasingly and from the late 1930s onwards – the Freudian unconscious is differentiated from the unconscious in general and is so because it is *other than* consciousness. It is maintained as such by the 'discharge' that 'repression' ejects into it. Thus the Lacanian unconscious conforms to the Freudian unconscious in fundamental respects. It is both inscrutable and dynamically kept away from consciousness by repression. (Lacan, [1964a] 1987)

It's worth noting that many of Freud's refinements of the notion of the unconscious and the process of repression have clear equivalents in Lacanian theory too. Freud eventually offered a more differentiated theoretical account of unconscious and pathological repression than the one provided in the preliminary communication. According to this account, traumatic memories – or otherwise over-cathected phenomena – are not *simply* repressed into and maintained in the unconscious by the disturbed subject. Specifically, it is only the traumatic (or disturbed) *idea* (or memory) that is sent and kept there. The affects associated with the idea (crudely, the traumatic feelings) are displaced onto the (typically hysterical) symptom.[18] Lacan claimed that his own theorisation of psychical function was in specific accord with Freud's on all of these points:

> I insisted on the fact that Freud emphasises that it is not the affect that is repressed. The affect...goes off somewhere else...what is repressed is not the represented of desire...but the *representative*. (Lacan, [1964a] 1987, p. 217)

Freudianism

Lacan's exposure to Freudian ideas was critical. It part-bypassed the ambivalences and impasses of his youthful development (or non-development) and set him off in a singular direction: that of psychoanalysis. From the early 1930s onwards, Lacan increasingly identified himself as a psychoanalyst (rather than as a psychiatrist, psychologist or a philosopher) and declared himself a Freudian.

Yet it has to be said that both Lacan's assumption of the role of analyst and his identification with Freud may have amounted to the assumption of an identity that, in psychoanalytic terms, was *egoistic*. That is to say that as well as having a unifying purpose, the said identity may have had a *dissimulative* and *defensive* one. More exactly, Lacan may have felt the need to assert that he was a single thing (a Freudian analyst) because he wasn't, exactly. In that case his Freudianism would have partly been a kind of act, imposture or performance, seeming to confer an integrity on his being that in reality it lacked. It's been shown that Lacan was enormously ambivalent about what he wanted to be (a philosopher, a doctor, a politician etc.). What if he chose to become something that seemed to assimilate all of these roles and even trumped them: a psychoanalyst, *the* psychoanalyst, Freud's heir? If this is the sort of thing that Lacan was doing, he wasn't the first. The idea that one might be an 'alpha-analyst' and that this might involve assimilation of all sorts of other professional and intellectual identities or roles (including anthropologist, linguist and philosopher as well as scientist and medic) was pioneered by Freud.[19] Wasn't Lacan just following his lead? Wasn't he, by accommodating so many different identities, just being a good Freudian?

This is a key question and it touches on one of the main issues that this book is grappling with, which has to do with whether Lacan's 'identity' was coherent. He was obviously multiply divided in significant ways. This means his desire was multiform and divided too. Was his choice to become an influential analyst – and to so strongly identify with Freud in doing so – a way of channelling his multiply identarian desire in the service of one supra-identarian form: the 'Superanalyst'? Might this not have been a good thing? Wasn't Lacan, the 'genius', the 'legatee', the leader of a psychoanalytic 'movement' and the worthy inheritor of Freud's mantle? A lot of Lacanians obviously think so. On the other hand, wasn't he just split and wasn't his desire to be a renaissance man, a great leader and a 'container of multitudes' a complex denial of his split personality and the fact that his conflicts were tearing him apart?[20]

To speculate about Lacan's motives – and about Lacan – in this way is to get a little ahead of the game. Yet the general proposition that his confident assumption of a secure identity (that is his identification of himself as a Freudian analyst) might be *questionable* and the particular suggestion that it might belie a more *fragmented* identity are of course not outrageous ones from a psychoanalytic point of view. During the period that roughly covered Lacan's medical and psychoanalytic training, both Anna Freud and Melanie Klein wrote different but comparable texts that showed that the ego's *apparent* integrity is a sham.[21] To assume or assert that 'I am this' is to repudiate or forget that 'I am (also) that' and is to do so for defensive reasons. Even Lacan himself proposed that the ego's self-identification (its constitution and view of itself) is illusory (even delusional) and that its seeming 'identity' is a sort of 'narcissism' that represses the many and more genuinely 'diversified images' that the 'self' properly contains. (Lacan, [1954–5] 1988, pp. 166–7)

Duplication

In any case, the psychoanalytic identity assumed by Lacan in the 1930s can be seen to have been split in a number of ways. Indeed, this chapter has been implicitly indicating what *one* of these splits was and consequently what *two* associated but conflicting strands of Lacan's identity were.

It's already been shown that Lacan's early information about psychoanalysis came from *two* sources: Freud's writing and Breton's surrealism. Lacan admired and identified with *both* phenomena. Yet his reasons for identification were *different* in each case, just as the sources themselves were. The differences in question correspond to the splits in Lacan's psychoanalytic identity.

Freud, of course, was a doctor. He had studied medicine at a highly reputable university (Vienna) and had originally developed psychoanalysis as a branch of neurology, which he practised throughout his life. For him, psychoanalysis was *ultimately* scientific. He hoped to show that the psyche obeys certain principles and laws, ones that are equivalent or even reducible to the laws of nature. For example, he saw the psyche as *dynamic*, just as organisms that live and die are. In other words he held that both psyches and organisms do what they do and are what they are because of the increasing or decreasing flow of energy through them (this is what causes them to grow, develop, decline and die). Psyches and organisms suppress and express aspects of what they are *energetically*. Furthermore, he held that psychical laws – and also their transgressions and aberrations (which account for *pathological* psychical phenomena) – are empirically observable and rationally understandable.

Freud observed all of these principles and laws in operation in his consulting room and reasoned about them in his theories. In other words he was a man of science, specifically an empirical and a rationalistic one. He was identifiably a figure of late Enlightenment scientism.

Of course, Freud wasn't just reducible to the figure he's just been described as and this fact isn't unimportant. His theories described perverse behaviours (sexual as well as hysterical ones) and irrational dimensions of the mind (for example the unconscious and later, the id). It's well known that Freud's theories were (and still are) controversial, both for their content (which was violent as well as sexual) and their argumentation (which has always seemed unscientific to some scientists). Still, Freud's ultimate aim was to wrest rational explanations of psychical (and psycho-physical) phenomena from their apparently irrational manifestations in mental illness. These explanations were ultimately to have a therapeutic effect for his patients and to return them to a state of 'normality'. Freud's lifestyle and personal values reflected this aim. In them all, he was conformist, bourgeois and conservative.

Lacan's life and aspirations reflected Freud's in many ways. As shown, his immediate family background was bourgeois. He pursued his ambitions as a career (rather than, say, an artistic enterprise). His broad career track (medicine) was conventional and respectable and the education that led him to it was too. He respected the classical medical tradition and cited it frequently and approvingly, even when he was turning it on its head. While he was training, his conservatism and career mindedness were especially apparent in his engagement with his primary discipline: psychiatry.

Some of Lacan's co-trainees (notably Henri Ey) immediately took to its liberal form: 'dynamic psychiatry'. By the 1920s, this practice included relaxed and open-ended therapies for patients in asylums. Dynamic treatments were benign and patients were regarded with sympathy and respect. By contrast, the young Lacan recommended strict disciplining of any 'protestation' or rebelliousness on the part of mental patients, whatever form it took. (Lacan, [1931a] 1988, pp. 437–45) His view had softened by the time he was writing his doctoral thesis when he was critical of incarceration of patients in prison. Yet even then he continued to favour the confinement – even the solitary confinement – of the 'criminally insane' in asylums. Where their re-adaption to conventional, respectable society seemed difficult, he recommended their isolation from it. (Lacan, [1932] 1975, Part III) In all of these respects his early attitude to mental disturbance was conservative if not reactionary and was at least as authoritarian as Freud's. In any case and in general, he initially shared Freud's conventional medical sense that psychical disturbances were *problems* to be eliminated, or isolated and contained, for the good of individuals and societies both.

Reduplication

Yet Lacan's Freudianism also came from somewhere *other* than Freud; a key specific source of it was Breton, which means that an important general source of it was surrealism. Lacan's encounter with Breton and his collaboration with Dalí have been noted. The transmission of psychoanalytic ideas to Lacan via surrealism was not neutral. Surrealism wasn't just a passive *conductor* of such ideas; it had its own agenda. Because the ends of surrealism were different from those of Freudian psychoanalysis *per se*, the latter was significantly altered in its adoption by the former. Thus Lacan's experience of psychoanalysis through surrealism was *mediated* by it and the psychoanalysis he adopted as a consequence was significantly, even *radically* different to psychoanalysis as Freud understood it. Because Lacan also embraced classical Freudianism (and did so in quite a conservative way), his Freudianism was split: it was conservative on the one hand and radical on the other. The phenomenon needs further explanation. This can be achieved by returning to the consideration of the origins and aims of surrealism and the matter of its engagement with psychoanalysis.

Radicalism

Surrealism had a *revolutionary* or radical aspect. The word 'radical' *comes from* the Latin word 'radic', or 'root'; the revolutionary aspect of Surrealism is evident at its source. The specifically historical source of surrealism was

Dada. The movement started by Tzara, Huelsenbeck and others was meant to shock and even destroy prevailing sensibilities. This meant attacking 'fine art' and the work of 'enculturation' that it did by promoting the values of the aristocracy, the church and the bourgeoisie. These were the groups that had, historically, commissioned, bought, owned and displayed such art, which consequently reflected their values. The bourgoisie – who were in the ascendancy in Europe in the early twentieth century – were a particular source of Dada ire. To the Dadaist they were cynical entrepreneurial or managerial exploiters of the working-classes, who maintained their power through the ideological exercise of convention along with participation in and manipulation of the agencies of state control: government, education, law. The artworks that they bought and/or commissioned – whether they were neo-classical allegories or self-portraits – reflected their self-regard, conservatism and hierarchical sensibilities. The galleries and parlours in which their art was displayed guaranteed its aesthetic and financial value and confirmed its social status. Thus 'fine art' was often paid for (and was sometimes even produced) by those whose values, power, dictates and taste it reflected: the bourgeoisie. Bourgeois art and the galleries in which it was presented became prime targets of Dada attack.

Dada 'anti-art' assaults were often carried out with little or no subtlety. At an exhibition at the Galerie Dada in Zurich in March 1917, Tzara openly and repeatedly insulted visitors. At the same gallery in May, Hugo Ball's incomprehensible sound poems were delivered to an audience so aggressively as to cause them to revolt. These sorts of provocations and responses had been common at earlier performance events organised by Ball and other Dadaists in the guise of the 'Cabaret Voltaire'. (Richter, pp. 18–28; 39–44) Of course, Dada actions weren't always straightfor- wardly or obviously *destructive*. This was even true about art that the Dadists *constructed*. The artist and photographer Man Ray attached a photograph of a human eye to the pendulum of a metronome. He called his work 'Object to be Destroyed'. A gallery-goer took him at his word and shot a version of it to pieces.[22]

Since its birth by his hand Breton saw surrealism as a continuation – more exactly a development – of Dada. This meant maintenance of its 'radical' ethos. Breton not only remembered his Dada roots, but also followed the Dadaist practice of 'uprooting' convention. He was a self-proclaimed 'revolutionary' in both art and politics. His aim was explicit and dogmatic throughout the 1920s and into the early 1930s, during which he founded journals entitled *La Révolution surréaliste* and *Le Surréalisme au service de la révolution*. (Nadeau, p. 185) Sometimes the revolution that

Breton advocated was social, sometimes it was artistic and often it was both. The period in which he was most stridently seditious was the one in which surrealism had its most direct and lasting effect on Lacan.

Although Surrealism's radicalism made it an heir to Dada, it was not exactly the same. Surrealism's aesthetic means were different, as were its points of political identification. The Surrealists were also writers rather than artists, so their output was self-consciously 'poetic'. Although they were not above committing aggressive or theatrical 'acts' (Benjamin Péret's habit of shouting at clerics is an obvious example) they often preferred literary and/or graphic interventions to performative ones.[23] Specifically, they more often collaborated on poems, journals, novels and pamphlets than 'performances' or 'actions'. Because it was 'written' rather than 'acted', surrealism's programme was more intellectual and thought through than Dada's. The surrealists more *explicitly and critically* questioned intellectual as well as cultural and political tendencies. Key among these tendencies was *reason,* which they abhorred quite as much as capitalism. Breton had come to be suspicious of reason by reading Marx as well as Freud. Lacan – following Breton following Marx and Freud – suspected reason too.

As many communists did and do, Breton believed Marx's claim that capitalism is produced and sustained by ideology. For him, as for Marx, ideology amounts to a representation of existence that makes apparent sense, but that only does so by concealing gaps and contradictions in the logic and functioning of capital. For example, a late nineteenth or early twentieth century factory worker who was working twelve hours a day five days a week and whose family subsisted in relative poverty and poor health might nevertheless accept that this was 'the way things are' even though 'life is hard', because 'that's life' and because 'nothing can be done about it'. He would also, importantly, be accepting that this state of affairs is 'real', that is a consequence of an immutable 'reality' that had to be come to terms with. In doing all of this, he would be deferring to the dictates of an ideology that covers over the truth of his situation. This truth – were it uncovered – would reveal that the worker concerned was being employed by someone who was overworking and underpaying him and who was thus profiting financially from his exploitation.

Now what makes the representation of the worker's situation as 'the way things are' ideological is that it occludes the truth of exploitation. This truth, if revealed, would *contradict* the account that obscures it. Ideology (ironically) obscures truth in order to *make sense* (or, once again, to *appear* to make sense). If it doesn't conceal the truth at the heart of it, ideology becomes contradictory and 'the way things are' starts to look like the way things aren't.

Two important conclusions can be drawn from this account of ideology. These conclusions may seem at odds, but in fact they are complementary and the latter can even be inferred from the former. First, ideology conceals truth. Secondly, it does so in order to 'make sense'. (Marx and Engels, [146–7] 1999, pp. 39–64)

Breton understood all of this. He also knew that there are correspondences between Marx's account of ideology and the Freudian account of psychical functioning. Lacan was also aware of these correspondences and pointed them out intermittently throughout his career. For example he noted that what is discoverable 'clinically' in psychoanalytic practice is a 'material...truth' which depends for its disclosure on a 'reversal' of the one that the patient initially holds to. The revelation of this truth corresponds with the ones that can be found in 'Marx's political writings'. (ES pp. 235, 368)

Yet the correspondences between Marx's ideas and Freud's are not decisive. They do not reveal any fundamental concordance between the two men's philosophies. Freud wasn't primarily a radical. Yet when Lacan inherited psychoanalytic thinking from the surrealists he inherited a Marxist sensibility with it. It possible to see how this sensibility took root (in both the surrealists and Lacan) yet it's important to note that *it wasn't Freud's*.

Still, Breton accepted Marx's argument that ideology, however dissimulative, is a kind of 'making sense' of things and concluded that is a crude if disingenuous kind of 'reason'. This 'reason' works in the interests of the bourgeoisie. It instructs the way bourgeois art is commissioned (by way of a rational judgement and an economic calculation), produced (by conventional means and with recognised skills) and understood (aesthetically). By contrast the revolutionary activity Breton advocated involved 'more awareness' of the world than 'ideology' permitted. This awareness was to be achieved 'beyond' reason in the 'poetic' products that access to the 'unconscious' allows.[24] Thus the surrealists celebrated the irrational in all of its forms and regarded doing so as a *revolutionary act*. Among the forms celebrated was hysteria, which Breton and Aragon described as 'the greatest poetic discovery of the Nineteenth Century'. They devoted a volume of *Le Surréalisme au service de la révolution* to it in 1928.

Of course Lacan developed his own interest in the irrational and the 'mad' products of it. This much is obvious in his fascination with Marcelle. As shown, this fascination was aware of and enthusiastic about its surrealistic parallel. Lacan and the Surrealists had a common interest in hysteria in particular and 'madness' in general and both he and they were absorbed by the same psychiatric cases in the early 1930s. They all discussed such cases and wrote about them in Surrealist journals. Sometimes interests were not just common between Lacan and the Surrealists, but interpersonal. What prompted the initial meeting between Lacan and Dalí in 1931 was their shared fascination with paranoia. (Dalí, 1949, p. 18; Roudinesco, 1990, p. 111) Lacan, always a voracious reader, had read Dalí's 'L'âne pourri' (The Rotting Donkey) in *Le Surréalisme au service de la révolution* and had also read other articles by him in other Surrealist journals. (Dalí 1930) He had been attracted by Dalí's idea that paranoia was 'pseudo-hallucinatory' and that it represented an alternative world for the paranoid subject, just as hallucinations do for the delusional one.

Dalí didn't just think that paranoid worlds differ from reality, he thought they actively contradict it. They represent a sort of 'criticism' of it that identifies and goes beyond its limitations and flaws. Dalí even claimed that paranoia does this because it has a perverse but rigorous 'logic'. (Dalí 1930) He was clearly following Breton's lead by suggesting that madness partook of a 'better' – or at least more 'perceptive' – reality 'beyond' reality as it is normally understood. This sur-reality was obviously represented in Dalí's paintings. More to the point, his claim about paranoia was very similar to one that Lacan made in his doctoral thesis. This was the claim that paranoia in particular (and even psychosis in general) can be understood in terms of the relation of its parts to each other, that is in terms of its total structure. This structure dictates its 'logic'. The action of the paranoid subject (or 'patient') will be instructed by such 'logic', even though s/he won't entirely know this. In order for the paranoid subject's 'illness' to make sense to her (or him) or even to her (or his) analyst (or 'doctor') its structure needs to be identified and understood. This is done through the relation of its elements to its whole. Lacan's argument generally conforms to Dalí's. For both men paranoia has a 'logic', which is subjective, structured and total. In another influential surrealist journal – *Minotaure* – Dalí wrote of Lacan that 'to his thesis, we are indebted for giving us, for the first time, a global and homogeneous idea of the [paranoid] phenomenon, beyond any of the abject notions in which psychiatry at present is mired.' (Dalí 1933)

Lacan published an article in the same surrealist journal in which Dalí praised him. In that article he stressed and repeated the assertions that significantly allied him with the surrealist cause. He said that madness is not best approached with reference to reality and that it is not best understood as involving any loss of a sense of that reality, or in terms of any 'insufficiency' in its 'function of relation with the world'. It is best understood in its own terms, which resemble linguistic ones. Lacan wrote of paranoia's 'original syntax' and the 'totality of the patient's lived experience', which that syntax indirectly but faithfully articulates. The decipherment of symptoms through the comprehension of paranoid syntax provides, he said, 'an indispensable introduction to comprehending the symbolic values of art'. In his first surrealist journal article Lacan was claiming that the psychoanalytic understanding of madness and the surrealistic approach to art are both anti-realistic and symbolically equivalent and are therefore, to a significant extent, the same. (Lacan, [1933a] 1988)

In the same article and just as radically, Lacan claimed that madness – even and especially when it involves criminal activity – is not best judged by rational moral means or by any general or specific 'penal code'. Even though the conception of madness has a 'juridical origin', it does not conform to reason or law, especially 'bourgeois' law. Lacan's point can be summed up as follows: madness is *defined* by convention – including and especially legal convention – but cannot accurately be *judged* by it. On this point, the surrealists couldn't have agreed with Lacan more.

Six months after the surrealists had published Lacan's article in *Minotaure*, they published another one. (Lacan, [1933b] 1988) This concerned the infamous crime and punishment of the Papin sisters, a pair of maids who killed their employer and her daughter on a February afternoon in 1933. The case attracted the attention of the national press, politicians, mental health professionals and writers (including, for example, Jean Genet, who based his 1947 play 'The Maids' on the Papin case). The sisters – Christine and Léa – had been assigned laundry duties while their mistresses – Mme and Genviève Lancelin – went shopping. A power failure had prevented them from completing these duties by the time their employers returned. Mme Lancelin scolded Christine for not having completed her work. Immediately Christine struck Mme Lancelin with a pewter pitcher. Genviève went to her mother's rescue, but received the same treatment. Christine then ordered Léa to set about Mme Lancelin and gouge out her eyes, which she expeditiously did. Genviève's left eye was then torn out by Christine. The two maids took a hammer and a knife to the Lancelins, braining and disembowelling them by turns. Once they had created enough carnage, the sisters bolted the front door, washed their hands, disposed of their soiled clothes and retired to the same bed together. The police found them huddled there together half an hour later.

The Papin case was obviously a dramatic and shocking one. It split public, professional and legal opinion. Most of the public abhorred the Papins' acts. A few psychiatrists, notably Benjamin Logre, pronounced the sisters mad and not responsible for their actions. Most others declared them sane – and hence responsible. Otherwise, they deemed them prone to psychical tendencies – like 'malingering' – that didn't mitigate their crime enough to render them innocent. It's no surprise that the case attracted the attention of the surrealists. Péret and Éluard cast the sisters as revolutionaries. Their act was apparently irrational but actually just. It violently overcame the rationalistic (and rationalised) power relations that kept the Papins as the Lancelins' slaves. The killing was also poetic, expressive of a primal revolutionary act that paid these peasant girls back for years of oppression by bourgeois employers. 'Six years in perfect submission, they endured criticism, demands, insults. Fear, fatigue and humiliation slowly gave birth within them to hatred, that very sweet liqueur which offers secret solace since it promises violence to grant it sooner or later physical force. When the day came, Léa and Christine paid evil back – in coins of red hot iron.'[25]

Lacan did not champion the Papin sisters as Péret and Éluard did. However, he effectively defended their actions by attributing a 'logic' to them that was beyond the sisters' wills. The atrocities they committed were caused by various tensions associated with their experiences and roles. Their experiences – which had included abandonment, exploitation, poverty and rape – had enraged them. When society had compelled them to assume subservient roles in which such rage couldn't be expressed, they had acted it out. More specifically, the 'delirium' that overcame them could be understood as 'a rational effort of the subject to explicate its experiences'. This effort was frustrated by the 'social tension' they felt because society demanded they adopt an 'ideal' of servitude. The tension between their 'social' oppression on the one hand and the 'repression' of their ire on the other was what led to their explosive act. The 'reasons' for this act were 'unconscious' when it was committed, but could be 'inferred psychoanalytically' after the (f)act.

Lacan was claiming that the Papins' 'crime' – though ostensibly irrational – was explicable and even rational. He was also saying that the explanations and reasons most appropriate to their 'act' were neither 'legal' nor 'moral'. They didn't accord with 'the punitive demands of public opinion' or 'the antique law regarding the crime of slaves'. (Lacan, [1933b] 1988) They conformed to a *pathology* of paranoid delusion. This was the same pathology that the surrealists attributed to societal oppression and mobilised in art.

Madness

A good amount of time and space has now been spent tracing the Freudian and surrealistic routes though which Lacan gained and developed his own psychoanalytic knowledge. There has been a simple and critical reason why this has been done. The routes concerned cross over, but they are also, in an important sense *distinct*. They represent significantly different interpretations and applications of psychoanalytic ideas.

It's true that Freud's ideas are richly interpretable (and therefore not entirely singular in their meaning and intent) but his own attitude towards and use of them was fairly clear and relatively unambiguous. Madness, he believed, is an illness to be treated if not cured. The aim of such treatment is to bring sick people back in touch with reality. This reality is a part-social reality, so successful treatment involves re-adaption to society and accommodation of social norms. Freud also believed that although madness is related to art, it is not the same as art. The latter is a human product; the former is a form of suffering. Thus madness is not inherently artistic and art is not a recipe for human happiness. Neither art nor madness are arguments for revolution. Freud wanted to treat his patients, he didn't want them to overthrow society, or even to provide a critique of it. He was a doctor in private practice and a social conservative.

In many respects, the young Lacan agreed with Freud. He saw madness as something to be treated and contained. He worked in institutions (like the Paris Préfecture de Police) that were designed to keep the public safe from mentally ill people. He thought that the latter should be confined and even punished when they misbehaved.

The surrealists, of course, were anti-establishment. They saw reason as a form of oppression and madness as a form of expression. For them, the irrational was poetic. Psychoanalysis was a means of appreciating and even encouraging madness and hence creativity. They also saw madness as a form of revolution. They did not believe that 'mad' people should be 'cured' or that they should adapt to society. They thought that society was the problem and that *it* should be changed by whatever means necessary. The surrealists '*Declaration of 27 January 1925*' asserted that 'We are specialists in Revolt. There is no means of action which we are not capable, when necessary, of employing.' (Nadeau, pp. 262–3) Breton made a call to violent revolution when he declared that 'The Simplest Surrealist act consists of dashing down into the street, pistol in hand, and firing blindly, as fast as you can pull the trigger, into the crowd.' (Breton, [1930] 1972, p. 125)

Like the surrealists, Lacan appreciated the 'irrationality' of madness, which he understood as its 'poetry'. He concluded that madness does have a 'logic', but it is not one that is in conformance with 'common sense', bourgeois ideology or any 'reality' that is understandable with reference to them.

In believing all of these things Lacan was effectively a surrealist. He was not a man of violence (at least not physical violence) but he was provocative and remained so throughout his life. In this sense he closely resembled Breton. Almost every article he wrote challenged some medical or philosophical presumption, just as every properly surrealist artwork challenges what conventionally 'makes sense'. Furthermore, he developed a style of writing – and later of speaking – that was dense, wilfully obscure and difficult to understand. His papers and lectures increasingly took on the appearance of surrealist performances. Much of the writing and the tiny amount of extant film of him that exists bears this out. People who experience it for the first time (and not only for the first time) are often utterly bemused by it. They don't understand what Lacan is saying, why he is saying it in such a convoluted and/or obscure manner and whether the eccentricity of his delivery is intentional (i.e. contrived) or involuntary (i.e. mad). Even if he didn't specifically see himself as an artist, Lacan saw himself as *avant-garde*. He aimed to make his audience *think differently* and shocked, baffled and confused them as a way of doing this. Overall, he was much more intentionally surrealistic than both his supporters and his critics have recognised. Yet this corresponded with an aspect of his approach that his supporters (at least) *have* recognised: he was a radical.

All of this is to make sense of Lacan and in some sense all of it does. Yet it also, obviously, points up a set of massive contradictions in the man and his ideas. Lacan was divided in all sorts of ways. He was strict Freudian and a surrealist, a social conservative with Marxist inclinations, a believer in social reform and social control, an appreciator of madness and a container of it, a scholar of medicine and a showman, a member of the establishment and of the avant-garde. In all significant respects (socially, politically, intellectually and psychologically) he was split. His splitting was not a folly of youth and did not diminish with development or age.

Duplicity

The paragraph above, which draws its conclusions from the long chapter
that precedes it, obviously represents 'Lacan' as multiply split. Yet it also
represents these splits in binary terms (conservative/Marxist; establish-
ment/avant-garde etc.). These terms disclose a *double* quality attributable
to Lacan. Yet taken together they also reflect his multiple personal,
intellectual, public, institutional and political investments and the multiple
splits that beset them. There is no contradiction between doubleness and
multiplicity here. One only needs to see the latter as the sum of more
than one instance of the former (Lacan's multiple splits comprise *all* the
bifurcations that beset him). This is an important point that has more than
logical and theoretical significance. Yet it's worth returning to the point
about Lacan's doubleness. Why is this so important?

One answer to this question is that thinking of Lacan *doubly* allows one
to identify his *duplicity*.

Lacan was concerned with *the truth*. He thought that psychoanalysis
should have the same concern and that its job (or as all analysts would
say, its 'work') was to do with revealing such truth. As the epigraph of this
book shows, he claimed to 'always speak the truth'. Yet as he also liked
to point out (and as Lacanians like to repeat) the truth is not 'simple' or
'whole'; one can't just assert it. By the same token, one can't just dismiss it
(or dismiss the significance of it).

A truth can't simply be absolute. If it were, it would apply everywhere
and there would be no possibility of falsity or error (because there would
be nowhere that the truth didn't hold or apply). In this case there would
be nothing to differentiate truth from and hence no way of telling what it
was. Two things follow from this, both of which are conditions of truth.
First, there needs to be falsity for there to be truth. Secondly (as stated
above) a truth can't simply be absolute.

What follows from all of *this?* When Lacan championed the truth – or
just as importantly 'told' the truth – it must have been credible at some
level. Yet this didn't mean that he was always consistent, or that he never
told lies.

This double-edged aspect of truth – that it can be genuine but also
questionable, is relevant to Lacan and his theories in more ways than one.
It is also pertinent to consideration of Lacan *himself*. He did tell the truth,
but he also often didn't.

Significant untruth did beset Lacan's life. This can be shown straightforwardly enough by returning to events and phenomena that have

already been part-described in this chapter: the personal and intellectual developments that Lacan underwent in the late 1920s and early 1930s.

Lacan completed his medical and psychiatric training in 1932. At the same time he began training as a psychoanalyst, a process that involved him undergoing psychoanalysis himself. He underwent psychoanalysis with Rudolph Loewenstein – a senior figure in the SPP. The analysis lasted about six years. During the course of it Lacan became an ordinary member of the SPP and began taking on patients himself (that is, he began practising as a psychoanalyst). None of this was unusual. There were, however, irregular and even highly questionable features of Lacan's training in general and his training analysis in particular. The first irregular feature had to do with Lacan's status and ambition during his training period. Although it is normal to seek to become an ordinary analyst during one's own training and analysis (as Lacan did) it is not (and never has been) normal to become a *training* analyst at that time. Lacan did seek this. He actively pursued a position as a *training analyst*, that is as a senior analyst in the institution he was training in. Having such a position would have meant that he would have had the same status as Loewenstein, the analyst who was training him. The second unusual feature of Lacan's psychoanalysis was that he didn't get on with his analyst. Now this is not in itself unprecedented. Patients don't always like their analysts (and vice versa). This is partly because their relation with them often involves a 'negative transference' of hostile feelings (from elsewhere) on to them. For example (and typically) a patient might 'transfer' his hatred of his father on to his analyst. In a successful analysis such hostile feelings are analysed, understood and dispelled in the course of treatment. This is called 'the dissolution of the transference'. Such dissolution *didn't* happen in Lacan's analysis by Loewenstein. Hostilities between the two men were not resolved. The analysis did not go well and it did not end well.

These two irregularities in Lacan's training analysis relate directly to an instance of duplicity that was both subsequent to and consequent on that analysis.

During the 1930s, Lacan's work was already being read, reviewed and discussed by a small Parisian intellectual coterie that included psychiatrists, psychoanalysts, artists, writers and philosophers. He had already gained some status as an exceptional thinker in both psychiatric and artistic worlds and as he entered the psychoanalytic one (which crossed over with the others) he made an impression there too. Yet this impression was not always a positive one. Lacan was known for being clever, but also perhaps for being too clever. Those who understood – or claimed to understand – him sometimes thought him brilliant. Yet his writing style and tone were obscure and high-handed. He was both dismissive and gnomic and sometimes savaged other thinkers – even whole disciplines – in a weirdly baroque way. For example in an early article he deemed 'institutional psychology' 'naive', 'bourgeois' and 'fabricated', but did so in a sentence that was so theoretically and syntactically complex that the charge could easily have been missed. (Lacan, [1933a] 1988 p. 4) Still, Lacan's precocity – some would say arrogance – *was* acted out by him and *wasn't* missed. He had a semi-public dispute with one of his professors, in which each accused the other of plagiarism.[26] In the small circle in which Lacan moved, this made him famous and infamous at the same time.

The role of training analysts in the SPP (not unusually) involved supervisory and teaching responsibilities as well as the analysis of other analysts in training. Lacan first applied for the role in 1936, when he was still undergoing his analysis with Loewenstein. Senior analysts who knew of Lacan (as many did) had become concerned about whether his ideas were compatible with the SPP's ethics, training programme and theoretical agenda. The training analyst appointing committee investigated both his work and his reputation. Because they were conservative in their views, they didn't fully understand either. However, they *did* end up worrying about the effect Lacan and his ideas would have on trainee analysts he might teach and supervise. They felt they had no way to control this influence. Their anxiety was naturally exacerbated by the knowledge that Lacan was still in analysis. He was seeking to train analysts – in an unpredictable way – when he still wasn't technically one himself.

There was one other serious problem with Lacan's application. Lacan's analyst Loewenstein was of the clear view that Lacan's analysis was incomplete and that he wasn't ready to become a training analyst. Lacan disagreed on both counts. In any case Loewenstein told the committee what he thought. After considering everything, they rejected Lacan's candidacy.

Lacan, typically, redoubled his efforts to apply. The position *was* eventually granted him in 1938, but not by unanimous agreement among the committee and not with the proper agreement of Loewenstein. Lacan's appointment came about as a result of him being the beneficiary of two deals: a political one and a personal one. Lacan didn't initiate the first deal, but he did take advantage of it. He was a party to the second one, which worked for him despite – and in fact because of – the fact that he reneged on it. It would not be inaccurate to say that Lacan engaged in double dealing.

The first deal was made among the committee of appointment and had to do with a historical and geopolitical situation that the SPP had found itself in. Throughout the 1930s, an increasing number of 'foreign' analysts were accepted by the appointing committee as training analysts. Their number had increased because more European Jewish psychoanalysts had begun to practice in Paris. Most were fleeing Nazism and some were quite senior in the psychoanalytic movement. Many were first and second generation analysts who had worked with Freud or his peers and their seniority and experience made them strong candidates for training analyst positions. Some of these analysts were appointed and quickly also made training analysts soon after they arrived in Paris (Loewenstein was one of these). Nationalistic French analysts complained. It was demanded that foreign appointments be replaced or offset by French ones. In this spirit the chauvinist Edouard Pichon supported Lacan's candidacy against that of Heinz Hartmann, an exiled Viennese Jew. To keep the political and institutional peace, the committee agreed both appointments. Yet this deal didn't meet Loewenstein's objection that Lacan was incompletely analysed and unfit as yet to be a trainer. In view of this an agreement was brokered, this time between Lacan and his analyst. Loewenstein agreed to recommend Lacan's appointment on condition that he continued his analysis after the appointment had been made. Lacan agreed and got appointed. He never returned to Loewenstein's couch. (Roudinesco, 1990, pp. 122–3 and 1997. pp. 69–87

Deficiency

By almost any measure, Lacan had been untruthful. He had promised to continue his analysis, but he had terminated it when he got what he wanted. Loewenstein, a much respected analyst, not only saw this as deceit, but also as reckless indulgence. 'One does not cheat on so important a point without dire consequences' he said. He not only deemed Lacan unanalysed, but (later) also claimed that his trainees were 'not analysed at all' either. (Roudinesco, 1990, p. 122).

If Loewenstein was right, the implications for much that Lacan subsequently did were profound. His duplicity and psychical immaturity would taint his career, relationships, ideas, institutional involvements and analyses. They would fatally complicate and limit his ability to be a good clinician, a thorough analytic trainer, a psychoanalytic pioneer, a man of intellectual integrity, the leader of a school and the inspiration of a movement. Loewenstein was saying that Lacan would not make a good analyst and that he was bad for psychoanalysis too. The fact that Lacanians – and not just Lacanians – would disagree with Loewenstein's charges might qualify them, but does not make them go away. They are no more subject to dissolution than the transference-relation was in Loewenstein's psychoanalysis of Lacan.

In view of this, it's not hard to see that Lacan's career-duplicity may have had an Oedipal cast, that it may have repeated the Oedipal conflicts that plagued his youth. Lacan had put his trust in an authority figure – Loewenstein – one who could not have helped being a paternal figure too. He had appeared – and probably initially intended – to return this trust in the hope that it would bring him what he desired: as much power as the 'father' he ostensibly trusted. He probably also desired – or even expected – eventually to exert more influence and fame than this 'father' would ever achieve. Yet in 'normal' Oedipal development the 'boy' does not accede to adulthood without loss. He gives up what he wants (the mother and the phantasy of absolute potency and satisfaction) in order to get something else (the 'other', incomplete love object and the possibility of a limited but realistic life). 'Normal' development was not something Lacan wanted or got. On the contrary, he desired and (in some sense) acquired everything, but did not do so without cost.

5

I and I

Decades

It was during the two decades between 1930 and 1950 that Lacan's adult life and work began to take shape. As suggested in previous chapters, he lived *various* (or *multiple*) lives (a number of these were *double lives*). Such lives involved *divisions* in and between the practices that took place in them, the institutions in which they were conducted, the appearances they gave rise to and the personae Lacan adopted in each case. Writing about all these divisions is no easy task. They are numerous but connected, discrete but homogenous and separate but implicated. It will take a while to show all of this clearly and rigorously.

One way to start exploring and explaining the divisions in Lacan's life (and lives) is to consider the different regions or *worlds* in which he operated. These could provisionally be 'categorised' as personal, professional and intellectual. During the decades covered in this and the next chapter, very significant changes took place in Lacan's life in each of these 'categories'. As indicated above, the changes were complicated by being multiple, contingent, related and conflicting both within categories and between them. Yet before this can be shown, the categories' particular contents need to be identified. This means registering what Lacan *was* and what he *did* professionally, intellectually and personally in the period at issue.

Professional

Lacan defended his doctoral thesis in 1932 (it was published in the same year). This meant he was qualified as a psychiatrist and was *almost* qualified to execute this role in state medical facilities. To attain this final privilege, he had to take a further examination, which he passed a few months after his thesis defence. Passing guaranteed Lacan a job in a state mental hospital, which he declined, preferring to expand his private practice, which already included psychoanalytic work. In order to continue with *this* in a registered and sanctioned manner, Lacan became a member of the SPP. As revealed in the last chapter he was only a member for six years before he manoeuvred himself into the position of training analyst.

Lacan networked vigorously with other French psychoanalysts, nearly all of whom were SPP members. Yet he also carried on associating professionally with psychiatrists and presenting his work (specifically his theories and case studies) in psychiatric (as well as psychoanalytic) fora. Intermittently, he courted academics, specifically philosophers, psychologists and psychiatrists who worked in universities full or part-time. For example, it was during the 1930s that his relatively well-known encounter and collaboration with the philosopher Alexandre Kojève took place. Through both that decade and the one that followed it, Lacan maintained his contacts with psychiatric, psychoanalytic, medical, psychological, philosophical contacts but also continued his associations with artists (including the Surrealists). In all cases he formed friendships as well as professional links with his Parisian peers.

Lacan's ambitions were never just local, or even national. He set about making international contacts, particularly in the psychoanalytic world. He wrote letters, collaborated on publications, met renowned analysts and spoke at conferences. Two such conferences provided platforms for key performances in his intellectual and public life. These were the IPA congresses in Marienbad, Czechoslovakia in 1936 and in Zurich, Switzerland in 1949. At these events Lacan delivered different versions of a paper about 'The Mirror Stage'. Both the notion and the paper would be closely associated with him for the rest of his life. 'The Mirror Stage' was triumphant, tragic and comic in equal measure. This is not only true of what the paper described, but also of Lacan's presentation of it to the IPA congress in Marienbad, which was an occasion, for him, of international exposure but also disappointment and farce. Lacan's second (and altered) presentation of the paper in Zurich was more of a success. It is the version of the paper that is well-known and influential. The two different presentations of 'The Mirror Stage' paper roughly bracket the historical period that is covered by this chapter: 1930s-50s. They will both be looked at in some detail.

Of course, during the decades just mentioned – and between the two congresses at which Lacan presented – a war broke out in Europe and France was occupied by German troops. Lacan's professional life both was and wasn't affected. Unlike some of his fellow countrymen (and women) he didn't collaborate with his occupiers. It's fair to note that in this case, he *wasn't* duplicitous. He acted in tandem and in good faith with the Société to which he belonged. Choosing inactivity over collaboration, the SPP ceased to function as an institution during the war. Like a number of his colleagues, Lacan discontinued his institutional activities (committee memberships, meetings, teaching etc.). He continued with privately arranged psychoanalyses, surviving on the meagre opportunities for psychoanalytic practice that wartime conditions allowed.

Intellectual

Lacan was no less active intellectually during the early part of his career. From his teens until the end of his life, he enthusiastically consumed and utilised others' ideas. He read voraciously. Because he moved in élite (psychiatric, psychoanalytic, artistic and academic) groups in which ideas were frequently discussed and exchanged, he was up-to-date with radical ideas and was informed about and responsive to the contingencies of intellectual fashion (which is why, obviously, he knew about and was interested in surrealism). Yet he was also well-read in and influenced by traditional and conventional medical – including psychiatric and psychological – thinking. It's worth mentioning which medico-psychological ideas – both traditional and fashionable – he was exposed to during his training and the early years of his practice. Unsurprisingly, these ideas sometimes conflicted with each other.

The psychological (as opposed to psychoanalytic) theories that were passed on to Lacan by his psychiatric teachers – particularly George Dumas – were mostly French and Cartesian in conception. They had often been sanctioned if not formulated by Pierre Janet, who had been Dumas' teacher. Janet was extremely influential, especially in France, where he had been a lecturer at the Sorbonne and the Collège de France throughout Lacan's youth. He had made discoveries about unconscious mental phenomena and processes that were not entirely dissimilar to Freud's and that had, in some cases, predated them. (Ellenburger, p. 182)

Technically, Janet was a psychologist rather than a psychiatrist. Lacan's teachers were psychiatrists. They taught him more specifically psychiatric ideas with reference to other figures like Paul Sérieux and Joseph Capgras, who had been most active and influential around the turn of the century. Both men were French. They met Lacan's teachers' preference for identifying their own compatriots as giants of their discipline. This chauvinism was entirely characteristic of French academic attitudes up until and including the early twentieth century. Yet psychiatry is a discipline that was pioneered by Germanic medics at least as much as by French ones. Lacan's teachers couldn't avoid having to teach him about the diagnostic and classificatory breakthroughs made by the likes of the Swiss Eugen Bleuler and the German Emil Kraeplin, who were Sérieux and Capgras' contemporaries. Lacan had become very open to influences from across the border by the mid-late 1920s in any case. By then he had developed a passion for Germanic ideas, as his fluency in German, study of German texts and enthusiastic pilgrimage to the Burghölzi clinic to acquaint himself with the practices of Bleuler and Jung demonstrated.

Indeed, among young intellectuals in Paris in the late 1920s and early 1930s Germanic ideas were *fashionable*. The larger effect of this other-national influence on French thought became evident in subsequent decades: the 1940s and 1950s. It was then manifest in a popular philosophical movement that came to be known as 'existentialism'. On account of this genealogy many people think of France as having been the intellectual 'home' of existentialism. They not only do so because of the weight of 'existential culture' that has emanated from that country but also because the French nationality of a famed philosopher associated with it: Jean Paul Sartre. Yet to think of existentialism as primarily or essentially or solely French is mistaken; to do so is to ignore – or to forget or repress – its German origins.

Existentialism hadn't been named as such in the late 1920s and early 1930s when Lacan was studying psychiatry. Yet he was aware of and engaged with some of the important ideas that *led* to it. This was precisely because, as mentioned, he was as enthusiastic about new intellectual trends as he was about established ones. Key among the proto-existential ideas that interested Lacan were *phenomenological* ones. Yet although his engagement with such ideas was enthusiastic, it was also indirect. He wasn't a philosopher, so he hadn't understood or even read the German philosophical texts that phenomenological (and later existential) ideas originated in (as, for example, Sartre had). Instead, his early interest in the relevant ideas came through the discipline whose texts he *was* reading in the late 1920s and early 1930s: psychiatry. He devoured the discipline's cutting-edge (as well as its approved) literature and it was thus that he became an enthusiast for 'dynamic psychiatry'. *This* movement absorbed phenomenological and (later) existential ideas and was the initial means by which Lacan drew on both.

The intellectual influences that came to Lacan in and through 'dynamic psychiatry' were *hybrid* ones. It thus makes sense, in the remainder of this section, to do three things. First: explain what dynamic psychiatry was;

secondly: to disclose the proto-existential, including the phenomenologi-cal aspect of it; thirdly, to show – in a general way – that Lacan adopted this aspect of dynamic psychiatry erratically and by combining it with yet other philosophical (and indeed psychoanalytic) ideas.

The term 'dynamic psychiatry' mostly refers to the non-organicist tendencies that have influenced psychiatry in Europe since the end of the nineteenth century. Broadly speaking, the movement takes account of psychical factors rather than physical ones in consideration of the cause and continuation of mental illness. Up until about the 1880s psychiatrists thought that such illness was 'caused' by bodily – most often neurological – breakdown of one sort or another. This breakdown might be hereditary (an inherited nervous illness or weak neurological constitution) or it might have an immediate organic cause (a nervous 'disease'). In any case mental breakdown was seen as the product of a physical infirmity, ailment or flaw. Dynamic psychiatrists abjured this view and concentrated on psychical processes. This meant looking at mental illness discretely, as a symptom of the functioning (or dysfunction) of the mind *itself*, rather than as a primary effect of physical malfunction. The approach took account of how a patient's illness might have been occasioned by what they had been forced to think, or how they had been made to feel – in other words what they had experienced and why this had led them to behave as they did. All this meant examining psychical processes rather than just physical effects. The processes might include reactions (for example fear or rage as reaction to a disturbing event) or repression or denial (forgetting or refusing to acknowledge an event and its emotional effect on one) or projection (erroneously or inaccurately blaming someone for one's own fault or misfortune). Because these phenomena involve psychical processes, they are *dynamic*. It follows that medical professionals who understood them in this way practised *dynamic psychiatry*.

Taking account of psychical dynamics is of course what Freud did. He showed that the psyche is a sort of energy system, in which psychical contents can be subject to particular fates by the forces that are or aren't exerted on them (ideas can be rendered unconscious by repression or can become conscious when this repression is lifted).[1] Thus dynamic psychiatry is broadly in line with discoveries made by Freud. A lot of Lacan's early psychiatric ideas were formed in the context of an increasing psychiatric acknowledgement – by him and others – of the importance of psychical dynamism. Thus the psychiatry he practised before during and after qualification was in broad conformance with the psychoanalysis that he read at that time and that he would practice in the decades to come.[2]

The above gloss reveals some of the specifically dynamic features of dynamic psychiatry. One can also identify other features of the approach that appealed to Lacan's particular intellectual sensibility. A particular Germanic and proto-existential approach adopted by some psychiatric dynamicists in the 1920s was *phenomenology*. *This* movement, like existentialism, was first pioneered by philosophers. It was *the* main precursor and contributor to existential philosophy *per se*. Like existentialism, it was transported into disciplines other than philosophy (for example literature as well as psychiatry) *after* having been pioneered philosophically. At first Lacan was not intellectually sophisticated or informed enough to know about or understand phenomenology's principles or origins. A small number of his academic contemporaries – *including* Sartre and Simone de Beauvoir – were. Lacan was aware of, but not *au fait* with, their researches. Instead, he came to phenomenology through psychiatric practitioners of it who did have some knowledge (including philosophical knowledge) of the field, like Ludwig Binswanger.

Lacan's adoption of phenomenology was not only mediated by psychiatry, but also extended in an unusual way. His 'take' on phenomenology was both abstract and ambiguous. This was especially marked in comparison with phenomenology's original philosophical formulation, which was strict, clear and rigorous. Anti-Lacanians – especially philosophical ones – would say that Lacanian phenomenology doesn't make sense. Lacanians, tellingly, don't refer to phenomenology much at all. The difficulty on both sides has to do with a use of phenomenology that is identifiable but eccentric.

In any case it was through phenomenology that Lacan's enthusiasm for philosophy was ignited. He began to engage with philosophical ideas in a more informed way in the mid-1930s. It was at that time that he attended the Paris seminars of Kojève, the Russian emigré philosopher. Kojève taught Lacan – and indeed a whole generation of young French intellectuals – about Hegel. His influence on Lacan's thought was extremely significant. Through Kojève, Lacan learned and adopted many of the ontological premises and arguments of Hegel's philosophy. These included claims about human evolution and development, subjectivity and intersubjectivity, unconsciousness and consciousness, conflict and recognition and need and desire.[3]

Lacan also encountered other major intellectual influences during the 1930s and 1940s. Principal among them was Henri Wallon, who gifted Lacan some of his key theoretical notions, including the mirror stage, the imaginary, the symbolic and the real. Lacan did acknowledge receipt of these extraordinary gifts, but did so – it has to be said – long after they had been received.

Personal

During the 1930s and 1940s Lacan obviously had a personal life as well as a professional and intellectual one. In fact, this life was relatively scandalous (or at least it would have been if it had been made public). Lacan married and then re-married. Before and between marriages he had lovers. He *wasn't* serially monogamous. Lacan was not only 'unfaithful' during his marriages, but before and between them as well. At all times he had primary 'partners' (married or not) *and* took 'mistresses'. One of the consequences of his complicated love life was that at one point he ended up with two families who knew little or nothing of each other. This fact alone – which clearly has psychoanalytic as well as moral significance – means that the story of Lacan's loves is worth re-telling for other than scandalous reasons. It is complex and revealing and obviously bears on the issue of his split constitution. Precisely *because* the story of Lacan's love life is a complex one, it's best to relate it at more length both in this and following chapters.

Thus all three categories of Lacan's life in the 1930s and 1940s mentioned above (professional, intellectual, personal) warrant more attention and examination. They will get such treatment in what follows, in which they will be dealt with alternately but within the context of a roughly historical account of what happened to Lacan during the decades concerned. This task can be begun by returning to a more detailed consideration of his intellectual development (which will focus on an aspect of Lacan's influences that has yet been underappreciated by commentators on his work: phenomenology).

Art

It was pointed out in the last chapter that Lacan understood Marcelle's symptoms and the symptoms of his abasiatic patient in a recognisably psychoanalytic fashion. In both cases he paid attention to the 'associative' rather than the literal qualities of symptoms. The paralyses of the abasiatic patient were not physical injuries as such. Although she had been caught in an explosion and briefly trapped under rubble, she had not broken any bones or suffered any long-term physical damage as a direct result of the blast. Her subsequent ailments had been occasioned by psychical rather than by physical trauma. The paralyses that tormented her were a *symbol* of this trauma. They were unconsciously *associated* with it rather than physically caused by it. This is why Lacan deemed her hysterical in the sense that the term would have been used by Freud. His treatment of Marcelle was similar. Her symptoms were also not viewed by him as direct results of organic (specifically neurological) infirmity or deterioration. On the contrary, he analysed her writing with a view to understanding its literary effects: its syntax, use of grammar, figures (such as metaphor and ellipsis) and symbols (such as ones of divinity and authority). Marcelle's delusions were a *symbolisation* of a trauma they indirectly expressed rather than an effect of neurological dysfunction. Thus the *symbolic* aspects of the symptoms of both Marcelle and the abasiatic patient allowed Lacan to discern the meaning or purpose – rather than the organic 'cause' – of each.

The specific phenomena analysed by Lacan in such cases, being symbolic, are arguably as *literary* or *artistic* as they are scientific. Lacan knew this. What's more, in valuing aesthetic effects and explanations alongside 'medical' ones, he was following Freud. It's fairly well known that Freud said: 'The poets and philosophers before me discovered the unconscious. What I discovered was the scientific method by which the unconscious can be studied.'[4] Some scientists have questioned whether Freud's method really is scientific, but no one doubts that it bears an appreciation of the arts and humanities and that it finds artistic, quasi-artistic, literary and quasi-literary phenomena among its pathological objects. It accordingly utilizes art-critical and literary-critical means to explore and make sense of the psyche. Lacan, like Freud was preoccupied with literature and language in general and the literary language of madness in particular. He utilised literary-critical methods in order to understand psychical phenomena, including *literary-linguistic* ones (as a later chapter will show in detail). These methods extended to aesthetic analyses that were not only literary but also *artistic* in both the specific and the general sense of the word. Thus Freud appealed to fine, classical and modern art and criticism in order to explain pathological phenomena where appropriate.

Examples of the ways in which art and literature can help explain the psyche – and vice versa – are easy to find in both Lacan and Freud's work. Lacan famously analysed a short story by Edgar Allen Poe which features a 'purloined letter' that bears a scandalous truth. In a key scene the letter is visible – but also invisible – among sheaths of other books and papers. According to Lacan this shows that psychical truth can be 'hidden in plain sight'. He was referring to a situation in which something can be barely apparent but very significant, or in which a message can be sent obliquely and almost indiscernibly in the context of normal communication (a 'letter' that contains a vital truth can be seen but remain unread). Lacan's analysis of Poe's tale is both a literary-linguistic explanation of the psyche and a psychoanalytic appreciation of literature. In the same way Freud's consideration of the 'The Uncanny' is both a psychoanalytic account of a literary device and a literary illustration of psychical phenomena. (EC, pp. 6–48; Freud [1919] 1985) In both cases literary and artistic and psycho-pathological phenomena are *mutually enlightening*.

For both Lacan and Freud the enlightenment concerned was clinical as well as theoretical. Freud and Breuer discerned artistic, literary and linguistic-type qualities in Anna O's mental disturbances, which they treated as *symbolic*. Her daydreams and night-dreams were understood as stories, her hallucinations as hieroglyphs and her multi-linguistic utterances as code. All symptoms and figures were analysed with a view to discovering the associative relations they had with each other that marked the meaningful trail that led back to the trauma that had produced them. To the extent that it was aesthetic, literary and linguistic, Freud and Breuer's approach to and understanding of Anna's symptoms strikingly prefigured Lacan's treatment of Marcelle (and indeed many others).

The general point to be grasped here is that the symbolic, associative, poetic and figurative qualities that Lacan focussed on from the outset in his theory and practice were not only fundamentally psychoanalytic but also essential to 'art' in general and literature in particular. Lacan loved the arts. His passions extended beyond his professional and intellectual lives into his personal one. Throughout it he collected painting and sculpture. He read assiduously. His 1931 encounter with Dalí was pivotal. The meeting he had with Joyce a decade earlier was inspirational too.[5] He was hyper-sensitive to the parallels between art, literature and madness and his enthusiasm for them all sustained his intellectual development from his youth until his death.

Individuality

Now there is a crucial *particular* point to be made in relation to this matter of Lacan's enthusiasm for art and literature. This has to do with a distinct and important element of both that he fully appreciated: *individuality*. This individuality is sometimes apparent in another artistic element: *style*. Lacan noted the significance of and connection between these two qualities in 'inspired' art. All this can be observed in the work of Dalí, who was an avant garde artist, whose art was intense and extreme. Thus his work was not only inspirational but also characterised by a distinctive painting (and writing) 'style', which is of course a manifestation of his individuality. The same could be said of Joyce (and *his* writing style and individuality). (Joyce, [1939] 2012) It's no mistake that individuality and style were properties that Lacan emphatically attributed to Marcelle's writing in his paper on 'Schizographie'. (Lacan, [1931b] 1975, p. 380) In a contemporary analysis of paranoia written for a surrealist journal, he emphasised what this attribution implies: that individuality and style are essential aspects of art *and* madness and that both of the latter involve both of the former. The style of paranoid speech and writing reflects an 'originality of… experience' expressed in an 'original syntax' that amounts to a 'personal signification'. Lacan was noting that style *is* a form of individuality and that madness, like art, is formulated and expressed in language that conveys both. Such language is thus highly expressive of the 'personality' of the person who uses it. Madness, like art, is *expressive* and *individual*. (Lacan, [1933a] 1988)

This realisation was crucial for Lacan. It would facilitate some of his greatest discoveries and theories. Most obviously, it would lead to a contention that psychoanalysis best understands the disturbed human being as a *subject*. Just as importantly (and not unrelatedly), Lacan's fascination with individual experience led him to appreciate and utilise an approach to the mind that valued and prioritised it: *phenomenology*.

Persons

The invocation of something like individuality and an identifiable phenomenological framing of it are clearly evident in much of Lacan's early writing on mental illness. It was in his first article on paranoia that he claimed that in any given case of it there is a 'unique reality' which is particular to the patient, that is felt *by* him and means something *for* him. (Lacan, [1931a] 1988, p. 8, my translation) That this 'reality' is *individual* is emphasised in the article he wrote for the surrealists mentioned above. In it, he stresses that paranoia bears an 'intentional signification' or 'personal signification'. The former term is specifically and technically phenomenological and the latter one is generally so. Both clearly signal the significance of 'individuality', 'subjectivity' or 'personality' for Lacan. *All* of these are unquestionably matters of concern for phenomenology. Lacan's enthusiasm for a 'phenomenological' and subject-oriented approach was confirmed in his article on paranoia in an approving reference to the 'phenomenologically inspired labours' of the psychiatrist Ludwig Binswanger.[6] This quote confirms two already-noted facts. Firstly, Lacan's intellectual exposure to phenomenology was initially through psychiatry, not philosophy, in which phenomenological thought originated; secondly – and consequently – it was indirect.

Some of the *personal* as well as the intellectual influence that led Lacan to phenomenology also came via Binswanger and some of *this* was indirect too. Lacan met Binswanger and was familiar with his work in a general way (he did not read it all, as he did Freud's). (Allouch, p. 246) The older man was of the previous psychiatric generation but his ideas had a marked influence on his antecedents, including Lacan. Binswanger's influence was even more personal and direct on some of Lacan's friends and peers than it was on him. These included Eugène Minkowski, Edouard Pichon and Henry Ey. It was through *these* men, as much as through Binswanger himself, that Lacan received phenomenologically inflected ideas.

It's worth sketching important aspects of Binswanger's ideas such that their effect on Lacan can be shown. This will involve revealing something of the historico-intellectual context in which Binswanger's ideas were developed.

Binswanger

Binswanger's influence on psychology, psychiatry, psychoanalysis and psychotherapy has been profound. He was not as well known as Freud, or even Lacan during his lifetime, but he is now recognised as a pioneer in his field. He is thought to have been one of the inventors of and key contributors to the movement known variously as 'existential psychoanalysis' or 'existential psychiatry' or 'existential psychology', all terms describing a key theoretical, therapeutic and clinical trend that has been active and influential in the psychological professions over the last century. Binswanger – like the philosophers who influenced him – came to existentialism through phenomenology. 'Phenomenological' psychologies developed into 'existential' psychologies and Binswanger was happy to be referred to as a 'phenomenological psychologist' before he was called an 'existential' one.

Other psychiatrists who were referred to and understood in similar ways to Binswanger included Amedeo Giorgi and Frederick Wertz. All three men became existentialists after having been phenomenologists. In this regard their *psychiatric* trajectory followed the historical development of twentieth-century European *philosophy*, in which phenomenology gave way to existentialism.

Sartre and his philosophical peers are also known as phenomenologists-turned-existentialists. Neither they nor their psychiatric equivalents were the first to have undergone this change. The *primary* transformation of phenomenology into existentialism took place in Germany and was then repeated in France (in line with the geo-traffic of early twentieth-century intellectual transformations mentioned earlier) when the ideas of the philosopher Edmund Husserl were taken up and transformed by the philosopher Martin Heidegger; *this* was when phenomenology first became existentialism.

It's important to have traced the origins of these forms of thinking, although it's not necessary to say more about this originary development *now*. What needs to be returned to here is the historical effect of Binswanger's ideas – and similar ideas – on Lacan. This *will* involve reference to Husserl because Binswanger's early intellectual principles were not only generally phenomenological but also specifically Husserlian.

None of this is to say that Binswanger was *just* a phenomenologist. Like Lacan, he was at first a psychiatrist. He identified himself with what was in effect a family profession. His uncle Otto was a professor of psychiatry at the University of Jena and his grandfather – also called Ludwig – was psychiatric founder of the Sanatorium Bellevue in Kreuzlingen where the younger Ludwig became the director in 1911. Four years before this he had gained his medical degree at the University of Zurich. As Lacan later was, he was fascinated by the crypto-psychoanalytic advances that were being made by psychiatrists in that city. Yet he was historically, physically and culturally closer to the people making the progress concerned than Lacan was and formed personal as well as professional relationhips with them. It's been mentioned that Lacan sought out Jung and Bleuler when he studied at the Burghölzi clinic in Zurich and that he remained sympathetic to their ideas from then on. Binswanger knew both men personally: he was mentored by Bleuler and was friends with Jung. He also became an intimate of the father of psychoanalysis, who was based elsewhere but who still lived in the German-speaking world. In March 1907 Binswanger travelled with Jung to visit Freud in Vienna. He and Freud became friends and colleagues from then on. On their return to Zurich, Jung and Binswanger founded a small psychoanalytic group. This led to the first International Congress of Psychoanalysis in Salzburg in 1909. (Ellenberger, p. 455)

It is not so much Binswanger's interest in psychoanalysis that is relevant to this book as his enthusiasm for phenomenology. After hinting at the advantages of a phenomenological orientation for psychiatry during the first two decades of the century, Binswanger made his preferences explicit in a paper he read to the Swiss Society for Neurology and Psychiatry 'On Phenomenology' in 1923. (Binswanger, 1923) In this paper he outlined the theoretical and clinical advantages to psychiatry of the adoption of phenomenological ways of thinking. He continued to make repeated phenomenological references in the books and the papers he published up until 1942. Then he systematised his primarily phenomenological – and by that time also existential – approach in one of his major works: *Grundformen und Erkenntnis menschlichen Daseins (Basic Forms and Realisation of Human Existence).* (Binswanger, [1942] 1962)

Objectivism

Following Husserl, Binswanger chose not to view the psyche 'objectively'. He thought that doing so amounted to 'reductivism', essentialism, 'positivism' and/or 'psychologism'. The argument will be detailed later, but to put it simply both Husserl and Binswanger were of the view that psychological objectivism reduces the psyche to common contents and functions in order to be able to generalise about it in a 'scientific' way. The putting of 'scientific' in scare quotes here is intended to register both men's scepticism about whether such a reduction is scientific at all and whether it doesn't instead depend on a debased and ultimately violent idea of what science is.

A 'science' often identifies its objects by virtue of their essences and does so by way of a reduction. Physics, for example, concerns itself with 'physical entities': ones that are material and occupy co-ordinates in time and space. These essences characterise all or most physical objects (bodies, chairs, rocks and so on) that are thus the objects of physics. Yet physical objects often contain other elements which are considered non-essential from the point of view of physics. For example the human being is physical, but can be said to contain – or at least feel and express – emotion. This is irrelevant from a strict physicist's point of view because s/he is only concerned with what s/he sees as the essence of the human object (and indeed most objects): matter, energy, time and space. Physics reduces human being to a physical entity or process or both.

A not dissimilar reduction often takes place in the 'science' of psychology, even though it is not a physical science. Psychology aims to be 'scientific' and employs objectivist principles and means in doing so. It tends to generalise about 'the human psyche' or 'people' rather than focus on the individual. This means excluding what isn't 'objective', specifically: 'the subject'.

By contrast Binswanger (following Husserl, but employing slightly different terminology) preferred to grant the psyche *particularity* as well as 'objectivity'. This meant treating the human being as a 'person'. This 'person' might have been considered in an 'embodied' way or not. In any case s/he would have been considered *individually*. As well as being individual, she would have been presumed to be complex. Among other things, this would mean that s/he would have neither been totally isolated nor entirely part of the mass. Instead, s/he would live in a 'world' that s/he related to. This world would include others who s/he both would and wouldn't be like. In relation to both them and the world s/he would have a 'world view'.

This recognisably phenomenological setup is obviously more nuanced than one that treats the psyche as a mere 'object' to be studied 'scientifically' and generalised about on that basis. It takes account of both the individual *and* his or her *perspective*. The setup was developed by Binswanger in various ways.

Concepts

Binswanger drew on a number of philosophical concepts to facilitate such developments. One such was was *lebenswelt* or 'lifeworld', which originated in the work of Husserl. 'Lifeworld' is not the world as it objectively exists, or even that world considered as a life-form. It is the world that exists *for* human life-forms.

Importantly *lebenswelt* has a discrete as well as a collective mode. There are not only 'group' lifeworlds, such as common beliefs, there are also singular ones, such as personal beliefs. The latter, of course, involve a type of individuality, or personality. In this mode, *lebenswelt* is *my* world (or, more abstractly, *his* or *her* world). This is the aspect of *lebenswelt* that most interested Binswanger and by extension Lacan. Both men increasingly investigated their patients' conditions through their *personal* histories, preferences, prejudices, preoccupations and even style. The investigation and what Lacan discovered as a consequence of it was of course what eventually led him to insist that the human being is a *subject*.

Throughout his professional and intellectual career, Binswanger maintained that there is a discrete mode of psychical being that is entirely specific to each being. This mode is even more subjective than *Lebenswelt*. It is the 'eigenwelt', or 'own world', which is the *particularly* subjective experience, including the relationship one has with oneself. This relationship is not simply insular, because it is projected beyond one, into the *'weltanschauung'*, or 'world-design'.

Binswanger sometimes employed *this term* to refer to flights of fancy which are clearly observable in the ideas and behaviour of neurotics and psychotics. Understood in this way, *weltanschauung* resembles 'psychic reality' as Freud conceived it. Lacan used the term *weltanschauung* too. He specified that the psychoanalytic consideration of it is 'the elaboration of the notion of the subject'. (Lacan, [1964a] 1987, p. 77)

Essentialism

It's clear from the above that phenomenology includes an appreciation – even a prioritisation – of 'subjectivity'. It is sceptical about the way in which objects in general are formulated, especially when this is done 'scientifically'. Such formulation is taken to involve a more or less violent reduction to essence and a presumption that such essence characterises *all* relevant objects.

It's worth putting all this more fully and explaining scientific (or scientistic) objectivism in more detail – including with reference to its *essentialist* qualities. Science presumes that given objects can always be identified by their essences. For example trees have branches and are made of wood; water is made up of hydrogen and oxygen. Such essences *characterise* objects. Other, more *particular* qualities of objects are deemed by science to be non-essential or 'contingent'. These (excluded) qualities often include subjectivity. Thus psychology and psychiatry can treat 'minds' as 'objects' of science yet make little or no reference to their particular subjective dimensions. In that case human beings are objectified as 'classes' or 'types', whether these be 'women', 'schizophrenics' or even 'people'.

The phenomenological approach of Binswanger and his colleagues contrasted with such 'scientism'. They considered 'objects' of enquiry (for example 'persons' or 'worlds') that weren't reducible to a single essence. They pondered non-objective – including subjective – aspects of these 'objects' too. Lacan followed Binswanger's phenomenological lead.

Deviation

Lacan's 'phenomenology' was of a non-standard sort. This was typical: he never reproduced an influence entirely accurately. He added, embellished and in one way or another *changed* every principle or argument he ever took from anywhere. His borrowed arguments were sometimes unattributed, often unfaithful, and nearly always overlaid with *others*. Thus his phenomenology was mixed up in his 'philosophy' with all sorts of other 'philosophies'. It wasn't just an interrogation of 'scientific psychology' (specifically its reductionism and essentialism) or a kind of 'subjectivism' (although it was this); it was also alternately combined – in a quite opaque and undifferentiated way – with dialectics and (later) structuralism. Lacan's phenomenology even partook of the scientism that phenomenology was supposed to eschew. Thus it was *variant* (if one wanted to be generous about it) or *delinquent* (if one wanted to be strict). Husserl (who founded phenomenological enquiry) would almost certainly have found Lacan's argument lacking in rigour. Heidegger, whose philosophy represented the key *development* of phenomenology in the twentieth century, found Lacan incomprehensible and even suggested that he was mad.[7] Still, Lacan's 'phenomenology' – should one wish to see it – *is* discernible as a derivation and alteration of its pure form and therefore *is* worth trying to understand.

As early as 1931 Lacan criticised 'institutional psychology' and its adoption of 'positivist science' as a model and method for the investigation of the human psyche. At the time, such a critique of such a science was undoubtedly phenomenological in inspiration if not in form. Lacan's argument included a charge that scientific psychology involves a 'naïve confidence in…mechanistic thought'. It held that such thought had produced an epistemological 'illusion'. (Lacan, [1933a] 1988, p. 4) Lacan's attack on 'mechanistic thought' included one on the logic of 'cause', which he took to inform the 'scientific' identification of 'essence'. He furthermore claimed that the 'illusion' propagated by such logic is one that seeks but fails to understand the world 'objectively'. While launching this critique of scientism, Lacan was also representing both mental illness and his patients in terms that were subjectivist. He was saying that a mental illness could be understood as a particular reaction to conflicts derived from and active in the history and actuality of an individual patient's life (beneath all of the baroque theorisation, dense argumentation and detailed medical terminology, this is the *exact* argument of Lacan's doctoral thesis). (Lacan, [1932] 1975) Thus there *were* significant parallels between Lacan's critique of psychology and an authentic phenomenological one. Lacan's exact 'phenomenological' argument can be laid out more clearly as follows.

Critique

What Lacan's critique of scientism attacked, broadly speaking, was conventional psychology in both its academic and its clinical incarnations. Such psychology sees the psyche as a repository of positively identifiable and observable objects and processes, specifically: thoughts and chains of thoughts. If it seems obvious that the mind and mental phenomena *should* be identified in this way then it's worth bearing in mind that the psyche and what's in it can't actually be *seen*. The mind is immaterial (it has ghost-like qualities, as a number of philosophers have pointed out). Technically, it can be represented as *absent* or *negative* – especially when considered from a physical point of view (this physical point of view is, after all, the view of the natural sciences).[8] To cast the mind as full of positively identifiable objects is thus to eschew the 'negative' quality of it and also the ambiguity that this causes for any objective account of it. How can something be positive, objective *and* negative? Yet psychological science, as Lacan pointed out, disavows this complication by *identifying* the mind objectively by way of a sort of *positivism*. This scientific (and scientistic) method needs some explaining.

A widespread approach in both modern philosophy and modern science, 'positivism' holds that objects can and should be positively identified. It argues that such objects need not be material – they may be mental, that is they may be ideas rather than things. Although they cannot be felt or seen, the existence of ideas is demonstrable by observation, experiment and logic. Thus even if only because they can be inferred, ideas are *there*. They therefore can and should be *posited*, and *positively* identified thereafter.

Once ideas are posited (and granted positivity as a consequence) they acquire another quality too. Positivity implies *objectivity* in so far as positively identifying objects means representing them truthfully and in an impartial and verifiable manner. The deductions made here (positivity = impartiality = truth) are of a particular logical sort. They have some validity but are also open to question as all deductions are. Yet they underlie much psychological analysis and experiment and are widely presumed to be 'scientific'. Indeed, some positivists argue that it is the positing of ideas as objects that renders them present for study (remember that from some points of view ideas are negative). They then claim that positivism is what allows ideas to be *observable at all*. Positivist approaches to mental entities thus clearly accord with scientific (or 'scientistic') ones that proceed by identifying their objects of study (see above) and then studying them.

Such approaches are of course open to phenomenological criticism. Lacan's early approach (and for that matter his later one) was explicitly *anti*-positivistic. Because positivism is in solidarity with objectivism *and* scientism, Lacan was critical of them too.

As indicated Lacan also opposed 'mechanism', which was a 'scientistic' approach that accorded with positivism and objectivism. Showing how he did this involves explaining exactly what 'mechanism' is.

The term 'mechanistic' originated in the natural sciences and was originally used to represent natural phenomena whose being or behaviour could be said to have been caused or determined. Causal and deterministic theories were developed by scientists and philosophers of science during the late nineteenth and early twentieth century. These thinkers' objects of study were largely those of the natural sciences and included plants, animals and, as a species of the latter, humans. Such objects were seen to be explicable in terms of prior causes, more exactly to be reducible to the *sum* of such causes, which were taken to be chemical, genetic, sexual, energetic, evolutionary and instrumental. Causes were taken to be successive – that is in a 'chain' in which one leads to another. Where causes were taken to strictly entail one another, organisms effected by them were said to be *determined*.

In many scientific theories organic cause has often been taken to have been occasioned by *need*. An organo-causal account of life sees it as a series of effects that are successively caused by such needs, which are at bottom the needs to survive or reproduce. The fish's gills allow it to breath; the giraffe's neck helps it reach food; their respective physiologies are effected by the needs that cause them. Where causes seem to effect each other in very strict chains, the life of organisms (including humans) is sometimes deemed *determined*. Where organisms are described as having evolved in a way that is determined, they can also be cast as *mechanical*. Thus some causal explanations of how organisms develop and behave are not only *deterministic*, but also *mechanistic*. Thinking this way involves a sort of analogy between organisms and machines. Natural functions are like the movements of the hands of a clock effected by the rotation of cogs activated by yet other cogs and so on.

Such accounts obviously *objectify* humans (as organisms, or animals, or machines) and obviously also diminish psycho-subjective aspects of human life. These aspects are arguably the *most* human ones; the ones in which *being* is most apparent. Representations of human life as mechanical are even evident in science and psychology *now*, in the twenty-first century. A popular contemporary example is cognitive behavioural therapy (CBT), which 'forces' patients to relinquish negative or self-destructive thought patterns and 'trains' them to adopt more positive ones. Such therapies presume that patients (specifically those suffering from obsessional neuroses or obsessive compulsive disorder) respond mechanically to thoughts that are themselves mechanical (that is repetitive and instrumental). They also presume that given symptoms have the same 'objective' meaning in all cases: they are learned and unhelpful thought patterns. Phenomenological – and for that matter psychoanalytic – analyses of the same symptoms would see them quite differently: as conscious or unconscious expressions of something subjectively significant about the person suffering from them. In any case, the conception of mental functioning held to by CBT is entirely mechanistic and objectivist and thus wide open to phenomenological – and psychoanalytic – critique.

Phenomenology, in interrogating scientism and its concomitant objectivism and determinism is thus also opposed (and continues to be opposed) to mechanism and positivism. Indeed it's precisely because mechanism and positivism *are* the object of Lacan's critique that this critique can be seen as having been phenomenological.

Humanism

It's worth noting in passing that the above analysis implies that in its anti-scientism, the psychiatry and psychoanalysis that Lacan advocated, at least early on, was *humanistic*. There is a strain of humanism in phenomenology (and in existentialism too).[9] This point is worth making because it disproves a common myth about Lacan: that he was unequivocally *anti*-humanistic. Although it's true that there were causal (and other scientistic) aspects to his thought, these were not apparent until he became inured by structuralism in the mid-1950s. Even then, he never advocated any kind of 'positivism' (and he can even be said to have advocated a kind of 'negativism'). On the contrary, he was always antipathetic to simplistic scientistic accounts of life. This was especially true early on, when he advocated a 'humane' attitude towards patients. (Lacan, [1975] 1988, p. 28) He continued to insist that patients' experience – including and especially their traumatic experience – be 'humanised' (ES, p. 75) by psychoanalysis.

Unnaturalness

Humanism aside, there is still more to say about the exact form that Lacan's critique of scientism took. Recall that he claimed that understanding nature scientistically involves a sort of 'projection'. What did he mean by this?

This projection that Lacan thought scientism guilty of was grafting unnatural processes onto natural processes. The unnatural processes in question are of course mechanical ones and the projection of them onto nature – including 'human nature' – constitutes precisely the 'illusion' of knowledge mentioned earlier that Lacan said was characteristic of conventional science. (Lacan, [1933] 1988) This argument needs unpacking.

During the late nineteenth and early twentieth century, according to Lacan, there was an 'illusion' of knowledge propagated in the natural sciences which was precisely in conformity with the misunderstandings of scientism. Scientists thought that nature could be understood as a collection of classifiable and comprehensible objects. Yet as shown, they *created* such objects through reduction of their qualities or components to measurable and/or consistent calculi (while also excluding phenomena that didn't 'fit the model'). Scientistic beliefs about 'objectively existing entities' ('objects' per se) was sustained and extended with reference to theories about *how* they existed and *worked*. These theories included the ones given in example above, concerning causalism, determinism and mechanism. *All* such scientistic accounts of existence amount to a sort of 'violence upon being'. This violence was repeated (and here is the crux) when the human sciences – including psychology – were invented. They were modelled on the natural sciences and took 'human nature' to be an extension or equivalent of 'nature' per se. This resulted, in 'institutional psychology...[becoming]...the last advent of positivist science'. Because such science saw mechanical processes in nature, psychology saw them in the mind too. It thus cast human nature as a 'fabricated second nature' that obeys the 'laws...of the machine'.[10]

Pavlov

The attribution of mechanism to human nature does indeed instruct many modern psychological descriptions of it. Indeed there were very influential psychological theories that *predated* CBT that held that humans react to stimuli in a way that is both 'natural' and 'automatic' and that were the object of Lacan's critique. In them, human psychology is taken to resemble animal behaviour in reacting mechanistically to instinctive impulses. Behavioural psychology, particularly, took (and still takes) this kind of positivistic and causal view of the human as a sort of animal that is also a sort of machine. It elides mentality, mechanism and biology in the process.[11] This point can usefully be made in more detail and with reference to a scientist intermittently referred to by Lacan: Pavlov. It can more particularly be clarified with reference to his renowned experiments with dogs.

Ivan Pavlov was a Russian neuropsychologist whose important work was more or less contemporary with Freud's. By the time of his death in 1936 Pavlov's ideas clearly warranted designation as 'institutional psychology'. Trotsky officially declared them complementary to materialist and hence communist philosophy. Yet Pavlovian theories were not only Soviet-sanctioned; they were and are accepted in the West too. Indeed, some of Pavlov's ideas have attained global status.

In the early years of the twentieth century Pavlov was conducting experiments intended to disclose the substrata of the digestive system. This turned out to be psycho-physiological. Pavlov demonstrated as much by experimenting on a fox terrier. He first of all affirmed an obvious fact: that when a dog is fed it salivates. He confirmed this by giving the dog meat and collecting its resultant saliva. The appearance of saliva is explicable in purely biological terms. A neurological impulse that is a response to the presence of nourishment produces an enzyme-based fluid that helps with digestion. Salivation when feeding is thus a straightforward organic consequence of a reaction to a stimulus. It is a natural, unmediated and hence 'unconditioned' reflex. Pavlov repeated his experiment a number of times with an added element: he rang a bell while he fed the dog. He then conducted it again, but eliminated rather than added an element. He rang the bell at the dog's meal times but deprived it of food. Interestingly, the dog continued to salivate. Pavlov concluded that its response during occasions of bell-ringing had not been to an organic stimulus but to a *situation*, in which a sound was associated with being fed. This response had developed and instituted as the situation concerned had been repeated. The response was thus a *learned* one. What had been learned continued to instruct behaviour even after the situation had changed. Pavlov concluded that the dog's response during 'bell-ringing' was a reflex, just as it had been when he had been fed and the bell was *not* rung. Yet unlike the original response, it was 'learned' and therefore a 'conditioned' rather than an unconditioned reflex. (Ellenberger, pp. 787–8; Roudinesco, 1990, pp. 35–9)

Pavlov's experiment involves an animal – let's not forget the human is such – having an involuntary reaction to an organic stimulus, then having the same reaction to a non-organic one. The second of these two reactions, having taken place in the absence of organic stimuli, must have involved a psychological process: the dog's salivation meant it must have *thought* that it was going to be fed. For Pavlov this did not so much show that dogs are like humans as that all animals, including humans, can have responses that are conditioned or induced.

Because Pavlov's approach takes account of learned behaviour as well as a biological impulse, it's subtler in its registration of human nature than deterministic biologism is. Yet it collapses psychology and nature nevertheless. Ultimately, both are taken to respond automatically to stimuli (whether this response is alterable or not). Because Pavlov 'verified' his speculations about human/animal reflexes experimentally, this gave them the status – or at least the veneer – of 'science'. Yet his whole approach was problematic, not least because of the presumptions that it involved. These were to do with being, objects, causes, nature, humanity and dogs. They were precisely the presumptions that Lacan was sceptical about from a phenomenological point of view – as well as from points of view that weren't phenomenological, notably psychoanalytic ones.

Behaviourisms

It should be clear that key characteristics of Pavlovian psychology are shared by certain contemporary psychologies that are very influential and commonly employed, including the psychologies that instruct cognitive behavioural therapies. Understanding Lacan's critique of Pavlovianism thus amounts to being able to reconstruct the kind of argument that he would have had *against* such psychologies and therapies (and that in fact *is now* deployed by Lacanian psychoanalysts against them). One can show this fairly straightforwardly by relaying what Lacan's criticism of Pavlovianism is and by also showing how it applies to CBT.

CBT helps patients identify their own negative or self-destructive thought patterns. It then prevails upon (one might say 'forces') them to relinquish such patterns while 'training' them to adopt more positive ones. (Beck, 1995) It might confront obsessive-compulsive patients with the manifest object of their fear by making them rub their hands around the inside of a toilet bowl when they have a compulsion to wash them because of a terror of dirt. The clinical aim of such treatment is to compel patients to confront the fact that their fears – which are apparent in their obsessive thought patterns – are irrational. Once this had been done, negative thoughts can be replaced by positive ones. The patient can qualify or change an ingrained habit of thinking of exposure to 'dirt' as disastrous.

S/he can even begin to think of it as good, by starting to accept that reasonable contact with bacteria builds immunity. If s/he can think this every time s/he is tempted to avoid 'dirt' and/or wash obsessively, s/he can gradually realise that bathroom facilities and the bacteria found there are relatively harmless. S/he can break the pathological habit of worrying and over-washing and adopt a more realistic, positive and healthy attitude to cleanliness (and health) in general.

It's notable that CBT, like Pavlovianism, reduces its subject to an object, or at most an objective variable. The obsessive CBT patient, like the dog, behaves in a given 'situation' in a certain way. The behaviours of both are 'automatic' or 'mechanical'. If nothing else happens, both dog and human will react to given stimuli predictably. They will even do so in different situations. They are like robots that have undergone 'programming'. It's true that the human, unlike the dog, *can* react in a different way after treatment by CBT, but this is because s/he can be *reprogrammed* by CBT. The CBT patient's different behaviour is still robotic. Thus from the point of view of both Pavlovianism and CBT, the status and potential of the human *and* the animal are understood in terms that are entirely mechanistic and scientistic. Human and dog think and react *mechanically* and in ways that are 'positive' (that is appropriate and/or measurable) or not.

One good way to appreciate the difference between a Lacanian approach to illnesses like obsession and a behavioural one (like CBT) is to understand the divergence in their approaches towards the *symptom*. Behavioural psychologies presume that given symptoms have the same 'objective' meaning for all subjects: they are unhelpful and learned thought patterns that can be unlearned. From a generally phenomenological, significantly psychoanalytic and specifically Lacanian point of view, the symptom is *not* simply unhelpful and common. It always has a *meaning* rather than just an effect or function. (Freud, [1917] 1986, pp. 429–33) This meaning is always subjective rather than objective and it will be different for different subjects (this way of understanding the symptom always holds for phenomenology and generally holds for psychoanalysis).

Indeed, it was precisely in relation to the question of the symptom that Lacan began to differentiate both his clinical practice and his theorisation of psychological disturbance from ones employed by what he called 'institutional psychology'. This meant showing that, although the symptom is mechanical, it is not best understood as 'effective', or more exactly as a 'mechanism of effect'. Such a mechanism might be something that *works* (by for example producing saliva as a 'by-product' or 'symptom' of eating) or it might be something that *doesn't* work (like the dysfunctional thought

identified by CBT). In any case the symptom *isn't* properly understandable in terms of its conflict or its correspondence with a physiological
need. It *is*, however, understandable in terms of its subjective meaning
and purpose – whether this purpose 'escapes' conscious thought or not.
(Lacan, [1933] 1988)

As noted, to understand symptoms in this way is to do so phenomenologically *and* psychoanalytically and Lacan's work did both. As a
young (fashionable and dynamic) psychiatrist he wore phenomenology
on his sleeve. As time wore on, his Freudian credentials and identifications became more manifest and he couched his arguments in more
explicitly psychoanalytic terms. In any case, he increasingly subjected
mainstream psychological accounts of both psychological and physical
phenomena to 'Lacanian' readings and came up with radical revisions of
them as a consequence. Symptoms, according to such readings, are not
the product of an impulse or habit but of a 'drive'. They are nevertheless
'isolated' from this drive and also from any 'metabolism of …function'.
Psychoanalysis should not be misled by a misguided psychological aim
of restoring proper function, but should aim to establish the *hidden and
subjective* links between drive and symptom that explain their relation/
detachment with and from each other. Such links are not only missing
in behavioural psychology, but in mainstream psychological theory and
experiment *per se*. Those who don't believe as much need only 'ask one of
Pavlov's dogs'. (ES, p. 314)

Dysfunction

What the last few sections have shown, hopefully with some rigour, is that
there are notable similarities and continuities between a classical phenomenological critique of scientism and Lacan's approach to mainstream and
cognitive psychology, which he took to be scientistic and mechanistic, just
as a phenomenological philosopher would.

Yet Lacan's ideas on this subject, though discernible and logically recon-
structible, aren't without contradiction. There is a discrepancy between
what he had to say about 'mechanism' and its ilk in the early thirties and
what he said about it in the late twenties. This isn't hard to see: all one need
do is note the anti-mechanism that he has been shown to have adopted in
this chapter (covering the 1930s) and contrast it with the enthusiasm for
automatism that he was shown to have displayed in the last one (covering
the 1920s). Lacan's attitude was different in each case even though the
object of his attention was similar. Here's why.

The sort of psychological automatism advocated by Freud and the surrealists *was* quite like the sort of psychological mechanism declared by turn-of-the century scientists. Both sorts of theories presumed that the mind functions in a mechanical fashion and more or less independently of the will of the 'thinking' subject. In the late 1920s Lacan was enamoured of the Freudian and part-surrealist idea that the mechanisms of psychical functioning were driven by unconscious and *automatic* forces to produce symptoms that offered clues to the motives that instructed them. Yet Lacan *didn't* fully carry over his enthusiasm for mechanism into his early 1930s phenomenology, where modelling the mind as machine-like was seen as an *error*. This would be fine if it were possible to say that Lacan had completely changed his view. However, the confusing – though not untypical – thing is that he didn't. He in fact never completely abandoned his earlier opinion, even though it contradicted his later one. This was most evident *much* later, in the 1950s, during his 'structuralist' period. Although, as indicated above, he never became a hard-line structuralist who treated mental and verbal events as having been *determined* by linguistic structures, he did see ideas as having been structurally 'caused' in some way. The most obvious example is once again the symptom, which Lacan saw as 'caused' by a problem that can be traced back through a verbal chain – or structure – of associations that run to it from the unconscious and that can be seen as having led the symptom to take the form that it has. This 1950s model of the mind *is* part mechanical in contradiction with Lacan's early 1930s anti-mechanism which isn't, but which itself contradicts his late 1920s automatism.

These sorts of apparent contradictions (in this case between an acknowledgement of mechanism and a denunciation of it) are not untypical of Lacan's theorisation of the mind and even of humanity in general. For example, one would have to admit that the ambiguity pointed up above affects Lacan's 'humanism' and further complicates what was said about it a few sections ago.

Putting all of these continuities and contradictions together one might say the following. Although it is true (despite appearance and popular understanding) that a type of humanism *does* infuse Lacan's work (particularly early on), it's also true that a certain kind of scientism sometimes does too (particularly late on – even though this is sometimes overstated). Now it's not necessarily fair to say that this means that Lacan's work is *just* contradictory because thinkers should surely be allowed to have varied and even different opinions about things. However, a major problem with Lacan's thought is that it is *always* contradictory in one way or another. This is the case irrespective of any changes and movements in his philosophy over time or overall. This persistent contradiction has something to do with the fact that Lacan was continually overlaying one idea or theory with another (psychoanalysis with surrealism, surrealism with phenomenology etc.) and something to do with his general inconsistency, which was both intellectual and personal.

Direction

Yet it's important (after that brief but significant aside) to continue with the thread of this chapter, which means returning to phenomenology and Lacan's enthusiasm for and use of it. What has been said so far undoubtedly shows that 'phenomenology' is discernible in Lacan's psychiatric and proto-psychoanalytic theories and analyses of mental disturbance in the 1930s; this can be shown again in relation to something else that has also already been referred to in this chapter: his 'Mirror Stage' paper.

As mentioned earlier, the first version of Lacan's 'Mirror Stage' paper was presented at an IPA conference in Marienbad in 1936, while the second was delivered at Zurich in 1949. The 1936 version isn't the best known one; the 1949 one is. One reason is that the 1936 paper was in truth only *part-delivered*. This was for unusual and circumstantial reasons. Of course nothing in psychoanalysis is entirely circumstantial and the failure of delivery of the paper turned out to have been emblematic of significant flaws in both it and Lacan (in other words the paper showed up Lacan's intellectual and personal shortcomings).

The first 'Mirror Stage' paper nevertheless *was* significant, partly because it was phenomenological, even though it's often not described as such. In any case, the first version of it will be summarised now. This summary/ explanation will be brief, because the first version of the paper *itself* only survives in a fragmentary/incomplete form.[12]

Lacan's first 'Mirror Stage' paper describes 'the subject's recognition of himself in a mirror [as] a phenomenon'. The recognition in question ostensibly takes place 'at the end of six months'. At that time the child's mirror image works to 'constitute the subject's reality because of its absolute similarity to the subject'. In other words the mirror image allows the child to recognise and have an image of himself. This self-image seems real and because of this, true. This is why the child's experience of self-recognition is accompanied by a 'feeling of understanding'.

Lacan's account here is entirely concomitant with the classical phenomenological description of the individual apprehension of thought.

In its original form, this account was presented by Edmund Husserl as an extension of the theories of Franz Brentano. It takes 'the idea' to be 'present' to an individual thinker of it, who is thereby directed to this idea *as* its thinker. This formulation might seem tautological (thought has a thinker who thinks it) but is in fact logical and discriminating. It expresses what the thought exists *for*: the individual (rather than, say, the purpose of the representation of reality); it also shows what this individual is directed *toward* (thought, rather than some *nominal* reality). In the moment of cogitation, individual thought and individual thinker coincide with and confirm each other (the moment is essentially a Cartesian one).

Thus in Lacan's first formulation of the Mirror Stage, the infant and the image that he has of himself in the mirror relate to each other in a way that is very similar to the way in which the 'phenomenological' thinker and his thought do. The mirror image exists 'for' the infant to recognise himself in. Yet it also 'facilitates' him. Because it is 'similar' to him it 'makes' him its 'subject', that is the individual who recognises himself in it. He is concomitantly directed towards the image as *the* image of himself (just as the phenomenological thinker is 'directed towards' his thought). There is clearly a 'process' of recognition here that involves an interaction between a mirror image and the subject in which each works to confirm the other. The psychoanalytic word for the self-image that results from this moment and process of apparent recognition is of course 'the ego'.

It's notable that both phenomenological and 'Lacanian' accounts of the constitution of the ego, unlike some scientistic psychological ones, don't identify it or the thoughts that it has in 'objective' or 'mechanical' terms. On the contrary, they represent the thinking self as *individual* and his thoughts as either spontaneous or self-directed.

Misdirection

On the face of it, or at least on a first reading of Lacan's first account of it, the image of himself that the child receives from the mirror seems coherent and robust. The 'specular image' that he encounters there has an 'integrative power' that brings about 'mental unity'. It is an image that allows him to properly – even truthfully – recognise himself. 'The unity of tendencies which it introduces...contribute to the ego's formation.' What the mirror-image confers on the child is no less than his identity.

This all sounds like a 'happy', holistic developmental account of the assumption of self. It even sounds like a logical one. Yet anyone who knows much about Lacan's general account of identity will know that it is not holistic *at all*.

The reason for the discrepancy between this account of the assumption of identity and the one more commonly associated with Lacan's theories is that in relation to the latter, the former is only *half the story*. This is not just the case if one compares Lacan's first Mirror Stage paper with his theories in general, but if one carefully considers the paper *itself*. The paper contains arguments that are at odds with 'holism' and that even directly contradict it. Thus the specular image isn't just a paradigm of unity but a 'double' that confers not truth, but 'illusion'. Because it is 'other' than the infant who sees it (remember that it is encountered elsewhere, in a mirror) it doesn't just unify his 'ego' 'but also profoundly alienates it'. It thereby facilitates 'fantasies of dismemberment, of dislocations of the body, of castration'. The relation of the child to his image in the mirror is also one of 'dissonance' which, furthermore, is 'characteristic of this stage'. (Lacan, [1938] 1988)

How can the mirror-image have this effect and still produce 'unity'; how can the ego be coherent and fragmented at the same time? The truth is that Lacan's first version of the 'Mirror Stage' paper doesn't provide a proper answer to these questions, it is as riven with contradictions as it is replete with clever ideas. In the later version of the paper, Lacan goes some way to addressing if not resolving these contradictions by offering a better argument for the mirror stage. The later argument is both more dialectical and more logical than the earlier one. Still, it isn't perfect and it doesn't mean that Lacan's ideas became paradox-free.

For now, it's most accurate and useful to notice that the first version of the 'Mirror Stage' paper *can* be read as a quasi-phenomenological explanation of the constitution of a coherent ego. It should also be noticed that it *can* be read in contradiction of this reading, in a way that suggests that the ego *isn't* coherent.

Succession

In 1936 Lacan was a medium-sized fish in a small French pond. He was still in analysis with Loewenstein in Paris. His urgent wish was to get this analysis over and done with so that he could improve the grade of his SPP membership and become a training analyst. He wouldn't succeed in his aim until 1938. Although Lacan's ambition to be a psychoanalytic 'player' hadn't come to fruition in 1936, it burned in him and he did everything he could to get himself known in the national analytic community. He sought friendship and support from his peers and their successors, who he already planned to influence once he had the training position that would allow him to teach. Some younger members of the SPP were already reading his published thesis and articles in anticipation of this moment. Lacan's 'flair for publicity' and profit from minor scandal kept him in their sights. In the long run it may have helped him that the older analysts who had their hands on the levers of power found him 'incomprehensible' and spurned his initial bid to be a trainer. Their resistance to his rise would provide a barrier for his young charges to kick over when the time came for revolt. (Roudinesco, 1997, pp. 25, 81)

Lacan determinedly worked to raise his profile. By the time he attended his first IPA Congress in 1936, he had begun to network internationally. Still, he only corresponded with and/or knew minor psychoanalytic figures outside France at that time. He would only meet major figures (or rather, they would only encounter *him)* later. Freud – the undisputed leader of the psychoanalytic movement – missed the Marienbad congress due to illness. He had suffered from cancer for more than a decade. Having just passed his eightieth year, he was not expected to live much longer (he died three years later). He was mostly loved and respected by the analytic community, but this did not mean that battles weren't being fought over his succession. Perhaps surprisingly, these weren't being directly fought over *international* positions of *institutional* power. In 1936 Ernest Jones (Freud's friend, confidante and biographer) was two years into a term of presidency of the IPA that continued until 1951. His tenure was interrupted by the war, but it was not his first and overall he served many more years as president than anyone else did. Thus the figurehead for psychoanalysis in Freud's absence (Jones) remained unchanged for years. The *real* battles for psychoanalysis, specifically for its *legacy* were fought elsewhere. These took place over psychoanalytic theory and practice. They were conducted during a number of 'storms', one of which broke out at Marienbad.

In the 1930s, psychoanalysis was subject to what became known as 'the controversial discussions'. Discussants – who were also combatants – tended to fall into one or other of two camps, each of them led by an influential post-Freudian woman analyst. One group took their inspiration from and declared their loyalty to Anna Freud, Sigmund's daughter. Another group fell in behind Melanie Klein, an analyst of Austrian birth who spent the latter part of her working life in London. Both Anna Freud and Melanie Klein accepted the basic precepts of psychoanalysis as they had been established by Sigmund Freud and both considered themselves Freudians. However, they each developed Freud's ideas in quite different directions. Anna Freud concentrated on the ego and its defences. She thought that these contained the cryptic clues to the unconscious content that causes the ego to become malformed in defence against recognition of it. None of this contradicted her father's work, which saw the ego as a site of symptoms that both repress and indirectly express psychical conflicts. Klein didn't explicitly dispute this account of the ego. Still, Sigmund Freud said that it is formed by and around the time of the Oedipus Complex. While Klein tacitly accepted this account of the developmental sequence and structure of ego formation, she nevertheless concentrated on psychical formations that appear earlier, in other words ones that are *pre-egoic*. Developing Freud's theories backwards – and in the process narrating a sort of prequel to the Oedipus Complex – Klein focussed on the pre-Oedipal period, particularly on the phases or stages that precede it. It's true that Freud had named and explained some of these (for example the oral and the anal phase) but Klein itemised some of her own (notably the paranoid-schizoid and the depressive phases).

It's not necessary to explain all of the differences between Anna Freudian and Kleinian theory right now. Still, this sketch should have been enough to show that each analyst was focussed on quite different psychical formations, phases, positions and dynamics. Anna Freud's focus was egoic and Oedipal, Klein's was pre-egoic and pre-Oedipal. This ended up being more than a fine distinction. The two women differed quite widely on theoretical matters and the differences between them on clinical matters were marked too. Anna Freud believed in spoken analyses of children and always included parents in their treatment; Klein developed a play technique which involved non-verbal communication through toys and treated children individually. The debate/dispute between the two women and their respective theoretical positions and clinical practices continued throughout the 1930s and raged with particular force in the Viennese and British societies (the British society eventually divided into three groups: Freudian, Kleinian and Independent). The 1936 IPA conference in Marienbad became another site of battle between Anna Freudians and Kleinians and so became another proxy for war.[13]

Humiliation

As it happened, Lacan eventually took ideas for his theories from both Kleinian and Anna Freudian positions (he also criticised both positions, as he was wont to do). Yet in 1936 he was not familiar enough with either of them to have an informed view or take a side (and he certainly wasn't knowledgeable enough to assume any judicious position *between* sides). Thus the key theoretical battles of 1936 went on above his head. They did not concern him and he was not *au fait* or powerful enough to participate in them. Instead, when he rose to deliver his first mirror-phase paper he expected the attendees to be interested in *him*. He declared himself to be delivering a theory that was 'established' in the French group (it wasn't) and sought to disseminate this theory worldwide.

Unsurprisingly, what happened during Lacan's paper was quite different to what he expected. The attendees of his group session were preoccupied with other theoretical and political matters and weren't interested in hearing an obscure Frenchman speak for longer than his allotted time. After ten minutes the chair of his session – Ernest Jones no less – interrupted Lacan to move on to more important business. The speaker barely got past his introduction. Lacan never forgave Jones for stealing his thunder. Later, he disparaged him, saying that he 'only qualified for the position [of president] by virtue of the fact that I never met one of his English colleagues who had a good word to say for him'. (Roudinesco, 1997, p. 153)

This would set a pattern. Lacan eventually fell out with quite a few of the most powerful figures in psychoanalysis (and/or they fell out with him). After a brief unsuccessful encounter with him in which he let her down, Melanie Klein ceased to trust Lacan. Anna Freud met him, but never liked him. Sigmund Freud's close friend and French psychoanalytic princess Marie Bonaparte hated Lacan. The feeling was mutual. In any case, Marienbad didn't especially raise Lacan's psychoanalytic standing. It just pointed up the difference between how other psychoanalysts saw him and how he saw himself.

Clandestinity

Of course Lacan, despite (or because of) his own arrogance, also had a very complicated view of his own position. He assigned himself various and quite different *social* registrations (aristocratic, bourgeois, radical, etc.) and lurched from one philosophical and/or political position (Nietzschean, Spinozan, Surrealist, Catholic, Chauvinist) to another in equal abandon and disarray. His personal life was just as conflicted and inconstant. He had sexual relationships with more than one woman at a time and assumed different versions of himself with each of them depending on who they were.

Between 1927 and 1930, when Lacan was an intern at the Hôpital Saint-Anne, he dated a sub-aristocratic widow fifteen years his senior who his friends called 'The princess'. Her name was Marie-Thérèse Bergerot. While he was seeing her he took another lover who was roughly his own age. Olesia Sienkiewicz was androgynous, Polish, bohemian and rich with new money (her father was a banker). Marie-Thérèse engaged Lacan in intellectual conversation, undertook study trips with him and paid for his doctoral thesis (which was dedicated to her) to be printed and bound. Meanwhile, Olesia accompanied him on holiday trips to a string of exotic locations on the European coast. The trips were made by plane and/or car. Olesia seems to have been perfectly relaxed about Lacan's driving, which was famously hazardous (and which, on the one occasion that Lacan had met Heidegger, near-drove the philosopher's wife to breakdown). (Roudinesco, 1997, p. 226)

It's probable that Lacan derived a reassuring sense of security and stability from Marie-Thérèse. Unlike him, she was emotionally constant and her position was secure. His own wasn't. Lacan's doctoral thesis did not get the reception he had hoped it would in psychiatric circles. On publication it garnered a few good reviews that mostly weren't by psychiatrists, but by people (artists, political philosophers, journalists) who couldn't help him progress in his primary profession. For a few years after its publication Lacan's analysis didn't advance much and neither did his psychoanalytic career. Amid all this uncertainty, Marie-Thérèse must have provided him with a feeling of stability, support and certain love; in other words she must have acted as a sort of mother figure for him. Of course, he was having sex with her, so he was gratifying an Oedipal need into the bargain. Still, Marie-Thérèse wasn't enough. When he vacationed with her in Spain in 1933 – apparently quite happily – he sent long passionate letters to Olesia. He loved her terribly, although he also confessed that he felt this most keenly in her absence. He intimated the break-up of their relationship and even seemed to encourage it by suggesting she might indulge her own passions with someone else. At the same time he suggested that he couldn't live without her and that she should wait for and be patient with him while he resolved other matters (including, presumably, his relationship with Marie-Thérèse). Lacan was arguably acting out a reluctance to undertake the sacrifice and commitment necessary to conduct an adult sexual relationship, but not with the woman who was offering it to him: Marie-Thérèse. He was showing his ambivalence about her to another: Olesia. Meanwhile, he was getting all the stable love he should have needed from Marie-Thérèse (and was taking it very much for granted). Of course, he spurned this love because it did not appease his insatiable desire. What a great model Lacan was for his own theories! He had to have two women because one was not enough for him, yet two were not enough for him either.

There was obviously a kind of bad faith, or duplicity, or double-dealing active in Lacan's triangular love life in the late twenties and early thirties. It's maybe even a common, immature sort of duplicity that's not hard to recognise in the general love-relations of young people who are still captivated by youthful passions and narcissisms and who haven't yet managed to accept that successful relationships often involve commitment and loss, including loss of *other* relationships. Yet this sort of view of Lacan's sexual behaviour (as common youthful behaviour) rather lets him off the hook for two reasons. Firstly: his double-dealing in matters of love was not restricted to the triangular relationship he had with Marie-Thérèse and Olesia (neither, for that matter, was it restricted to matters of love). Secondly: the type of amorous double-dealing he habitually indulged in is specifically identified and theorised by Freud in a paper that Lacan not only read, but absorbed into his own psychoanalytic theories in a significant way.

Ichspaltung

The split ego in general – and Lacan's split ego in particular – can be accounted for in Freudian terms. In 'The Splitting of the Ego In The Process of Defence' Freud tried to explain why some psychoanalytic patients *have* a 'split' ego, more specifically why they have an ego that at once accepts and denies a fact of reality. An example might be someone who knows that a relationship is damaged, damaging and hopeless but carries on with it as if it is healthy, happy and permanent. This kind of splitting involves a part-recognition of a reality (unhappiness) but also a part-denial of it. The part-denial includes fantasy (that a relationship is perfect). These two positions (reality and fantasy) can sometimes appear to be resolved by a 'disavowal', that is an acceptance that the disagreeable reality *is* real, but a concomitant declaration that it doesn't matter. Yet a disavowal is no more than a complex denial. Opposite positions held in the mind are ultimately contradictory however one holds them. This is true whether the split subject alternately denies and affirms reality or maintains 'the two contrary reactions' at the same time via 'a splitting of the ego'. (Freud, [1940] 1984, p. 462)

Freud traced such splitting back to a sexual infantile situation, more specifically an Oedipal one. He gives an example of a fetishistic boy. The boy has had a proto-sexual relationship with an older girl. His Oedipal phantasy of being able to sexually own his mother has been kept alive by this experience. As all boys directly or indirectly do, he eventually experiences a castration threat, which he perceives to be coming from his father, the rival for his mother's affection. He associates this threat with his memory of the girl's genitals. In other words he thinks that *the girl* has been castrated. By extension, he 'reasons' that all females must have suffered this fate and that his mother must have been castrated too. This thought is as unbearable as the thought of his own castration.

In the early Oedipal situation the boy has experienced his mother, his ultimate love object, as perfect, as 'whole'. He either identifies with her in a very primal way – experiencing himself as 'whole' too – or he imagines himself to own her as he would own an extremely beautiful and valuable object. In any case the thought of damage having been done to this object is intolerable to him, especially because it represents a kind of reality (the reality of female sexual difference, the reality of loss, etc). Yet this reality, once encountered, cannot be forgotten (the boy has seen the 'castrated' girl). The boy thus assumes a psychic position that allowed the reality but denies it at the same time. He imagined his mother *not* to have been castrated by transferring his desire onto another part of her body. He develops a 'fetish' (for her hair, say, or her feet). His fetish object acts as a 'substitute' for the penis that he cannot entirely bring himself to admit she has 'lost' (the fetish is persistent and continues into adult life as a denial of realities of all sorts, but specifically the reality of loss). Yet although the fetish denies reality, it also allows it to be represented in some way. In the case of the boy, fetishism does not preclude the possibility of an at least minimal admission of what is real. Because he has *transferred* desire onto a different part of the mother's body and can believe that the female has 'something like' a penis somewhere else, he can begin to believe that she *doesn't* have a penis between her legs. He can thus part-tolerate the idea that his mother (and by implication he) is 'castrated'. The boy denies and accepts castration *at the same time*. It is in exactly this sense that his ego is *split*. (Freud, [1940] 1984, pp. 462–4)

Freud clearly identified the Oedipal situation and the castration complex as the two circumstantial factors in the splitting of the ego. He obviously also took the presence of the penis to mean wholeness or power for the Oedipal subject, while its absence marked the reality of loss. Once his theories were properly developed, Lacan often focussed on ego-splitting.

In fact he took it into account from the outset, as the tensions between egoic coherence and fragmentation in his first description of the 'Mirror Stage' testifies. Following Freud, he also identified the Oedipal Structure as the exact one in which psychosexual development *takes place*. The castration threat, he said, is the successful catalyst for such development, but also the traumatic complication of it when it fails. Lacan didn't take the penis as literally as Freud did, which is why he called it 'the phallus' and thought of it *symbolising* plenitude or loss rather than amounting to it. Thus although the differences between Lacan and Freud's theorisations of psychosexual development are not insignificant, it should be clear from the above that the former were significantly *derived from* and *extensive of* the latter. As Jacqueline Rose put it: 'Lacan returns to the key concepts of the debate, to the castration complex and, within its terms, the meaning of the phallus.' (Rose and Mitchell, p. 7) Lacan avowedly received and utilised a certain developmental structure and genealogy laid down by Freud and he even emphasised that the *perversion* of such development proceeded as Freud had said: maternal love – castration threat – disavowal of reality – ego-splitting. Like Freud, he even took there to be a lot of common ground *between* the perversion and the norm. In other words he took *all* egos to be *at least minimally* split (this is of course what he demonstrated rather better in the *second* account of his Mirror Stage theory).

Multidimensional

What conclusions can be derived from all this? As well as stressing the significance of the splitting of the ego in Freud's theories, Lacan acted it out in his own life. This can be seen from the details of the love triangle that he concocted in the late 1920s and early 1930s, and can be explained as follows.

Lacan took two lovers because no one woman could live up to the phantasy of what he wanted her to be. She couldn't be a loving and stable mother (Marie-Thérèse) and a dangerous and racy androgyne (Olesia) at the same time. Committing himself to *one* woman would have meant facing the loss of what another could offer him. How could he avoid this loss? The answer must have seemed to Lacan to be to have *both* women, or at least to try to maintain the phantasy that this was possible. Yet his unhappiness in his *ménage à trois* was testament to the fact that the reality of loss persisted in it and that it couldn't, ultimately, be repudiated.[14] When one of Lacan's women was present the other one was absent; if the other one was present either or both were inadequate. Both women couldn't be present and adequate at the same time. The reality of loss wouldn't go away, but neither did Lacan avow it. Instead, he split himself in two. The splitting took various forms, including idealisation and denigration. Lacan idealised Marie-Thérèse as maternal and forgot Olesia, or he thrilled to Olesia's subversive charm and acted as if he'd never have to give up Marie-Thérèse. It didn't work. Neither 'solution' made him happy because loss pervaded both.

Of course the mature way for Lacan to have resolved his conflict over who to love (at least according to orthodox psychoanalytic theory and practice) would have been for him to give up one of his 'objects' and face the reality of the loss of it so that he could have a realistically-conducted relationship with the other. He did no such thing. Instead, he found *another* woman.

Marie-Louise Blondin was the sister of one of Lacan's medical-student friends. Sylvain Blondin attracted Lacan before Marie-Louise did. Like his whole family, he was 'haute-bourgeois', beautiful, elegant and brilliant (he came second in the final interns' exams at Saint-Anne). Through him, Lacan fell in love with his sister. One could of course make something of a kind of double desire *here*, by speculating whether Lacan transferred a homosexual attraction to Sylvain onto Marie-Louise to supplement a heterosexual desire that he might or might not have felt for her in any case. Whatever was true, he fell for Marie-Louise and this gave him temporary relief from his entanglements with Marie-Thérèse and Olesia.

Marie-Louise wasn't really like the other two women with whom Lacan had been having sexual relations with and he almost certainly didn't weigh up the prospect of life with her, which would be an entirely different ball-game. She had some artistic inclinations, even gifts (she could paint) and generally had an aesthetic sensibility. Lacan's intelligence and appreciation of art clearly attracted her. Yet art was not her passion or her destiny (she would never have accepted being poor for it) and she didn't have Lacan's obscure interests or avant-garde tastes. Ultimately, she wanted a respectable bourgeois life with beautiful children and enough wealth to sustain a comfortable and elegant existence. Lacan was ambitious, qualified, well-connected, handsome and well dressed enough to be able to promise that he could provide these things. Unsurprisingly, the question of marriage came up quickly and the couple wed, with all due Catholic ceremony. At first, Lacan seemed to take to marriage willingly and with evident satisfaction. Yet although he was married, he continued to act like a bachelor. He communicated with Olesia and had clandestine meetings with her. One guesses that when they met they did more than discuss the Lacans' furnishings.

Just as he had wanted contradictory things (stability and excitement) in his previous love-triangle, Lacan lived by opposite principles in his current one. With Marie-Louise he played the faithful, respectable bourgeois husband. He clearly had some investment in this role, which provided him with emotional security. It did so within a familial context, which included children. The first, Caroline, was born in 1937. A second, Thibaut, followed in 1939. Lacan apparently loved his children and was ostensibly committed to his family. Yet the same family could also see that he wasn't *just* a family man, that he was consumed by other things. Lacan worked hard, spoke at increasingly high-profile events, socialised intensively, drank, travelled and flirted openly and frequently with other women. He remained an intellectual and a libertine and was still a psychical and sensual adventurer. In multiple and marked ways he clearly *wasn't* a family man. Instead he was *absent* from his family much of the time. As if to act all of this out definitively, he embarked on a new affair.

Bataille

Sylvia Bataille must have appeared to Lacan, consciously or not, as a means of subverting the comfort and respectability of his marriage to Marie-Louise. To be sure, this subversion would be subtle and invisible at first. Sylvia was not openly revolutionary. She was slim and pretty if mischievous and her feminism was one of accomplishment rather than provocation. When Lacan met her in 1938 she was twenty and had begun establishing herself as a film actress, most notably in Jean Renoir's *Partie de campagne* (1936). Yet she already bore the traces of a personal history that was other than the impeccably bourgeois and French one that Marie-Louise had enjoyed. Sylvie's father Henri Maklès was an Eastern-European Jewish travelling salesman who had not done especially well from his trade. The family was often in debt and Henri's wife Nathalie was anxious to marry their four daughters off to respectable husbands with good incomes. By becoming an actress Sylvie put herself in the position of potentially being able to fulfil her mother's dreams. Yet her trade kept her in contact with men who were respectable and ones that weren't. She consorted with artists, and other irregular and inconstant inhabitants of the bohemian demi-monde that both nurtured and wasted the early twentieth-century Parisian avant-garde. Sylvia's elder sister Bianca was married to Théodore Fraenkel, a medic who, like Breton, was also a surrealist. Fraenkel knew

Breton well within a social circle that included other aesthetes and intellectuals. This circle included a writer who also temporarily embraced
the surrealist cause before devising a radical, negative and scandalous
philosophy of his own: Georges Bataille.

Although it was dismissed by some of his contemporaries (notably
Sartre), Bataille's thought increased in significance and effect throughout
the twentieth century. By the end of it, his name and ideas had not only
been heard beyond France, but beyond Europe, particularly in the United
States.

Bataille was fascinated by the sacred, but also saw it as inseparable
from the profane. The most debased states, he claimed, are also ones
of joy. Drunkenness, violence and scatological practice bring pleasure,
even ecstasy of a quasi-religious sort. Such propositions are seemingly
dialectical and Bataille was avowedly indebted to Hegel. Yet his arguments
were not synthetic and the opposite states that Bataille invoked were
mostly confounded, rather than resolved, by their common ground.
In other words he showed that defilement might bring thrills and that
violence might feel like transcendence but the coming together of these
states never brings peace or understanding. Thus Bataille's sensibility was
less akin to Hegel's and more like that of Nietzsche, whose influence he
readily acknowledged. He further resembled Nietzsche in his *style* in so far
as his brilliant, violent and scandalous propositions *didn't* take standard
philosophical form. Bataille wrote literature, art, anthropology, sociology,
history and economy *as well as* 'philosophy'.[15] He also lived an extreme,
sexually perverse and drunken life. Unsurprisingly, the avant-garde
tradition in art and thought loved him (they still do). Needless to say,
respectable bourgeois society found him obscene.

There's no good evidence that Sylvia was either obscene *or* perverse
in herself. She did have left-wing politics and had been a member of a
fairly successful 'working-class' theatre troupe: The Octobrists. Yet none
of her activities involved any really scandalous or radical aesthetic or
political action. She did nothing that might get her arrested or shunned in
respectable society.

Yet the fact that Sylvia's parents were relatively loving didn't mean
that they weren't naive. They thought that Georges would make a good
husband for Sylvia and erroneously sanctioned their marriage. Georges'
friends – equally naively – thought Sylvia might save him from himself.
They were wrong and he continued to drink, gamble, womanize and
develop his auto-destructive and apocalyptic philosophy as before.

Sylvia quickly worked out that her best bet with regard to Bataille was to leave him, which she did in 1932, four years after they had wed. Lacan had known both of them since before the marriage and remained friends with both after it had collapsed. His friendship with Georges – which was intellectual as much as it was emotional – persisted throughout their lives. His relationship with Sylvie became intimate and sexual some time before 1936.

Absorption

Lacan read Bataille's work, absorbed it and recycled it much later in a different form that became associated with him rather than with its source. More exactly, he took up Bataille's theme of the non-mediative elision of the divine and debased and noted the ambiguous horror, pleasure and incomprehension that accompanies it. Instances of horrific but enjoyable states take place in what Lacan would come to call 'the real'. This isn't so much 'reality' normally understood as the experience of being sunk in it *without* being able to understand it. 'The real' is how one experiences reality when it *doesn't* make sense. This is why Lacan so often described it as 'the unrepresentable'. In strict Lacanian terms 'the real' is the *absence* of 'the symbolic'. Yet what kind of experience *is* that, exactly? It might help to say that the real is nakedly experienced in both the psychopathological symptom and the existential angst that one is confronted with each day.[16] Both of these states are 'real' states that are fundamental to human being but both also involve a failure or lack of meaning or understanding. The 'symptom' is concomitant with a lack of understanding of the unconscious conflict that is at the root of it. 'Angst' is precisely the psychical and emotional irresolution of a conflict or doubt about meaning – most obviously 'the meaning of life'. Thus both the symptom in general and anxiety in particular operate in the dimension of 'the real' as it was formulated by Lacan (but not in 'reality' or 'the real' as it is understood by everyone else).

The establishment of 'the real' as a uniquely 'Lacanian' notion didn't really take place until the 1960s, when Lacan started to set it alongside the other key notions of his (anti-) metaphysics: the imaginary and the symbolic. At the beginning of the next decade he borrowed from Bataille again. He took an observation from the latter's *Eroticism*, concerning the coincidence of spiritual transcendence and female pleasure (specifically the female orgasm). Then he worked the argument into a new account of female sexuality. His specific example of an instance of the coincidence

in question was the ecstasy of St Teresa. The example came directly from
Bataille, but has since been popularly associated with Lacan.[17]

Liaisons

None of the appropriation of Bataille's arguments by Lacan is clearly
evident in his work of the 1930s although there are equivalences between
Bataille's ideas and Lacan's surrealist-inflected disquisitions of the period.
In the 1930s, Lacan had ears for what Bataille had to say, but eyes for his
wife. Thus his habit of multiplying and splitting his love-objects resurfaced.
Sylvie and Jacques' affair split Lacan's libidinal *and* his social life. It caused
him to have to co-occupy quite different worlds. While he was with the
Blondins he inhabited a haute-bourgeois world which was wealthy, elegant
and securely tied to the institutions of French society: the élite hospitals,
the universities, the aristocracy, business, parliament. At the same time he
frequented bohemia and the 'underground' world of the avant-garde. He
traversed the 'Right Bank' as well as the 'Left Bank' of the Seine.

Marie-Louise was pregnant with Thibaut, the Lacans' second child,
when she found out about the affair. Typically, Jacques did nothing to
rectify the situation. Just as he had prevaricated between Marie-Thérèse
and Olesia, he couldn't make up his mind between Marie-Louise and
Sylvia. Unsurprisingly Marie-Louise utterly disapproved. Yet she couldn't
quite bear to shatter the facade of her successful bourgeois marriage
to a 'genius' (her words) and rising star in the high-status world she so
comfortably occupied. Sylvia, entirely at home in bohemia, continued with
the affair without demands of divorce or re-marriage. She was able to
tolerate her position longer than Marie-Louise. After years of pain and
dissimulation the latter confronted Lacan in the summer of 1940, asking
him to break off with Sylvia. She gave him a year to make up his mind,
or, she said, she would make it up for him. A few months later Lacan
discovered that *Sylvia* was pregnant. Extraordinarily, he shared this news
with Marie-Louise in the expectation that she would be pleased about it.
The difference between his expectation and her response was of course
exacerbated by the fact that Marie-Louise was pregnant too (and had been
so for eight months by then). What was he thinking? Whatever it was, it
obviously didn't involve any proper or entirely sane acknowledgment of
reality. For that matter – and for the Freudian reasons given above, it also
didn't involve any true recognition of *the reality of loss* which was more
inevitable in the situation at hand than in any other amorous one than

Lacan had been in so far. Marie-Louise petitioned for and was eventually granted a divorce, which was finalised in December 1941.

Three months before this date Sylvie gave birth to Lacan's daughter, named Judith. She already had a daughter by Bataille named Laurence. Georges and Sylvie were amicably separated, but still married. There were practical and political reasons for this. Sylvia was a Jew living in occupied France. She received a certain amount of protection from persecution by the Nazis through marriage to a non-Jew (Georges). Lacan couldn't marry Sylvia (he wasn't yet divorced) and Georges was happy to oblige. For these reasons Sylvie gave Lacan's daughter Georges' surname. She was called Judith Bataille.

Even beyond Lacan's divorce, this absurdly complex situation continued. If anything, it got worse. Lacan and Marie-Louise agreed that their children should know nothing about the fact that their father had divorced their mother and taken up with another woman. This was done despite the fact that Lacan, at Marie-Louise's insistence, had legally renounced his parental authority over them. He lived elsewhere, but continued to visit his children by Marie-Louise regularly and to 'act' as their father. The situation came to a head that was surreally awful (especially for the children) in 1949. One afternoon Caroline and Thibaut had visited the zoo and were returning home from it. They saw Lacan at the wheel of a car that was stopped at a crossing. A woman was beside him and a child was in the back seat. Lacan's children (by Marie Louise) ran towards him shouting 'Papa, Papa'. Lacan saw them but pretended that he hadn't and drove off without looking.

Suffice to say that Lacan's capacity for splitting and disavowal are fully in evidence in the episode described above. He kept his second family apart from his first. When he was no longer physically able to do this, he acted as if the separation held nevertheless and as if his first family didn't exist. Yet he was of course already accepting that they did exist by visiting them regularly. Lacan's actions involved both the denial of a reality and the denial of a reality of loss. In other words he displayed exactly the characteristics of a subject whose psyche is split in the way that Freud described in his 'Splitting of the Ego' paper.

Eventuality

The type of split behaviour that Lacan exhibited was not only explicable in Freudian terms but was also eventually theorised by Lacan himself. From about 1950 onwards (that is from after the time of his *second* Mirror Phase paper) Lacan identified splitting as being typical of ego functioning and (thereafter) as being pre-dispositional to certain severe psychopathological conditions. More exactly he described the ego as being constitutionally split and deemed this split to involve a denial of reality that could lead to psychosis. He gave this proto-psychotic denial a name: *foreclosure*.

Lacan's argument about foreclosure was both an extension and an alteration of Freud's one about splitting. It *comprehended* Freud's argument but also overlaid it with one that was Lacanian. Technically, according to Lacan, foreclosure amounts to denial of the possibility of castration rather than denial of reality *per se*. The boy undergoing the Oedipus Complex doesn't so much fear the real as he fears losing the means of being able to master it, or have what he wants from it (notably his mother). The imaginary agent of his mastery (that which he 'holds on to' as a way of convincing himself that he is in control of the real) is 'the phallus'. Lacan preferred this term to 'penis', not least because it designates something that wields power symbolically rather than actually.[18] In any case the 'castration threat' isn't a real threat. It doesn't (really) threaten the (real) penis and it is conveyed in a medium or order which is not that of reality as such. Rather the castration threat is transmitted *in* language. Even more specifically (and significantly) it is implicit in language. This is because language itself involves a kind of separation – in fact it involves various kinds of separation but most obviously it involves differentiations between concepts, or words. The world is known through words, so the encounter with language ensures that the world is divided into parts, that it is cut up, that it is not 'whole' and that the one who encounters it (in the first instance the child) can no longer *feel* 'whole' *in* it (as s/he might have done in the pre-Oedipal maternal universe and/or the womb). In a sense, language *per se* bears a 'castration threat'. Now of course language also involves and is even a form of *symbolisation*. Thus when the child resists language (and its differentiating force) s/he denies symbolisation *as such*. This is the 'foreclosure of the symbolic' that prompts psychosis.

Lacan accounted for these phenomena and processes in a typically intermittent, abstruse and gnomic way. Yet they *were* brought together by him in at least one context, albeit a large one: his annual seminar of 1955–6, which dealt, somewhat loosely, with psychosis. (Lacan, [1955–6] 1993, esp. pp. 3–157; 247–32) This date is of course considerably later than the date of Freud's paper on splitting [1940], it is also much later than Lacan's first Mirror Phase paper [1936] and even post-dates his second one [1949]. If Lacan did understand the theoretical significance of the phenomenon of splitting, he only did *so eventually*. To put it another way, he didn't realise the implications, ramifications or significance of the 'splitting of the subject' at once or at first.

Paper

A closer look at Lacan's early work confirms this. Although there are relations between his first Mirror Stage paper and the arguments that Freud developed around disavowal and the division of the ego, they are not straightforward or faithful ones. Even if Lacan's *later* writing *did* demonstrate his comprehension of Freud's ideas, his 1936 paper indicates that he *hadn't* then understood them. More exactly, he hadn't yet grasped Freud's argument about splitting. Even more specifically – he hadn't appreciated the *logic* of it. It's even true to say that Lacan's early paper on the ego, compared with Freud's paper on splitting, wasn't logical at all.

The Mirror Stage paper was a testament to Lacan's interest in phenomenology, yet it presented the phenomenological agent – the ego – *illogically*. It described it as coherent on the one hand and divided on the other. These contrasting observations were made separately – in different phrases, sentences and paragraphs. At no point in the first Mirror Phase paper did Lacan explicitly or meaningfully link the ego's coherence and its division. Yet why should he need to do this, one might ask? Aren't coherence and division opposite and therefore mutually exclusive characteristics in any case? In fact they aren't, or at least they aren't *always* so. This much is apparent in *Freud's* paper on 'the Splitting of the Ego' and one only need recall the *logic* of that paper to understand the point. In the Oedipal scenario that Freud describes, the boy is split in his attitude towards the mother precisely to *maintain* a contradictory view of her. He fetishises her (or part of her) as a way of denying that she doesn't have a penis (and in order to mitigate his fear that he might lose his own). Yet his need to do this *is* a tacit acknowledgement *that* she doesn't have a penis (and that he might *indeed* lose his own). The boy holds two opposite ideas in his mind at the same time: the denial of loss and the admission that loss is real. The two ideas are correlative as well as contradictory. Thus even though one can say that there is a discrepancy between them, there is a logic to the way that they're both believed. This logic, to be exact, is one of *disavowal*.

Freud's account thus explains the *logic* of the link between splitting and contradiction and thereby the *necessary* connection between the two. Lacan's first Mirror Phase paper manifestly *doesn't* do this. It's true that by 1949, when Lacan's paper was re-written and re-delivered, he had understood something of *dialectical* logic and was able to describe the formation of the ego in terms of a process and a structure that was both constitutionally split *and* integrated (this will be shown shortly). Yet in 1936 his paper looked more like a symptom of what it was describing than an account of it. It wasn't so much about egoistic contradiction as it was contradictory itself. Rather than adequately describing the ego's fragmentation, it *was* fragmented. It was an example of the splitting it couldn't yet properly describe.

Life

All of this was equally and obviously true about Lacan's life at the time. It was split and contradictory in a way that he hadn't realised – or rather *symbolised*. His view of himself (as an influential analyst) differed from others' view of him (as not especially important). He required two lovers, but could only cope with one; he wooed both and each supplemented the other.[19] When this didn't work he married a third woman without sacrificing either of the first two. Then he married a fourth who represented a bohemian transgression of the bourgeois respectability of the third. This fourth woman, who was a second wife, was both the apotheosis and the completion of her predecessor. In matters of love Lacan acted as if he could have everything and as if loss could be avoided. This was effectively a denial that he had to lose anything at all. His life and work continued in the 1930s and 40s, but he gave no sign of *fully* understanding splitting and loss at the time. This was as true in practice as it was in theory and held for Lacan's personal life as well as for his intellectual one.

Had things changed by the time that Lacan wrote and delivered his *second* Mirror Phase paper in 1949? In order to begin to address this question, that paper is explained and summarised below.

Between six and eighteen months the child is captivated by his image in the mirror. He plays with this image, gains some control over it and begins to recognize it as 'his'. This 'ownership' of his image is the child's first experience of a sense of 'identity'. He sees and has some influence over an image that he can think of as his own and as himself.

Prior to the moment of recognition in the mirror, the child has no secure or singular-seeming sense of identity. He exists – or rather subsists – in a continuum in which he doesn't have a clear sense of his own separateness from either the world or his mother. He hasn't yet fully accepted or adjusted to the fact that he has left the womb.

Yet it's true that from the outset the infant also feels separate from *as well as* merged with his 'umwelt' – not least because he *is* separate from it – he has, after all, experienced the trauma of birth. Yet this separateness is uncomfortable and is primarily experienced as vulnerability that is felt in a number of bodily as well as psychical forms. Thus the child experiences 'organic insufficiency': the need for sustenance that only another can provide. He exhibits 'motor incapacity and nursling dependence': his central nervous system and motor skills are not yet integrated and this accentuates his dependence on his mother. Concomitantly, he is subject to 'turbulent movements', which are a result of both his un-coordination and his primal distress.

Despite, or rather because of all the turbulence and dissension that he feels, the child seeks a 'symmetry' in the image in the mirror. He 'fixes' it. The fixed image is held in the head as much as in the field of vision and the mirror and is *held to* anxiously against the contingencies that characterise both the child's environment and his sense of his place (a displaced place) in it. In the fixity it opposes to its environment, the self-image becomes a sort of 'statue'. Ostensibly, it is secure; actually, it is immobile. Because the self-image (and hence the nascent self) doesn't move or change in a world that does, it also amounts to something else that is non-concrete but equally fixed: an illusion. This illusion promises something safe and sustaining but is of course not real. It is misleading and is therefore also a *delusion*. In other words it is a 'mirage'. In general, the self-image is a phantasy in which the child misrepresents his circumstances and himself *to* himself. It has only a 'willed' and besieged contact with itself and with the world it is sunk in. Consequently, it ossifies. All it then provides by way of security is 'the armour of an alienating identity'.

The most important aspect of the mirror image in Lacan's formulation is that it is *other* than what it reflects. This point can usefully be made in the first person singular. The mirror image is other than me as well as being me. This is literally and obviously true because it is *in* something other than me: the mirror. Yet the 'otherness' of the image isn't just a physical, spatial or even visual fact. It holds for my 'mental' image of myself too – the image I have of myself in my mind. *That* image is *also* other than me. In order to appreciate both the implications and the consequences of this situation, it might help to indulge a short digression relating to a philosopher who is nevertheless mentioned in the Mirror Stage paper: Descartes.

Descartes

The self's imagistic 'alterity' conforms to a formulation of it that, according to Lacan, 'sets us at odds with any philosophy of the cogito'.

(EC, p. 94) By saying this, Lacan was suggesting that his understanding of the formation of the self (in particular) and identity (in general) is the *opposite* of the one made famous by Descartes. This is true in some respects, but is also an oversimplification of what is actually the case. The formulation of 'identity' proposed by Lacan's second Mirror Phase paper is both opposed and not opposed to the one proposed by Descartes. It contradicts and conforms to Descartes' account of selfhood at the same time. This is best shown by way of deconstruction of both arguments at issue: Lacan's and Descartes'.

In order to enable this deconstruction, it's worth first recalling how Descartes formulated the self. This happened while he was attempting to satisfy a philosophical need to find something that he could be sure of, something that promised some 'certainty' and hence a foundation for the establishment of everything else. In short, he was trying to discover the conditions for knowledge, to establish how we know what we know.

First of all he wondered whether sense impressions might provide such foundation. Since evidence of the world seems to be provided through the senses, he asked whether those senses can be trusted as being absolutely reliable. Could his eyesight and his hearing, for example, always be relied on to show and tell him what was really going on, really existing and happening in the world? Had he been able to show this, Descartes would have been able to argue that sense perceptions were sound conditions for knowledge, at least of the external world. Yet he was unable to demonstrate the soundness of perceptual evidence. This was because sense perceptions can be deceptive. It's possible to think that you hear sounds when you don't. A twig sticking out of a pool of water can appear bent when, in fact, it is not. Sense perceptions may provide *some* reliable evidence of what can be known, but they can never be *absolutely* secure foundations for knowledge.

Besides, Descartes said, it's at least conceivable that *all* of one's apparent perceptions are misleading. Still considering his own apprehension of things, he conceded that he could be dreaming everything that he thought he perceived. Alternatively, it's conceivable that one's apprehension of the world could have been induced in one by some 'evil demon' and that one could have no notion that this had happened.

Still looking for a scientific and philosophical guarantee for knowledge, Descartes turned his attention inward, to his thought. He noted that he was aware of his own thoughts. He then reasoned that this awareness of his own thoughts implied consciousness, and knowledge, in the following way. The thoughts which he recognised *as* thoughts must have had a thinker, who, he concluded, was himself. He was thus conscious of both his thought and himself at the same time.

Conscious thought implies a thinker who can recognise himself as the thinker of the thought he has. Consciousness is thus a kind of self-consciousness. It is also a kind of self-knowledge, since to think is to know that one is doing the thinking and so to know oneself. Descartes had (or at least thought he had) established, in thought, the foundation of the self, knowledge and knowledge of the self at the same time. *Cogito ergo sum:* I think therefore I am. He considered such reasoned self-knowledge in thought (otherwise known as rational self-consciousness) to be a kind of condition or bottom line of knowledge in general. Furthermore, he suggested that if one can know oneself, one can extend this knowledge in order to include facts about (and hence knowledge of) the external world. It's true that this knowledge would be subjective (and that the world would hence be 'my world') but Descartes would argue that it was knowledge based on a prior and secure premise (self-knowledge) nevertheless.

Gap

Yet Descartes' argument contains a 'logical gap' (that is a gap in logic that is also logical), which can be explained thus. The image that I see of myself in my thought is *other* than me. Indeed, it *must* be thus, otherwise I wouldn't be able to see it. In the same way that I can't see my own face except in a mirror, I can't recognise my own thought unless I 'see' it in my mind (or in my 'mind's eye') as something other than me that *can* be seen. *Only then* can I recognise myself. Otherwise, I would only be recognizing myself as something I already know myself to be (and would be doing so tautologically and even autistically, or one might say 'tautistically'). The alterity of the image is the logical (or reasonable) condition for the recognition of the self in it *at all.*

Yet Descartes didn't acknowledge this. He effaced the alterity of the self-image. He did so, significantly, in order to maintain the appearance of the autonomy and integrity of the 'I'. For him, self-recognition and selfhood (in thought) had to be complete and secure and even assured enough to confirm perception of the world. Otherwise, how could it be the foundation of *all* knowledge? Now in order for the self to be secure (or at least to seem convincing) self-recognition had to be total, so the gap between the seer and the seen in thought in the moment of self-recognition had to disappear. Only thus could the self become *one*, such that it 'may be able to know its own nature with perfect distinctness'. Descartes 'eliminated' the gap between the subject that recognises himself in his own thought and the *other* that he recognises himself as and did so in order to produce a subject that seemed *whole*.

Yet, as shown above, it is the very alterity of self-recognition that allows the subject to be. It is what permits Descartes to recognise himself *as* himself in thought *at all*. Once again: *the self that is recognised must be other than the self that recognises itself in it.* Of course Lacan knew this. It's why he thought of his 'Mirror Stage' formulation of identity as being 'opposed' to any Cartesian one. Descartes claimed that the self recognises itself in thought, while Lacan claimed that the subject recognises himself *as another* in thought. This is why when Descartes said: 'I think therefore I am', Lacan replied: 'I think where I am not, therefore I am where I do not think.'

In seeking to securely establish identity in self-recognition, Descartes worked to occlude the gap between the self that recognises and the self that is recognised. Lacan saw his own formulation of selfhood as being *in opposition* to Descartes' because it acknowledged the very gap that Descartes dis-acknowledged and stressed that the self only ever finds itself in *another* representation of it, one that only ever secures it insecurely and by way of an alienation.

Inversion

Yet Lacan failed to see that a reverse formulation is also true (in other words that a formulation that is opposite to *his*, whether or not it is Cartesian, is also true). In order for there to be an 'other' to the self (in thought) there has to be a self in terms of which it is apprehended as such (as 'other'). The other *always already* presumes a self that might recognise – or for that matter misrecognise – it. Just as Descartes' formulation occludes alterity, Lacan's effaces the selfhood that alterity allows. This is incidentally (although not insignificantly) why Lacan's account of selfhood often seems *tragic*. For Lacan absence – of fulfilment, of *self*-fulfilment, of full selfhood – is the very condition for the possibility of the self. *Yet an opposite truth still holds*. The otherness of the self *requires* a self if it is to be apprehended at all.

The upshot of all this is that alterity and unity are mutual conditions of the formation of the self. The self needs an other to recognise itself in and this other already implies that such a self exists. Lacan's position and Descartes' *complement* as much as oppose each other.

On this sort of basis one could say that Lacan's formulation of the constitution of the subject doesn't strictly contradict or correct Descartes' argument about the self. It just shows *the other side* of that argument. Logically, the constitution of the self is explained by *both sides* of the argument: the other and the self imply and require each other. If Descartes' formulation is erroneous then Lacan's is too; if it isn't, then Lacan's isn't either.

There are all sorts of significant general and particular implications that follow from both Lacan's theory of the subject and from its articulation (and disarticulation) with Descartes'. Many of these implications will be teased out in the material that constitutes the rest of this book.[20]

Unconstitutional

Yet for now, it's important to continue to articulate Lacan's account of the reflective constitution of the ego *as he understood it*. More specifically, it's necessary to emphasise and understand the implications, for Lacan, of the self-image's 'alterity' as it is described in the second Mirror Stage paper.

A number of significant – and even well-known – aspects of 'the self' as it is described by Lacan follow from its constitution 'otherwise' and 'in the mirror'. These 'characteristics' all have to do with the ego's formation by way of an image that is 'other'.

Most obviously, the ego is *alienated*. Why wouldn't it be? It has to seek and find itself 'elsewhere'; it is not 'at home' in itself. The entirety of Lacan's work – from its beginning to its end – describes or presumes a human self that is foreign to itself. It is displaced in self-recognition, or caught up in the network of words that give it voice but exceed it (the 'defiles of the signifier') or hidden in the unconscious, or ejected into projection, or buried in the transference, or dispersed in the fragmentation of psychosis, or unsure of its sexual identity, or lost in 'the real'. The ego *is* an alien. More exactly it is alien 'to itself'…'in its own land'.

Additionally the ego, precisely in so far as it is constituted 'in the mirror' is *imaginary*. It has no material substance and is not 'a thing' in the ordinary sense. It is imagistic and is, at best, a *representation* (of a person or thing, rather than *being* a person or thing). Consequently, it is suffused with the subject's wishes, most obviously his wish to be whole. The very stuff of the making of the ego (its memories, its identifications, its idealisations, its 'dreams', its 'wishes to be') is the stuff of phantasy, as psychoanalysts since Freud have pointed out and as Shakespeare intuited when he wrote: 'we are such stuff/as dreams are made on'. (The Tempest, Act IV scene I) The ego is *phantasmatic* and Lacan's account of the mirror phase is really the beginning of his formulation of the ontological category of 'The Imaginary' per se.

Finally, the ego is part-unconscious.[21] This is best explained in the first person and with reference to the constitutive gap in the ego. Because the image that I have of myself is other than me as well as being me there is a gap in me or between me and myself. This gap both allows my self to be (minimally) constituted and prevents it from being (ideally) constituted (or to put it as it has been put above), allows for the Cartesian constitution of the self *and* the Lacanian one). Now if the self isn't an ideal one because it is constituted over a gap (which is the Lacanian point of view) then this gap isn't only constitutional, but also representative of what the *ideal* self *isn't*. In other words the gap not only marks the self, but also the gulf between its ideal and its actual constitution – between what I think I am and what I actually am. This holds in both theoretical and personal terms. If the ideal self is unified and conscious, then the gap in the self marks its disunity and unconsciousness (I like to think of myself in a certain way, but I don't really know who I am). Furthermore, if the gap-free self is ideal, then what comes up in the gap *isn't* (my errors and flaws show me as I wouldn't, rather than would, like to be seen). Because the gap marks the limitation of how I (can) consciously think of myself, because it is what my inadmissible wishes fall into, because it represents the rupture in thought of my pathologies and the route out for my desires, the gap in my thinking, indeed the gap in *me, is* my *unconscious*.

Ideal

For some, Lacan's 1949 Mirror Phase paper has come to represent his work as a whole. It is undoubtedly the most read, quoted and studied of all of his writings. The paper often seems the most manageable work to present to students. It's not easily comprehensible (not much of Lacan's work is) but it does allow one to get a grip on one of the key axes of his thought: the constitution of the ego in so far as it oriented towards the Imaginary. Above all, it is short.

Yet the Mirror Phase paper is not just the lowest-pain/highest-impact work by Lacan. It really does represent a significant step forward in the development of his ideas. In many ways it summarises and crystallises the observations and discoveries that he made in the 1930s and 1940s. It presents an ego that conforms to the one described by Freud, that is set in consciousness but is also unconscious, that accedes to selfhood but is also delusory. This ego, furthermore, has a paranoid caste that part-derives from its constitution by way of another, which it both needs and fears and which in many ways resembles the relation to the 'object' described by Klein, which also involves a distinctly paranoid dimension. (Klein, [1930] 1986; [1940] 1986)

Yet the paper not only collates Lacan's influences and intellectual past, it anticipates his future. To be exact, it calls for concentration by analysts on an ego whose shape and limitations are significantly instructed by its rootedness in unconsciousness. This means no truck with any form of analysis that holds that the bulk of the ego is conscious and that declares that it can be modified and improved by *changing* that consciousness, either by remodelling it on the analyst's consciousness (that is his conscious ego) *or* by adapting it to *reality*. Lacan thought that such strategies that can be attributed to 'ego-psychology', were misguided, misleading and above all *un-Freudian*. He would spend much of the early 1950s discrediting them and directly and indirectly berating US analysts (who practised them) and his own analyst Loewenstein (who moved to the US in 1942) for betraying what he saw as Freud's message in their practice.[22] Yet perhaps the most significant anticipation of Lacan's future that the 1949 Mirror Phase paper contained was in its rudimentary but basically sound use of dialectical thought. *Unlike* the 1936 paper, it managed to provide an account of the ego as something that *contained* opposite tendencies and it succeeded in doing so *logically*. Lacan *did* describe the ego as conscious *and* unconscious, singular *and* split, assertive *and* defensive (and so on) and did so in a way that *wasn't* contradictory.

Redevelopment

In short, the 1949 Mirror Phase paper is a powerful recapitulation of Lacan's early and continuing position. It is more comprehensive and makes much more sense than his 1936 paper. This is not to say that it's without contradiction. If nothing else, Lacan's confusion about the relation of his own argument to Descartes' shows as much. Indeed, Lacan's arguments would *never* be entirely contradiction-free. Still, this doesn't mean that he never made progress, that his thought never developed. The better quality of his 1949 paper compared with his 1936 paper confirms that it did.

Yet what kind of development *was* this exactly? We have seen that the 1936 version of the Mirror Phase paper *didn't* make sense. Lacan clearly *had* developed by 1949 and this development had involved a quite sophisticated *intellectual* understanding of splitting. Yet intellectual development doesn't necessarily include personal development. Was Lacan developing personally?

Knowledge

As suggested above, the 'splitting of the ego' that Freud identified was increasingly emphasised in Lacan's *theories*, which eventually took it as fundamental to the constitution and functioning of the human ego. The 1949 Mirror Phase paper is exemplary in this regard. Thereafter Lacan often stressed the 'split the subject undergoes by virtue of being a subject'. (EC, p. 530) Did he see this split in himself?

It's clear that as Lacan developed intellectually he was also theorising a condition that he was 'acting out'. Recall that he had unilaterally terminated his own psychoanalysis, against the advice of (and in breach of an agreement with) his analyst. Thus his views on splitting weren't primarily developed out of a completed personal psychoanalysis. They were intellectual and theoretical views, formulated in Lacan's persona as a psychiatrist and analyst (of course, Lacan sometimes adopted the persona of a philosopher too). Little or none of his opinion came from his personal analytic experience *per se*. All of this is really to say the following: Lacan's understanding and knowledge of splitting came from his ego rather than his unconscious. It was clever, but it didn't contain much insight. Specifically, it didn't show that Lacan had insight *about himself*. How could it? His behaviour contradicted any sense that insight was what he had. As he was beginning, in 1949, to chart the myriad divisions of 'human nature', his own 'nature' was still utterly divided. Hadn't his familial and sexual relations shown this?

It's arguable that not only Lacan's life, but also his practice and even his theories are significantly compromised by him not having completed his personal analysis. His preoccupation with splitting might look more sincere, less unconscious in its motivation and less ambiguous if one could take it as having been a product of his comprehension that he *was* split and that he had, via analysis, understood the origins of, reasons for and effects of this splitting *in himself* as well as having identified splitting as a phenomenon otherwise, via theoretical understanding and speculation and/or observation of his patients. Yet Lacan terminated his own analysis and one therefore has to wonder whether his interest in splitting was pathological as much as it was clinical and that his theories relating to it were as symptomatic of his personal pathologies as they were reflective of his professional and intellectual insights.

For his part, Lacan claimed to have completed a *self*-analysis, as Freud did[23] He claimed that this happened *after* he had fled Lowenstein's couch. To be precise, it had happened 'in his own Seminar'. This is a strange claim. It suggests that Lacan was analysed by his own public interpretations in a context in which he was the master of interpretation and in which by all accounts he delighted in passing on pearls of wisdom and truth to his eager and besotted disciples. Does this sound like truth derived from a psychoanalysis or does it sound like a narcissistic phantasy? (Schneidermann, Roudinesco and Roustang, 1997, p. 75)

It's fair to speculate that even if Lacan understood (Freud's account of) splitting and even if he increasingly understood himself, this didn't mean that he was able to see the splits in himself honestly enough to be able to mitigate them entirely or to transform himself into someone who *wasn't* split.

6

Fight and Flight

By the early 1950s, the Second World War was over and so was more than half of Lacan's life. His Mirror Stage paper had had a mixed reception at the 1949 IPA conference. Responses varied from enthusiastic to dismissive, with many positions including acceptance and indifference adopted in-between. Some psychoanalysts received Lacan's paper positively. Others at least acknowledged that he was a force to be reckoned with, whether they understood him, agreed with him, liked him, or not. Most analysts respected Lacan's psychiatric training and/or recognised that he understood Freud. Some even sought tentative alliances with him to further their own ambitions. The best known of these was Melanie Klein.

There was an affinity between the ideas of Lacan and Klein that each instantly recognised. In the great struggle to produce theoretical dogma and gain institutional power that beset psychoanalysis in the 1930s and 1940s, Klein initially saw Lacan as someone who could help her. Like her, he claimed Freud's inheritance but expanded on the master's theories in a novel way. His ideas, like Klein's, *were* Freudian derivatives, yet they also involved concepts and categories of being that were different from – and difficult to recognise as – orthodox Freudian ones. This was precisely why Klein saw Lacan as a possible ally against conservative Freudianism, which was personified for her by Anna Freud. In the 1940s Lacan courted Klein, letting her know how much he admired her work. Klein encouraged him in his interest, suggesting that he translate her work into French. This way, she thought, she could solicit the attention of young French analysts (many of whom admired Lacan) and add a French wing to the troop of international analysts that supported her bids for institutional power. Lacan undertook to co-translate 'The Psycho-Analysis of Children' with an associate, René Diatkine. (Klein, [1932] 1997) The latter completed the first half and gave it to the former. Lacan promptly lost the manuscript, possibly betraying his ambivalence about Klein in the process (he must have seen her as a rival as well as an ally). Klein had little to do with Lacan after that.

Some analysts disliked, distrusted and discredited him from the start. Among these were some very influential figures, including Anna Freud herself. Princess Marie Bonaparte, Freud's friend and confidante and a major psychoanalytic player, also immediately felt enmity for Lacan. Both of these extremely influential and powerful women called Lacan 'paranoid'.

Despite all this, throughout the 1930s and 1940s, Lacan built up a network of international analytic allies who engaged with his ideas and sought to gain him a global hearing. A notable number of French analysts were colleagues and friends of Lacan's and had leverage in the IPA. Lacan also had domestic supporters who were analytic trainees and who would make up the next generation of French analysts. Many of them were loyal to him by virtue of being his analysands.

Thus although it's true that Lacan alienated people, he also had admirers. He was sometimes dishonest and his intellectual worth has always been disputed, but he was charming, charismatic and intelligent. He built himself a following that continued to grow. Some of his supporters had real power; others didn't, but were able to give him something that enabled *him* to feel empowered: love. He may have been exaggerating when he opened his [1949] Mirror Stage paper by claiming that 'The concept of the mirror stage [has] been more or less adopted by the French group', but he wasn't telling an outright lie.[1]

Disruption

It was in such a concatenation of sympathetic and unsympathetic, national and international, political and personal forces that Lacan's life would play out in the 1950s and 1960s. This was the time during which he most closely engaged with international institutional psychoanalysis in the form of the IPA. Because of his mixed reputation and ambiguous character, he spent much of the period battling with the institution concerned, one might even say *at war* with it. Yet the IPA/Lacan war wasn't all-out from the outset. Lacan first wanted to be a *member* of the IPA; he wanted to *belong* to it. Given his ambition, he almost certainly wanted to occupy a position of *influence* in it too. Still, Lacan and the IPA couldn't sustain good relations and their engagement became and remained combative. It ended up in a sort of fight to the death, like the one that Eteocles and Polynices conducted over Thebes, or the one that Hegel described in his

Phänomenologie des Geistes. Lacan had much to say about both fights from a psychoanalytic point of view, but was nevertheless unable to learn from either, at least not enough to be able to transcend recurrent and deathly conflict with an institution he both resented and wanted to conquer. (Sophocles, 1984; Hegel, [1807] 1977)

The 1950s and 1960s were also the period in which Lacan's most eye-catching, best-known and most influential ideas developed. His writings were published and spread *beyond* the community of registered psycho-analysts. Trainee analysts, academics, critics, students and anyone who encountered Lacan's increasingly translated and published work pored over it. He was *idealised.* Yet he was also widely *criticised* and personally and intellectually attacked. This first of all happened in France and then (in the '70s and '80s) in the UK and US. Some of Lacan's readers declared him a genius, others a fraud. Many confessed to not understanding what he had to say at all.

Lacan's extremely mixed history, contribution, reputation and fate during the 1950s and 1960s will be described in this and the next chapter. The description will be historical and biographical, but also theoretical as this book is of course about Lacan's ideas as well as his life. Material will mostly be treated in historical sequence, although one brief return to the 1930s will have to be made. Lacan might have forgiven this return, in principle if not in fact, for he recognised, as all analysts do, that progress forward requires some steps back.

Establishment

To sum up: Lacan has the reputation among some of having been a disruptive force in world psychoanalysis – this view of him largely prevails among members of the IPA. Yet Lacanians obviously demur, seeing the IPA as establishmentarian in its administration, conservative in its practices and authoritarian in its edicts. They see Lacan as having been the hero who challenged all of this. In order to understand this polarisation in perception of Lacan's worth, it's necessary to sketch out the orthodox institutions and relations of power that hold (and have long held) in global and local psychoanalysis. Doing this will reveal the world in which psycho-analysts have operated since the beginning of the twentieth century.

The IPA's roots were in meetings between Freud and other analysts in 1908 in Vienna. The group they convened conducted a congress in Salzburg in the same year and consolidated their association at a further meeting in Nuremburg in 1910, at which they named themselves the International Psychoanalytic Association. The organisation bought together various European analysts and associations and pledged to consolidate, develop and spread the word of its founder and the 'science' and practice of psychoanalysis that he bequeathed to it.

Psychoanalysis' European roots are much commented on, but its constitution is no longer exclusively European. Indeed, much of Lacan's conflict with the IPA had to do with his quite valid view that, throughout the twentieth century, it became Americanised. In the year before Freud established the IPA, he travelled to the USA with the aim of disseminating his ideas there.[2] By mid-century, psychoanalysis had become a global practice, one which some say was (and is) dominated by North Americans.

The Americanisation of the IPA is arguably apparent in its past and current constitution, organisation and membership. It administers three regions: North America, South America and Europe. Institutions that are associated with it mostly fall into two categories: societies, which tend to be national, and associations, which are supra-national (for example continental). Bodies that organise training for societies and associations – sometimes called 'Institutes' – are not only regulated by local or regional grandees, but also overseen by a central IPA committee. In most cases analysts who 'qualify' via their national or regional training body (or 'Institute') are also – in effect – approved by the IPA. Thus many members of (national) societies and (trans-national) associations are *default* members of the IPA too.

The administrative details of global psychoanalytic training and regulation might seem a little over-technical to be relaying here, but they are relevant for at least two reasons. Firstly, they bear directly on Lacan's story, specifically on the history of his (and his societies') tortuous and conflictual relations with the IPA. Secondly, they relate to the North American presence in the psychoanalytic world, which is very considerable and which exercises significant power because of the structure of association outlined above, more specifically because of the arrangements afforded the North American part of this structure. The North American region of IPA administration is so massive and so populated by analysts that the association that represents it – the American Psychoanalytic Association (APA) – has a unique institutional autonomy. It is left to administer and approve training in the USA *without* the specific oversight of the IPA. At the same time the number of its qualified and successful analysts is so great that its members also occupy significant positions *within* the IPA. According to its critics, North American analysts are too numerous, too-powerful and too-privileged members of the global institution that regulates the practice of all others.

By the early 1950s 'ego-psychology' was a popular and influential psychoanalytic form among IPA members that had been developed by analysts who were citizens of, and/or migrants to, the US. It represented what Lacan took to be an errant form of Freudianism, one that de-emphasised the influence of the id and the unconscious on human being and that misguidedly sought to put patients in touch with a perceived 'reality'. Lacan thought this 'reality' was nothing of the sort but was instead a sort of ideological fiction. He saw the 'ego-psychologist' trying to adapt their patients' egos *to* this 'fiction' and saw them doing so by modelling their patients' egos on their own – which they of course took to be 'realistic'. For Lacan such analysts not only failed to understand that their self-perceptions were delusional, but also that their perceptions of reality were too. Both the perception and the experience of the 'reality' invoked in ego-psychology conformed to a norm rather than anything real. Specifically, it equated to no more or less than 'the American way of life'.[3]

Lacan made his criticisms explicit. They were strident and appeared in his public pronouncements and addresses as well as in his personal conversations and correspondences.[4] Yet – at least at first – his complaints went against the grain of his general engagement with the institution concerned. He didn't criticise the IPA at its colloquia and wasn't generally unfriendly with its members. Indeed, he seemed to want not only to *be* an active IPA member, but also to *rise up* in its ranks. Thus his behaviour and attitude seemed anomalous. It looks less anomalous and more explicable if his split 'nature' is recalled.

Society

Before that, though, it's necessary to provide a description of the *national* institutional situation in which Lacan operated. This means saying something about the SPP. The SPP was founded in 1925, significantly later than some other European societies. Some founding SPP members were medics and many of these were psychiatrists. Others, like Marie Bonaparte, advocated lay-analysis. There was no single 'type'. Bonaparte was a French princess (although a liberal-minded one) while members like Edouard Pichon were bourgoise and chauvinistic. Still others, like Rudolph Loewenstein, were Jewish, migrant and liberal. The society was healthily diverse. Despite or perhaps because of this diversity, SPP members managed broadly to agree on a way of understanding Freud's ideas and they devised statutes and processes to enshrine this under-standing for the purposes of qualification and training. They received Freud's endorsement in 1926 and were made collective and individual IPA members from then on.

Much of the recognition of the SPP was negotiated by Sacha Nacht, an ambitious but fiercely respectable Hungarian émigré analyst who had forged international links, including ones with Freud. Nacht's approach to psychoanalytic theory and training was conservative and his attitude towards both institutional matters and individual analyses might be described as authoritarian, or at least authoritative. He didn't sanction any bending of institutional rules and he believed that in the end the analyst (or President, or 'father') was always right. He was head of the society from 1949.

Lacan was not among this first generation of analysts when the SPP was founded, but of course he consorted with them when he joined their ranks in 1932. They were trained, intelligent and experienced – in life as well as in medicine. Lacan wanted to sit in power beside them, but this was easier said than done. He couldn't simply win them over with his extreme cleverness and charm (they were psychoanalysts, after all) and he sometimes had to resort to disingenuousness to get what he wanted.

Yet by 1949 Lacan had managed to garner some respect or at least acceptance from his colleagues, however grudging. It helped that the power-dynamic within the institution had shifted in his favour. Nacht was President, but Lacan had become very involved in administrative matters. When Nacht set up a commission on instruction to examine how to train analysts, Lacan drew up the rules of the commission and advised on the doctrine that the commission should pursue. Nacht then formed an Institute in which to organise training and swiftly appointed himself Director of it (he was at least as ambitious as Lacan was). Lacan was as involved in the setting up of the Institute as he had been in the drafting of the commission. Although he didn't at first have Nacht's titles or authority, Lacan had got his hands on the key administrative and executive levers of the Institute – and eventually the Society. He wasn't in overall charge, but he did write the rules. No procedures were implemented that hadn't been formulated or at least sanctioned by Lacan and no laws were made that hadn't been made by him. This formidable *instrumental* power eventually gained him both a position and a title: that of Vice-President.

The set-up described was one in which there was some stability in the SPP, however temporary. Rules were made, written, implemented and held to by all analysts. Yet there was also considerable tension beneath the surface. Nacht held many of the positions of power within the institution. Other analysts were unhappy about this. Lacan played along with Nacht, but he was not entirely content with the set-up either, most obviously because he had big ambitions of his own.

A 'break' would have to come sooner or later. Lacan's ideas were fundamentally different from Nacht's and in any case he wanted more power. Neither man fully realised this in 1949 at which time, in any case, both men benefitted from the status quo.

Thus between 1949 and 1953 Nacht oversaw a society and an institute whose administrative, doctrinal and pedagogic functions were managed – at least on the face of it – in a professional manner. This was specifically true with regard to the training and appointment of analysts. Candidates would present themselves to a committee, all of whom were 'titular' members of the society and who would decide whether said candidates were suitable to become analysts. If so, they were given a list of possible training analysts who were 'titular' members too. They would then receive training analysis and also academic instruction, as organised by the Institute. Once they were deemed, by their analyst and the commission, to be ready to practice, they could then do so as 'adhering members', at which point they could call themselves 'psychoanalysts'. If, during the course of training or later, they were deemed to be suitable to train or instruct analysts themselves, they would then become 'titular' members like their mentors.

On the face of it, the arrangement looked fair and judicious, but it was very hierarchical and conservative. The titular members had absolute power not only to decide who would train, but also who would qualify and then possibly go on to join their ranks (to then decide who could train – and so on). The process tended towards elitism and the nepotism. Titular members held all of the official positions in the Society, for example Nacht as President, Bonaparte as Honorary President and Lacan as Vice-President. The structures of both the Society and the Institute consolidated power and discouraged change. (Roudinesco, 1990, pp. 207–8; 223)

Regulation

The SPP set-up wasn't the only one that was relevant to Lacan's position and fate. The IPA's character and constitution affected him too, directly (for example through its *Americanism*), but also indirectly, via its influence on the SPP. This was exemplified in a small but important way in Lacan's membership of the IPA, granted by default because he was a member of the SPP. The implications of this dual membership and the fact that part of it had been gained by default would end up being very significant for him (and also for others).

The wider politics and constitution of the IPA were also significant with respect to Lacan's position too. By the 1930s it had, by necessity, become a broad church. The 'controversial discussions' between Kleinians and Anna Freudians were just one example of significant differences of opinion that had arisen over Freud's doctrine. Lacan's own difference of opinion with the IPA – over the metapsychological pre-eminence of the ego in American psychoanalytic doctrine – was another. In order to be a functioning institution, the IPA had to keep its member societies and associations together, which meant finding something they could *agree* on and organising around that. It's clear that theoretical and doctrinal differences between different associations were significant – sometimes huge. In view of this, IPA officers looked for agreement *somewhere else*. Specifically, they looked for it with respect to *technique*. Luckily for them, they managed to find – and then continue to impose – such *technical agreement*. Specifically, they determined that psychoanalytic sessions should be conducted for a 'fifty minute hour'. This meant that patients' sessions ended after fifty minutes, (usually) ten minutes before the next one. Other guidelines were also upheld, specifically that analysis should take place 3–5 times a week and that it should normally last 3–4 years. These other guidelines were both more loosely formulated and more loosely adhered to than the one regarding session-length, which became the one on the basis of which psychoanalytic practice was modelled *per se*. The fifty-minute hour was imposed internationally and almost universally held to by IPA members, including SFP ones.

Nonconformity

It's now well known that one notable member did not obey the fifty-minute 'rule'. Lacan practised what he called a 'variable length' session. In contravention of the guideline, he elected not to predetermine the length of the session before it started and decided *within* the session when it should end. This was almost never after fifty minutes. More often than not, the sessions were *shorter* (which is why Lacanian practice is often said to involve 'short sessions').

Lacan's idea was that the fifty-minute hour was a norm that the patient came to expect and that he or she could use defensively. Most obviously, the patient could stay silent near the end of session – if difficult issues presented themselves – and just wait for the session to end. Lacan reasoned that leaving the length of the session indeterminate would destabilise the patient so that s/he couldn't get comfortable enough to use silence and patience as a way to avoid difficult material. Ending the session abruptly would provoke an unconscious reaction and hence *engage* the unconscious, which is where such difficult – and significant – material would come from. Such apparently arbitrary action could also wrong-foot the ego, which uses knowledge of the session length to *avoid* tricky material. Lacan's technique took account of his own sense of the importance of the unconscious. It also de-emphasised the importance of the ego, which the ego-psychologists, of course, had been choosing to refocus their attention on. (Roudinesco 1990, pp. 227–32; Roudinesco, 1997, p. 203) This all meant that his innovation not only broke what had become the cardinal psychoanalytic rule and principle psychoanalytic practice, it also set him against dominant international psychoanalytic theory.

Unsurprisingly, Lacan's dissident practice became a bone of contention in the IPA. It also made waves in the SPP. Nevertheless, it took a while for this to happen and for the 'short session' to become the political football it did. *Different* tensions surfaced in the SPP beforehand.

To recap and clarify: the sequence was roughly as follows. Nacht became powerful in the SPP. Lacan did too, but to a lesser extent. He co-operated with Nacht, partly because it benefitted him to do so. Eventually, however, differences of opinion and ambition surfaced between Nacht (the President) and Lacan (the Vice-President). Once these disagreements had emerged, Lacan's practice of conducting 'variable-length' sessions also became an issue, first in the SPP, then in the IPA. All of the relevant doctrinal, personal, professional, theoretical, practical, political issues then became entangled in a way that meant they became difficult to separate.

Combatants

The power struggles in the SPP that took place shortly after 1949 mostly seemed as if they were played out in conflicts between SPP members *other* than Lacan. This meant that he came out of early fights relatively unscathed and even without seeming to have been involved in them. As a consequence, he managed to turn them to his advantage.

A long-term friend and colleague of Lacan's – Daniel Lagache – found himself opposing Nacht's rule. Lagache had medical and psychiatric training at the École normale supérieure, where he had studied alongside Sartre. He respected and employed medicine and psychiatry in his practice, but he considered the treatment of mental illness to be primarily the job of *psychology*. For him, psychiatry, medicine and indeed psychoanalysis were *tools* of psychology broadly conceived.

Yet Lagache's approach differed from local and global psychoanalytic ones in two very significant ways. Firstly, his attempted integration of psychoanalysis into psychology tended to neuter the former and distort the latter. Most psychology is cognitive and hence focussed on what is in consciousness (or at least just behind it, in something like the 'subconscious'). Psychoanalysis – at least in its purest and most radical form, is directed towards the *un*conscious (as Freud conceived it), of which the conscious knows little or nothing. The consideration and treatment of individuals in each discipline is quite different. Lacan disagreed with Lagache's perspective, although his disagreement was always diplomatically voiced.

Thus in some significant sense Lagache's approach contradicted classical Freudian theory. He was an academic and a liberal. His broad conception of psychology included an idea that its practitioners might vary. They might be doctors, or psychologists, or psychoanalysts, or any or all of these. He didn't take the view, as some psychoanalysts did, that psychoanalysts should be *medics*. Freud, intriguingly, didn't take this view either, or at least he was agnostic about it. Marie Bonaparte championed Freud's view and argued on its behalf even more strongly than he did. Thus it wasn't from the princess that Lagache met with opposition in the SPP. It was from the President: Nacht. In line with his predilection for orthodoxy, authority and hierarchy, Nacht thought that all psychoanalysts should be doctors, or at least ideally should be so. If that wasn't possible (and it wasn't really possible, given Freud's views) then medical psychoanalysts should have more power. This is why Nacht proposed that the rank of titular analysts should be reserved for medics within the SPP.

Fights

In 1952, Nacht proposed a series of statutes to regularise both psychoanalytic training and the relation between the Society and the Institute. Yet the proposed arrangements were not just administrative. They afforded Nacht more power and shaped the institution according to his will. They made him Head of the Commission as well as Director of the Institute and President of the Society. Furthermore, they solidified the privilege and exclusivity of titular membership – reserving it for medics. Acting in the absence of a number of members at a key meeting, Nacht pushed the changes through. Lagache stood up to him, demanding that the statutes be withdrawn and re-drawn. Nacht demurred and stood down. In the void,

Lacan saw an opportunity and proposed himself as interim President. This was accepted and he set about altering the statutes to engineer a compromise.

The new statutes allowed the President of the Society to sit on the boards of both the Commission and of the Institute. Nacht could still be very powerful, although not King of all he surveyed. Titular members still had power, although not absolute power. They regulated the training of analysts, but not their titles or status. The liberal wing of the psychoanalytic corpus – Lagache and his associates – was appeased. Because Lacan had negotiated the compromise, they saw him as an ally. Nacht also seemed happy – Lacan had brokered him a good deal. All that remained was for him to regain his position as President of the Society – or for one of his allies to take the position – and for Lacan to step down. Yet Lacan had got the taste for power himself. On 21 January he forced a Presidential vote, which went in his favour. He had won the day and (not for the first time) benefitted from conflict among others. At first Nacht and his followers seemed to accept this. Yet in truth they were displeased and even wanted revenge. The eventual vehicle of this would be a questioning of Lacan's 'technique'. *This* was when the variable length sessions *really* became an object of contention in the SPP. (Roudinesco, 1990, pp. 205–40; Freud [1926] 1986)

Insurrection

Other events followed Lacan's accession to President that would intensify the institutional drama surrounding his appointment and that would eventually have a 'tragic' end. The new statutes were established in January 1953; by May, they were causing disquiet among the younger generation of trainees. They required that all such were approved by the Commission before they could practice as 'psychoanalysts'. Yet some had already been approved by the society and did not want to have to resubmit their applications. To add insult to injury, training and tuition fees were hiked up. The nascent analysts began to feel that they were being unfairly oppressed by an authoritarian and demanding parent and began to rebel. In theory, Lacan, as President, was in a key position to be on the receiving end of the students' ire. Yet they understood that the constitutional changes had not been his idea, but Nacht's. Besides, a considerable number of them were Lacan's trainee analysands and so had very positive transferential feelings towards him. They saw him as a rebel too and therefore as on their side. Although Lacan's rebellious status made the students like him, it also made the SPP establishment see him as the representative of the rebels and hence as a problem. When the students rebelled, the grandees suspected that Lacan had instigated it, or at least been involved. Crucially, they began to see the 'short' sessions as more evidence of his insurrectionary character and deviance. In various fora, Lacan was publicly challenged by senior analysts to regularise his technique. Motions were passed that standard analytic procedures should be universal. Lacan promised that his analyses were reverting to standard practice. In truth, they were not.

At the end of May the students held a public meeting in which they denounced the constitutional changes and expressed no confidence in the management of the Society and the Institute. Subsequently, many of the older generation openly declared their allegiance to Nacht. This now-formed conservative faction also announced their opposition to Lacan's presidency. A vote of no confidence in him was tabled at an institutional meeting. Lacan survived it because he had support from the liberal faction led by Lagache. Yet *this* faction didn't exactly love Lacan. They by no means considered him their *leader* and mostly supported him because his presidency was a bulwark against conservatism. He had the support of students, for sure, but his practice was beginning to look toxic from a political point of view. The conservative faction was beginning openly to accuse Lacan of malpractice and the IPA was beginning to sit up and take notice.

Eventually, however, the liberals began to see the fight differently, probably because they realised that they couldn't win it, at least not in the form that it was being fought. They wanted changes that had the students' support (less medicalisation, looser regulatory structures, lower fees) but that couldn't be effected unless the conservative faction agreed them, which they wouldn't, precisely because the changes weren't conservative ones. Coincidentally, or perhaps not, Lacan and Lagache came up with exactly the same solution at the same time: they should form an alternative society called the Société française de psychoanalyse (SFP). Lagache would bring the qualified analysts and Lacan would bring the students. The enemies of Lacan and Lagache finally gave them the opportunity they needed to realise this dream. At a (truly) extraordinary SPP assembly on 16 June, The princess tabled a motion of no confidence in Lacan. It was carried and Lacan resigned, not only from the Presidency but also from the Institute. Ironically, Lagache was then immediately promoted from Vice-President to President, at which point *he* resigned, tendering the resignations of his allies at the same time.

Yet in the heat of battle the secessionists had made an error, possibly a fatal one. They had not realised that resignation of their memberships of the SFP also effectively curtailed their membership of the IPA. The group that they would go on to form would have no international recognition. This was an eventuality that they had not bargained for, or wanted.

Proxy

Lacan's irregular technique was clearly a catalyst for the SPP/SFP split and was even a vehicle for it. International conflicts involving the issue would erupt twice more during Lacan's lifetime. They were really about far more than the sanctity of the fifty-minute hour; they were also about the way in which both the establishment and non-Lacanian analysts saw Lacan. His claim to be Freudian was hugely at odds with the way a lot of other analysts saw him. He used metapsychological (even extra-psychological) terms that they had never heard of and did so frequently and abstractly. Many psychoanalysts simply didn't understand him and thought he was doing something very different to them. This situation hasn't changed much, even now.

Lacanians might claim that IPA members don't understand Lacan because they don't *want* to or rather because they *want not* to. In other words they might say that non-Lacanians' incomprehension is a form of denial of the truth of what Lacan had to say – about psychoanalysis in general and its US incarnation in particular. There might be some merit in this claim. Yet some of the lack of comprehension of Lacan's version of Freudianism has to be put down to him, not just to resistance to him. This is apparent in any dispassionate and/or impartial account of the style of his lectures and seminars. Lacan used 'Lacanisms' in both his Seminars and his more formal addresses, but in neither context did he explain very clearly what they meant. The Seminars *did* have a pedagogic remit and Lacan *did* concentrate on identifiable themes in them: 'Freud's technique' and 'the ego' in the first two seminars, for example. Yet he continually used alien ideas and terminology in his treatment of these themes without explaining them in anything other than an abstract way.

From a political point of view, the complexity of Lacan's ideas and mode of address worked against him. It was just one more reason for the IPA members and grandees *not* to engage with him. Why, after all, should they take on *his* dissident ideas and practices on *his* terms? Why should they accept – or even listen to – his explanation of himself when he was giving it in a language they couldn't understand and why should they bother about whether his ideas were valid as long as he was excluded from the association? The situation was double-edged, but neither edge cut in Lacan's favour. His exclusion was cemented via a row over his *technique,* yet the war couldn't really have been fought over the other 'real' issue – the theory – in any case.

As far as Lacan's character and fate is concerned, one can view this double bind in two ways. On the one hand, one can see Lacan as a victim of a sort of aggressive displacement, whereby an incidental aspect of his work (his clinical technique) was demonised by the psychoanalytic establishment as a way of sidestepping and disabling the greater (theoretical) challenge that his work represented. On the other hand one can see Lacan as a sort of (tragic) fool, for continuing with a practice that was clearly unacceptable to the establishment while attempting to seduce them with a philosophy they didn't want or understand.

Cracks

Thus what the history of Lacan's engagements with and disengagements from psychoanalytic orthodoxy begin to reveal is something very similar to what his personal and intellectual biographies reveal: splitting. Lacan varied in his practice from the standard technique. When challenged by SFP grandees, he defended this practice on theoretical grounds. When he was told to cease his irregular practice, he didn't. Instead, he stopped theorising it and carried on practising it, while claiming that he wasn't. Later, he again sought theoretical approval and respect from the IPA. He didn't really get it and the IPA again prevailed upon him to regularise his session-length, which he didn't. And so on...

Lacan continually engaged in evasion of institutional authority and was constantly disingenuous about what he was doing. The shifting nature of his behaviour contrasted with what he was actually evading, which was relatively fixed, and was so because it was a traditional and conservative form of authority. Just like the 'parental figures' they were, the SPP and IPA authorities told Lacan what he needed to do to avoid their ire and to win their approval and love. Lacan agreed and did no such thing. Instead, he behaved like a precocious and rebellious teenager: he made arguments that were both formal and querulous, he explained himself but didn't tell the truth, he hid and revealed his practice. In a very striking way, his situation was a classically Oedipal one in which the subject inhabits shifting or multiple positions in relation to an authoritative structure (whether it is familial or institutional) as a way of repeatedly *refusing* that structure, rather than accepting its presence and coming to terms with the position to which one was ascribed in it.

Division now not only beset Lacan's personal life, but also his institutional affiliations, his ambitions and his intellectual projects and pronouncements. Of course, it also presented itself as a *theme* in his work. This was shown very clearly in the previous chapter with reference to the Mirror Stage. It emerges again now with respect to another very important dimension of Lacan's work. This is one that might broadly be called 'dialectical' and that engages with a certain tradition of Continental thought that developed via an engagement with the philosophy of Hegel.

Kojève

It's already been shown that young French artists and thinkers of the 1930s welcomed Germanic ideas into their country's cultural and intellectual life. Young French philosophers (like Sartre and de Beauvoir) and their correspondents in related fields (like Lacan and Bataille) also looked back further into German intellectual history to the work of a philosopher who, among other things, had *anticipated* modern phenomenology and who, his devotees might say, even superseded it. That philosopher was Georg Wilhelm Friedrich Hegel.

Lacan did not come to Hegel alone or without help. He came to know and understand Hegelian philosophy through Alexandre Kojève. Kojève's account of Hegel's philosophy was of a very particular sort. It concentrated on one aspect (indeed one book) of Hegel's oeuvre and interpreted it in a particular, non-standard way. Specifically, it focussed on Hegel's 'phenomenology', especially that part of it which is often referred to as 'the master/slave dialectic' and did so in a non-synthetic (rather than synthetic) way. It is sometimes said that Lacan's understanding of Freud is a dialectical and Hegelian one. It would be even more accurate to say that it is dialectical and *Kojèvian*.

Alexandre Kojève (non-Gallicised name Kojevnikov) was born into a bourgeois Moscow family in 1902. He became interested in philosophy from quite a young age, and had early ambitions to be a professional philosopher. However his mid-teens coincided with the 1917 Russian revolution. According to post-revolutionary ideology and policy, his class origins were regarded as antipathetic to involvement in education, so he was prohibited from continuing his studies. He escaped, illegally, through Poland, to Germany, where he studied (particularly Hegelian) philosophy, at the University of Heidelberg. In 1928 he moved to Paris, and later became a naturalised French citizen. In Paris he taught philosophy. Despite having become partly exiled, or alienated, from Russia, his political allegiances remained Marxist, and he returned to the Soviet Union every year.

Kojève's most important philosophical work was conveyed orally, in lecture form, at the École practique des haute études. His lectures were attended by Sartre, Merleau-Ponty, Bataille and Breton. Other young French thinkers who would later make a mark were also listening. They included Louis Althusser, Raymond Queneau and Raymond Aron. Lacan was frequently in attendance too. Kojève's lectures were mostly devoted to an analysis of one of Hegel's great texts, a sort of summary of his entire philosophical system, which is usually referred to as the *Phenomenology of Spirit* or the *Phenomenology of Mind,* published in 1807. (Hegel, [1807] 1997) His lectures were transcribed and assembled by Queneau and published in 1969. (Kojève, 1969)

Kojève's account of Hegel's great text is essentially a sort of exposition of it. In other words he seeks to explain Hegel's ideas step by step and in conformance with the way in which they are laid out. Crucially, he seeks to convey the *logic* of these ideas in a clear and progressive way (and Hegel's logic is certainly progressive, if not always clear). In doing so he employs a form of argumentation that is the same as Hegel's and is indeed the argumentative form for which Hegel is known: dialectics. This form is a complex one. Before trying to relay how Kojève uncovers it in Hegel, it's worth saying a little about it. This should help make arguments made by Hegel, Kojève and Lacan all the clearer later on.

Dialectics

Dialectics are not easy to understand, at least not immediately. This is because, in whatever form they are manifest they are significantly unlike other ways of thinking. More specifically, they are unlike ordinary and apparently useful ways of thinking. Even more specifically, they are not commonsensical. They do not begin by accepting what is most *obvious* about any state of affairs. Neither do they take experience, or at least immediate, direct or unreflective experience, to be authoritative. At the same time, however, they do not unquestioningly advocate reflection. They do not presuppose that thinking about things can, in itself, solve problems, or that it can, in itself, achieve any adequate resolution of conflict, in the mind or in the world. Thus dialectics neither take the world to be straight-forward and self-evident, nor do they take reflection or thought to be what makes sense of the world.

One implication of the suggestion that dialectics are neither one thing nor another (in this case neither commonsensical nor rational) is that they work by means of a sort of consideration of *alternatives*. They might treat these alternatives negatively (for example by saying that one thing is not another) or positively (for example by saying that one thing *is* or at least *is related to*, another). Indeed, they might even do these things *together* (in which case they would be taking a very sophisticated – and incidentally Hegelian – form). In any case dialectics *always* take account of alternatives.

Such consideration of alternatives, at least on Hegel's part, can be seen as a reaction against *singular* philosophies. Many of these preceded Hegel's work and were inclined to view 'life' or 'existence' as *one* sort of thing (from one point of view). Such philosophies also scotomised (that is didn't see, or de-emphasised) any *other* sort of thing (from any other point of view). In pre-Hegelian – particularly *Enlightenment* – philosophies, this eschewing of alternatives and emphasising of singularity tended to take a particular form. Rational and human entities were generally seen as more important and meaningful than organic or natural ones. For example Descartes, whose work in many ways instituted and typified Enlightenment thinking, claimed that the origin of meaning is to be found in the self, because the self is what can first of all be known. It followed for him that the world, or nature, is *not* meaningful in itself; it is only meaningful in so far as it is comprehended (mentally) by humans (who only know the world because they first of all know themselves). Hegel thought this sort of argument placed too much emphasis on human knowledge and meaning, and acted as if nature had no purpose or sense independent of humanity. Apart from being quite arrogant, it also had the disadvantage of cutting humanity off from nature and of describing it as something which can have no direct access to nature, but only to a sort of image of it that complements humanity's image of itself. Hegel did not go along with this Cartesian account. He always represented ideas and the self as *not* independent of real or natural things. His consideration of the self, the mind and ideas was *dialectical*, rather than singular.[5]

What is central to Hegel's sort of dialectical argument is that all sorts of apparently opposite things in ostensibly different categories – self and world, thought and thing, humanity and nature – are not, and should not be considered as, mutually exclusive. None of them should be seen as being completely isolatable from any other – as a *pure* self, for example, or as a *purely* physical thing. Neither should any one thing be thought of as being a primary possibility of meaning for, or cause of, any other thing. For: example the world should not be thought of as produced by the mind. Such presumptions of non-mutual exclusivity are *essential* to dialectical thought.

Organism

It's already possible to see how Lacan might have been attracted to such thought. It must have appealed to his scepticism about the integrity of the self or ego. His Mirror Stage paper was avowedly pro-Freudian and anti-Cartesian, and could easily also be seen as implicitly Hegelian. Later, Lacan would make his own 'Hegelianism' explicit.[6] Yet he would not have been able to *be* Hegelian without Kojève. This is all the more reason to return to Kojève's reading of Hegel.

It's with an Hegelian presumption of the non-mutual exclusivity of mind and matter that Kojève sets out, via the *Phenomenology of Spirit*, to give an account of human existence. For him, and in an appropriately dialectical fashion, this involves making a link between organic life and consciousness.

Kojève's account begins by considering organic life and by noting the importance of *consumption* in the organic world. Organic life (for example animal life) lives by consuming other organisms. There is a fundamental sense in which life is *about* consumption: organisms live by consuming other organisms. This primitive sort of consumption seems to be to do with the pre-human, the primal, the animal, the *natural* (in so far as one thinks of 'nature' as a state which is in some sense *before* humanity, or that humanity transcends or dominates or 'comes out of'). Yet there is *something other* than a strictly primal urge in organic life. This is because organic consumption isn't just autonomous. It implies and in a sense creates and certainly takes place in conjunction with *something else*. This something else is a rudimentary *self;* more exactly a *self that consumes*. The organic urge to consume something, in other words, implies a *self* that *has* such an urge. What's more, this self senses *itself* as such, as something that lacks nourishment, as something that has to eat to live, as something that has *need*. Rather than coming before or being cut off from nature, the self is already minimally apparent *in* nature, *in* natural organic states as soon as they need to sustain themselves, as they nearly always do. Thus the (animal) organism is not just something that consumes, it is something that, via its need, has a sense of itself *as* something that consumes and hence has a sense (however crude) of itself *as such*.

Need

Before showing where this argument takes Kojève (via Hegel) it's worth briefly signalling that it already anticipates Lacan's work. The 'consumption' mentioned above is borne out of a 'natural' urge that Lacan described, simply, as 'need'. Lacan saw this need as being basic to human life and as impelled by what Freud called 'trieb' – which English Freudians would translate as 'instinct' and English Lacanians would translate as 'drive'. This need 'does not sicken and die' and is fundamental to 'the organism itself'. (EC, p. 431) That it corresponds with a rudimentary self, one that *feels* such need, is apparent in all of Lacan's theories from 1949 on, when this self is cast as first encountering itself in the mirror.

Thus Lacan's ontological schema, like Kojève's, involves both a differentiation and a link between something that is primal (or pre-human) and something that is like a self (or prototypically human). Because this 'link' maintains a continuity *and* a difference between the two entities concerned it is, as shown, a dialectical one.

The continuity concerned allows Kojève to speak of both entities by using the same word: 'beings'. As shown, these beings, whether they are 'human' or 'animal', both feel need and have a sense of self. Now *because* it is formed via 'organic' need, this sense of self, or more precisely this 'sentiment of self' (which is something less developed for example, than 'identity' or 'knowledge of self'), is formed through its opposite. It is shaped in terms of what it both has need of and is opposed to. This 'fact' has all sorts of implications and consequences, for both Kojève and Lacan, many of which are explained below. (Kojève, pp. 3–4, 13, 15)

Object

Need – and also the self that needs – always has an *object*. The breast is the object of the baby's hunger, just as the gazelle is the lion's. It is in terms of this object that the rudimentary sense of self *is formed*: thus the relation with the breast is formative of the sense of self, just as Klein claimed. The affinity between Klein's thought and Lacan's – mentioned earlier – is immediately apparent in this example, as is a more indirect link between the thought of Klein and that of Hegel, a link of which Lacan would have been aware, but of which Klein arguably wasn't.[7] In any case Lacan's adoption of Kojève's explanation of Hegel's account of human development concludes that need requires an *object* and that 'the self' becomes that which *specifically* needs this object.

All three accounts (Lacan's, Kojève's, Hegel's) intermittently employ a different and more general term to cover the object-end of this dialectical process. The 'object' of self and need is *sometimes* described in a *non*-specific way and is subsumed by and included in a broader category of that which the self needs, namely 'the other'. The self's object, in other words, *is* 'the other', which the self is thus essentially formed in relation to.

Other

Anyone who has read Lacan's work at all closely will recognise his use of the category of 'the other' and will see immediately that this use derives from Kojève and – at another remove – from Hegel. However, Lacan sometimes employed his own emphasis; or one should say *emphases*. He tended to use the term in two ways. Both carried a Kojèvian/Hegelian sense, but each bore a Lacanian inflection.

Lacan capitalised the term 'other' in some cases but not in others. Hence he tended to either refer to 'the Other' or 'the other'; in French: 'l'Autre' or 'l'autre'. This second 'autre' was sometimes referred to in a slightly more elaborate way as: 'l'objet petit à' or 'l'objet à'.

L'Autre

The Lacanian 'Other' is probably best defined as that which, *in general*, the self or subject is both opposed to and defined in terms of. This definition accommodates the Kojèvian (and Hegelian) premise that the self needs the other and is formed *by* (needing) it. A psychoanalytic example of this – which has already been given – is found in the child's need for the mother. This need – and its consequences – are obviously formative of the child's personality, or self. Lacan, as well as Klein, argued that good mothering renders the child's ego stable. Maternal privation, on the other hand, renders it insecure and can give rise to what Lacan called the 'Weaning Complex'.[8] In both cases, the (m)other *is* the Other and this other is clearly both a part-function of need and formative of the self. By pointing this out, Lacan was just taking a philosophical (Kojèvian/Hegelian) argument and extending it so that it had a psychoanalytic (Freudian/Kleinian) use.

There are still other psychoanalytic and psychoanalysis-related senses in which the term 'Other' was used by Lacan. Perhaps most importantly, if not most obviously, Lacan used the term to signal *the unconscious*. As always, he understood this unconscious in a Freudian sense. That is, he took it to be a part of the self that is very important (even crucial) to it, but that is also inaccessible. The unconscious – as the Other – is vital but invisible. For example, repressed material *is* in the pathological symptom but can't immediately be *seen* in it – more exactly, it is *implied* or *hidden* in it and has to be drawn out by psychoanalysis (as explained in Chapter Four).[9]

Thus when Lacan famously said that 'the unconscious is the discourse of the Other', he was claiming that the Other is the place where the unconscious is being spoken but can't be heard, just as it is the place where it is manifest but can't be seen (at least not without psychoanalysis). (ES, p. 172) Putting aside the strictly linguistic aspect of this situation (which will be dealt with in the next chapter) one can see that it involves a remarkable claim. In so far as one is 'defined' via 'the Other' and in so far as 'the Other' is the unconscious, everything that one sees and hears *involves one's unconscious*, even though one isn't aware of it. This can be put even more sharply and in more strictly psychoanalytic terms. The way one sees the world involves an enormous *projection*.

Psychosis

By describing the unconscious as Other, Lacan was casting its functioning as external and projective as much as internal and repressed. This view doesn't oppose Freud's, but it does differ from the standard or default model employed by many psychoanalysts, in which the unconscious is imagined as something that functions *within* the psyche (moreover at a *buried* level) rather than at its *outer* limits (or even *beyond* them).

Indeed, Lacan's conception of the unconscious as Other corresponds with a psychoanalytic model that is even more unusual than this. It includes an understanding of the formation of the ego that casts it as *psychotic* as well as neurotic. Once again, such a view is not anti-Freudian, but it does go against the orthodox psychoanalytic grain. This can be explained as follows.

In his best-known clinical analysis of psychosis, Freud made a link between projection and paranoia. He first of all showed (as he had done before) that projection is the externalisation and displacement of an unconscious impulse into someone or something else, that is *into an other* (whether that other is an acquaintance, stranger or thing). (Freud, [1911] 1984) This displacement allows the impulse to be disowned. Thus rather than hating someone, the subject can accuse them of being hateful ('the other *hates me*'). He casts his aggression into the other and thinks that he does not have to take responsibility for it himself. If there is further (internal or external) pressure for him to take responsibility and he continues to resist this, he can do so by imagining the aggressions as coming back towards himself *from* the other ('the other is *attacking me*'). The projective subject turns into the paranoid subject. In sum, his fear of the other is his aggression *expelled into and returned from the other* where both the expulsion and the return are for the purpose of *defence*.

Lacan accepted this Freudian link between paranoia and projection and worked it into his account of ego formation. Because, according to this account, the ego is formed via the Other, it constitutionally involves projection. In so far as projection can lead to paranoia, the ego is paranoid *as such*. This is exactly what Lacan meant when he spoke, as he sometimes did, of the paranoid constitution of the ego, which takes the shape it does because it knows itself *Otherwise* and thus via knowledge that is 'paranoiac knowledge'. (Lacan, 1973, pp. 109–193; EC, pp. 91)

Lingua

As well as a generalised 'object' (in terms of which the subject knows itself) and the (externalised as well as internalised) unconscious, the Other can be defined in a third way. This is as language (or more broadly as representation). The Other is (in some respect) the unconscious and the unconscious is (according to Lacan) 'structured like a language'. It therefore must be the case that the Other (at least in some sense) *is* language (or is *in* language, or comes *from* or *out of* language). Exactly what this means and how it works will be explained in the next chapter.

L'autre

Once the Other – l'Autre' has been thus and triply defined, it remains to say what 'l'autre', or 'l'objet petit à' or 'l'objet à' is. The definition of *this* is not exactly simple, but there *is* a way of defining it – provisionally but accurately (and fairly briefly), as follows.

'L'objet petit à' is that other that the subject yearns for which he thinks might complete him. It may be personified in a real person (a 'love object') but it is significantly *psychical*. Unlike the Other, it is not broad or multiple; it is specific. It is what 'I' want to complete 'myself'. It's not surprising, from a Lacanian point of view, that the 'I' (or ego, or subject) should want such completion. After all it is constitutionally incomplete. It longs for the image in the mirror, wanting it to be fixed and to return its gaze in a reassuring way, a way that might promise that it will never be wanting. (Lacan, [1954–5] 1988, pp. 243–7)

That last sentence signalled something obvious but important about 'l'objet petit à', namely that it is the product (or object) or a sort of desire. Very shortly, the general but essential question of the relation between 'desire' and 'the other' will be taken up and this will help define 'l'objet petit à even more fully. Currently, however, a comparison can be made between it and another sort of object. This comparison was made, indirectly, by Lacan. He did this by indicating that 'l'objet petit à' is like the fetish as Freud explained it. Freud's explanation was summarised earlier: in Freudian terms the fetish is an indirect representation of something that the subject feels is missing from his mother, namely the penis; or in Lacanian terms, the phallus, which the fetish acts as a substitute for. (Lacan, [1972–3] 1999, pp. 71–7 The latter is the subject's ultimate phantasy object, the one that he thinks will satisfy him completely and make up for the loss he feels: of his mother, his phallus and his omnipotence. In all cases the fetish is an object of desire. Given that it is what desire is concentrated *on,* it is even *the* object of desire. Lacan sometimes represented it algebraically, thus: s ◊ a: the 'formula' for 'l'objet petit à'.

Indefinite

What the previous section should have shown is that there are two general senses in which Lacan used the term that he got from Kojève (and that *he* got from Hegel): 'the other'. These two senses – 'L'Autre' and 'l'autre' – themselves include other senses.

It would be fair to say that Lacan didn't work especially hard to differentiate these different senses and/or to explain them very well. His account of each term and of both terms was allusive and ambiguous. There is even a logical problem that is *prior* to his imprecise uses of the various senses of the term(s) concerned, which is that some of them contradict each other, or at least *seem* to contradict each other. Thus the Lacanian other is visible but unconscious, or linguistic but personified, or a 'lack' but an object. Lacan offered no clear explanation of these contradictions. Unsurprisingly, all this has led to misunderstanding(s) about the meaning(s) of the term(s).

Distinctions

Thus exegesis of Lacan's ideas is inevitable and continuing. Clarification is a necessary part of this. It's therefore worth noting an important point of both similarity and discrepancy between the Kojèvian and Lacanian terminology referred to above. The word 'need' has been used above to signify that which the organism feels for the other that renders it a nascent self or subject. Lacan does use this term ('need') although Kojève generally doesn't. In fact, Kojève tends to use the term 'desire' in the same context. (Kojève, pp. 3–9) The term 'need' has been employed above not only because Lacan used it, but also because this use relates to what is felt at the mostly-organic level. It is equivalent to what Kojève would call 'animal desire'. (Kojève, p. 4) However, when this is felt *as* or *for* something that *goes beyond* the animal level, Lacan uses the term that Kojève uses at all levels: desire.

Differentiations

The distinction requires a little refinement. It isn't entirely the case that for Lacan 'need' corresponds to animal or organic sentiment and desire corresponds to human sentiment. Things are a little bit more complicated than this. Lacan introduced a third term: demand, which helps differentiate need and desire from each other.

Need *seems* only to correspond to animal life because when it is felt, it is prompted by something like a 'real dependency'. For example, it is occasioned by the organism's dependence on food. However, where the 'being' that is hungry is 'human', or 'proto-human', his need is expressed in language 'by [virtue of] the fact that he speaks'. (EC, p. 579) Even the newborn baby, as the Lacanian analyst Moustafa Safouan notes, emits a cry and therefore always *articulates* his need, however crudely. (Safouan, p. 9) In other words, humans (of whatever age) express their need through a demand, in language. Because this is a representation of an organic urge (rather than the urge itself), it is, according to Lacan, 'a deviation of man's needs due to the fact that he speaks'.

As the next chapter will make very clear, language is not the object (needed), it is only the representation of that object (expressed in a demand *for* it). It thus does not necessarily *get* one what's needed. As Lacan put it: 'demand in itself bears on something other than the satisfaction it calls for'. In a significant sense, language is *empty* of what it requests. Hence 'to the extent that….[man's]…needs are subjected to demand, they come back to him in an alienated form'. In other words, because language can never entirely realise what it invokes or represents, demand always falls short of the need expressed in it. This 'falling short', which is of course a negative function, or more exactly a lack, is *desire* as Lacan understood it. This is precisely why 'desire is neither the appetite for satisfaction nor the demand for love, but the difference that results from the subtraction of the first from the second'. (EC, pp. 579–80)

Desire

As well as establishing and explaining the Lacanian distinctions between the terms 'need', 'demand' and 'desire', the previous two sections have also begun to hint at the importance, for Lacan, of the last of these terms. 'Desire' has a significant place in the Lacanian lexicon, one that is both ontological and epistemological. Its importance can be registered with reference to a key terminological nexus that has recently been exposed, namely the one that surrounds and includes the term 'other'. A more concise way of saying this is to say that Lacan was much preoccupied by what he called 'the desire of the other'. What is this?

'The desire of the other', like 'the other', can be understood in more than one way. Once again, it's best to try to distinguish between some of the different usages – or rather sets of usages – of the phrase. These usages can be overlaid and, unsurprisingly Lacan did overlay them. They will be separated out as follows. One set of usages will be explained here. Another will be dealt with later, after a return to Kojève's argument. Before that, as stated, a first clutch of usages of 'the desire of the other' will be clarified immediately below.

Lacan's use of the phrase 'desire of the other' can be usefully understood as one that enlightens the Oedipus Complex – both as Freud imagined it and Lacan understood it. As noted in an earlier chapter, Lacan both accepted the *general* principles of Oedipal sexuality and development *and* had his own 'take' on the phenomenon. For him, the Oedipal scenario is a structure. This implies that there are positions designated in it, ones that can be taken up by those for whom such positions *are* designated (for example: mother, father, child) but also ones that can be taken up, or related to, by others. All of these positions are craved or occupied via desire, which, it's now been established, always implies an other. Here are some examples.

Quite obviously, in the conventional and prototypical Oedipal scenario, the young boy desires the mother. Equally obviously, because she is other than him, his desire is a 'desire *of* the other' (his mother is what his desire is *of*, she is *what* he desires). It's worth noting that this desire is predicated on a separation that is actual if not acknowledged by the boy. He desires his mother because he *lacks* her (which he was able to feel he did not do when he was in her womb, or which he is able to forget he does do when he phantasises about union with her). In any case desire is clearly a negative term (compared, for example, with 'libido' or 'instinct' as used by Freud).

An important implication is worth teasing out here. For Lacan, desire only comes about when one *doesn't have* something. It is even *created* in such lack: one formulates one's object *by* wanting it. This point corresponds with one made earlier in this book, where it was suggested that one *can* only want something that one doesn't have because if one already had it there would be no point wanting it. Psychical objects always contain or imply or anticipate some kind of lack or loss and the desire of them, that is 'the desire of the other', always does too.

It follows from this that that even *occupation* of *any* of the available positions of the Oedipal scenario (not just the position of the son) involves desire, the desire of the other and the lack that is coextensive with both of them. There are obviously ways in which this all corresponds with basic Lacanian theory. *Any* assumption of identity will be an identification with *something else*, that will always require a gap to remain open between oneself and what one identifies with (even and especially if it is oneself). Hence the father in the Oedipal scenario is never fully the father, he is identifying himself *as* the father – as long as he sees himself in the paternal *role*. The same is obviously true of the mother. She 'is' the mother in so far as she wants to be and identifies with this role. Even in situations where they act 'as themselves', characters in the Oedipal drama are always subject to 'the desire of the other'.

Phallus

Thus the 'desire of the other', subsists in *and* between *all* Oedipal positions. It can be even more complex than in the examples given above and can be active in Oedipal matrices involving more than two positions. This is probably most apparent, in Lacanian theory, with respect to the phallus.

In one instance, Lacan referred to the phallus as 'the signifier of the desire of the other?' (Lacan in Rose and Mitchell, p. 84) This is a complex and quite ambiguous phrase, which can be taken to mean a number of different but related things. In so far as a boy might want the phallus, it would be the *object* of his desire (the other that he desires). It would *represent* his desire too and be 'the signifier of the desire of the other in this sense. This implies a further sense. The phallus is a symbolic entity. As such, it can represent two different (even opposite) things, or feelings. On the one hand, to the extent that the boy 'has' it, he feels potent, even omnipotent (it represents his ability to 'have' his mother). On the other hand, to the extent that he can always be deprived of it (or as Freud would have it, can be castrated) it represents the possibility of loss. The phallus is something that might be had or might be lost and in this sense is precisely (even ontologically) something that is desired *as such*. It is an object of desire *whether one has it or not*. Because it *is* an object of desire – and given that desire *is* always 'of the other' – desire for the phallus *is* also always the desire of the other. Yet because (once again) it is symbolic, it is also always 'the signifier of the desire of the other' too.

Yet that the phallus is 'the signifier of the desire of the other' can also mean something else. The phallus can be desired by the mother. This might involve the mother *identifying* with it. Lacan is here referring to the Freudian figure of the 'phallic woman' or "the 'phallus-girls of Fenichel'" who, for example, adopt typically 'male' attitudes, gestures or dress, particularly where these might signify a sort of potency. (Lacan in Rose and Mitchell, p. 94) Now of course the boy – or for that matter the girl – can desire the mother *because* s/he thinks that she has (or because s/he wants her to have) the phallus. In that case the boy or girl would not only be desiring, but also desiring the desire of the other. This could mean either wishing to *have* the mother and have her desire, or wishing to *be* the mother and have her desire. In a last eventuality, it's possible that the mother might want the child to be a sort of phallus for her, to complete *her* as it were (this possibility echoes Freud's claim that the mother, acknowledging that she is 'castrated', might accept the child, specifically the boy, as a substitute for the penis). Yet this desire might also become the child's, who might then want to meet the mother's desire and be the desire of the mother in the sense of being what the mother wants him to be. In that case he might be being a sort of phallus for the mother and a sort of fetish for himself.

As noted above, of course, it can be the father who desires the phallus (because having a penis – or even a phallus – does not preclude him from this). Of course if the child identifies with the father (or *as* the father, or as the father wants him to be) he would then be subject to the desire of the other in one or other of its registrations along the paternal axis. In all cases and in any case, the desire of the other would be paramount.

Development

All of these permutations of desire are generated by and acted out in both the structure and the phenomenal field that is the Oedipus Complex. It is important to recall that Freud considered passage through this complex as a form of *development* – just as he saw capture in it, or regression to it, as a sort of failure of development.

This raises the question of Lacan's view of Oedipality. Did he see it as developmental or not? Lacan was insistent that the Oedipus Complex (including the Castration complex) was of primary significance for human being and the Oedipus Complex *is* a developmental model. What's more, Lacan's understanding of it was instructed by another way of thinking that was also implicitly developmental too. This was *Hegel's philosophy*. Lacan also proffered *other* theories that were developmental, at least in principle. The obvious example is the theory of the Mirror Phase, or as it is sometimes translated: Mirror *Stage*. Given all of this and also what's just been explained regarding desire, it makes sense to return to Kojève's account of Hegel's description of *human development*. It might then be possible to understand where Lacan stood on the question of development in general. Doing all this will involve returning once again in a different way to the question of the desire of the other.

Autodestruction

It is through need, for example hunger, that the organism begins to get a primary sense of itself. This sense of self (or more precisely 'sentiment of self') comes about via an object.

Three important aspects of this process are worth spelling out very clearly. Firstly, self becomes apparent by *being opposed to* an object. Secondly – and conversely – it is formed *in terms of* that object (one might say that it is negatively as well as positively formed). Thirdly, it becomes apparent in terms of what it is *lacking*; more precisely, it gets a sense of itself *as* lacking. The condition of 'sentiment of self' is 1. relational, 2. negative, and 3. needy.

An important aspect of the third of these functions should be concentrated on here. If 'sentiment of self' cannot be had without need, then self is something which might always feel *unsafe*. Need might not always be met and the self that is needy might always feel at risk because of this. It might be *fearful*. What's more, this fear might very well be directed towards the object that it is opposed to, the very object that has indirectly formed it. The organism might feel that this object is a threat to it. After all, the other can eat the organism just as it can eat the other.

In its fear, and perhaps in panic, the rudimentary, organic self might act to try to resolve this situation of possible threat and diminish its anxiety. However, precisely *because* it is rudimentary, it might do so in a very crude and unthinking way. It might feel that consuming its object would eliminate its need for that object, and that it (the organism) might thus cease to feel needy or vulnerable if it did so. Why shouldn't it think this? It would only be following the logic of *hunger*, after all; it would just be *eating* its object to sate its need. However, if the organism acted in this way, it would be doing something *fatal and* that fatality would not only effect its object, but also itself. Because the organism's sense of self depends on needing an object – which it senses *itself as* needing – elimination of the object would ultimately eliminate this sense of self. What the organism thinks will make it more secure (consumption) does away with the *very possibility* of its own self-consciousness (the organism's attempt to consume and eliminate its enemy ends up eliminating *itself*).

Progression

This is essentially an exposition of Kojève's account of the first stage of Hegel's account of 'human development', more specifically (and accurately) the early stage of the master/slave dialectic in *The Phenomenology of Spirit* (Kojève, pp. 3–5) It's already been shown that Lacan applied some of the ideas and principles in this account to psychoanalytic theory, specifically Freudian theory, even more specifically, the Oedipus Complex. In fact, Lacan borrowed quite liberally from Kojève and Hegel in other ways too.

It is fairly unarguable, for example, that Lacan synthesised the argument summarised above with some key aspects of Kleinian theory to arrive at his own account of 'Aggressiveness in Psychoanalysis'. Anyone who is at all familiar with Klein's theories will be able to recognise how the primal processes above recall primitive object relations, specifically in their 'aggressivity'. That is they will see how the opposition to, fear of and consumption of 'the other' on the part of the rudimentary subject resemble the violent psychical cycles of projective identification and destruction that make up the infant's psychical relations with the breast. Lacan perhaps acknowledges this when he says that 'Before Darwin... Hegel has provided the definitive theory of the specific function of aggressiveness in human ontology, seeming to prophesy the iron law of our time.' (EC, p. 98)

The Lacanian and developmental link between psychoanalysis and Hegelian philosophy seems even clearer when it's known that Kojève – who was of course Lacan's teacher – is generally thought to have interpreted Hegel in an *anthropological way*. His focus was more narrowly *human* than Hegel's (which was also historical and universal). It's thus not difficult to see how Lacan, in taking from both Kojève and Freud (or Kojève and Klein), might have been able to combine an argument about the development of humans out of animals with one about the development of adults out of children.

Yet having said all of this – and even given his acceptance of Oedipality – its still not entirely clear that Lacan *unambiguously* subscribed to the ideas that people *can* or *do* develop. In this, interestingly, he followed Kojève, rather than Hegel (or Freud, or Klein). Kojève's dialectic did not exactly end up in the same (developed) place that Hegel's did. It's necessary to return to both of their arguments to show this.

Hegel

This is how *Hegel* continues with his own argument about rudimentary selfhood. At the organic level, selfhood is caught in a vicious cycle of need and satiation. Self sees itself as needy, eliminates need, and loses its sense of self. This cycle seems inescapable as long as the satisfaction of need and the attainment of selfhood are mutually exclusive. According to Hegel and for rather obvious reasons, the first of these (need) cannot be completely done away with, at least not while the organism is alive. As long as it lives, it needs, even if that need is only for food. Yet if it is to *develop* it must also find a way to sustain 'itself', or more exactly 'its self'. Need and satiation on the one hand and selfhood and development on the other *don't* seem compatible.

The only way in which this circle could be squared would be if need could be met *without* an obliteration of selfhood. According to Hegel, this *is* possible and comes about when the organism chooses not to obliterate the object that opposes it, but instead decides to *acknowledge* it. In doing this, it must forgo its immediate *organic* need (it will have to direct its desire to eat *somewhere else*) and instead *recognise* its object. This recognition, in not destroying its object, allows the organism to continue to be reflected and hence recognised *itself*. This is possible because the organism's object is *also* an organism that in being acknowledged by *its* other can also acknowledge that other *itself*. Mutual recognition secures individual selfhood: each being recognises the other, recognises the other recognising it and recognises the other recognising itself.

Both beings avoid the 'fight to the death' that would have characterised their primitive state and in fact the 'dialectic of master and slave' which would have been no more than a quasi-human substitute for that. Instead, in their mutual recognition, both 'organisms' become human. (Hegel, pp. 111–9)

Equivocation

A great deal could now be written about whether and to what extent the versions of Hegel's philosophy deployed by Lacan and Kojève correspond with the one glossed above. However, it's not necessary to write at length to state the following, which is accepted by a good number of philosophers and critics. Lacan and Kojève's ideas both *do and don't* correspond with Hegel's.

Both Lacan and Kojève signal – and sometimes even state – something like the possibility of human development. Yet both of them also eschew this possibility. One could put this more particularly by saying that both thinkers place more emphasis on and are more influenced by the argument made by Hegel about the *first stage* of the dialectic – the one in which desire allows for the possibility of developed 'life', but also regularly confounds the possibility that it might be sustained. For Kojève this is essentially because desire is always 'directed towards another desire' rather than *primarily* directed towards the recognition of the other. (Kojève, p. 7) Desire is oriented towards its own need, where simple satisfaction of this need is self-destructive. Lacan, for his part, might say that the organism's (or infant's, or human's) desire is either misdirected and/or 'caught up' in 'the desire of the other' without precisely its *recognising this.*

What can one conclude from this? Simply, one can say that Lacan, at least in so far as he followed Kojève, did not believe in the possibility of development as much as Hegel did.

Yet of course Lacan was not simple, or single, or unambiguous. He contradicted himself; he believed in development and didn't; he developed and didn't. Some more of this will be shown, if not settled, in the space that remains.

7

Word and Wish

Negotiation

By mid-1953 the truth had sunk in for the senior members of the SFP. Because it had broken away from the SPP, the new society was no longer affiliated with the IPA; and SFP members were no longer IPA members. The seniors, including Lacan and Lagache, had to give their students the bad news. Because they were in training with the seniors, because they had trusted them to engineer an exit from the SPP and because IPA membership was not their main priority, the juniors largely accepted the situation, with a proviso that they expected IPA affiliation to be arranged as soon as possible.

Yet the IPA, on the advice of SPP grandees, made it clear that there would be no easy or quick route back to affiliation or membership. The SFP would be subject to investigation, so that it could be established whether its training, practices and processes conformed to official international standards.

A juridical and interrogative process for re-admission was lobbied for heavily by Marie Bonaparte. She hated Lacan even more than she disparaged his SFP colleagues, who she saw as dissidents. Unfortunately for the SFP, the princess had enormous influence in the IPA. She wrote to the President Heinz Hartmann to recommend that the most thorough investigation and the most stringent tests be undertaken before SFP affiliation were granted. She also wrote to the IPA vice-presidents and to Anna Freud. Fatally – especially for Lacan – she insisted that the SFP assessment take full account of its members' *techniques*. She knew that Lacan was deviating from the norm and she sensed that his deviation was the best stick to beat him with. On 26 July, 1953 at the IPA congress in London, Hartmann announced that a committee would be set up to examine the SPP's request for affiliation and also to look into allegations of its deviant practices.

The members of the SFP wanted affiliation for their society and themselves, but at the same time they wanted to have Lacan as a member, nay, *a leader*. The situation was one of conflicting forces. The IPA was growing rapidly in terms of size and influence. As it did so, it was becoming a sort of administrative machine, controlling many societies with quite different cultures and orientations by holding them to certain standard rules and procedures, including and especially the fifty-minute hour. Lacan was a counterforce. It was not just that his theories was dense, arcane and idiosyncratic. He would not conform by observing the few rules that were sacrosanct. These rules were the *compromise* that allowed different practices to find common ground. Yet Lacan *wouldn't* and *couldn't* compromise. Either he had to change or the IPA did; he would either have to submit to them or conquer them. It's clear that he didn't realise how hopeless his chances of winning were. Perhaps more to the point, nor did his colleagues and students.

Many SFP members were enthralled by Lacan. By the early to mid-1950s, his training seminars were full. He was courting the attention of academics and had begun to deliver public addresses in prestigious locations at the invitation of national intellectual figures. His SFP colleagues looked on approvingly; how could his pupils not do the same?[1] Lacan had power in the society, attention in academia, a controlling influence over the training programme and wide popularity. The SFP *was* hard to imagine without him. Yet even if only because of his technique, Lacan had broken from international orthodoxy.

For a long time, the SFP sought affiliation while trying to convince the IPA that Lacan presented no obstacle to it. This was the general tactic employed when the IPA began to interview SFP members. Lacan wasn't interviewed, but wrote to various IPA figures and falsely claimed that he had regularised his technique in any case. What's more he encouraged his students, when interviewed, to say the same. The SFP negotiators downplayed Lacan's influence in the society. He agreed that this was a good approach and kept a low profile. Some of his best and most trusted colleagues took up the negotiations instead. These included Wladimir Granoff, Serge Leclaire and François Perrier. All were respected analysts and skilful diplomats. When they were asked about Lacan, they noted his brilliance and integrity. They declared the SFP to be beyond reproach in all other respects too.

The committee didn't believe them. They found that Lacan's technique was errant and furthermore deplored his influence over younger analysts. He used his charisma, they said, to influence his analysands and colleagues and coercively to alter the nature of the SPP to suit his preferences and whims. The decision to refuse affiliation was made official in 1954. This was the international association's first clear and explicit rejection, not only of Lacan, but of *Lacanianism* per se. (Roudinesco, 1990, 277–94; 318–20)

Renegotiation

The SFP didn't re-attempt affiliation at the 1956 IPA Congress in Geneva. In theory at least, their inaction could have been a sign that they were genuinely reflecting on their situation. They could have been taking stock and could have been thinking about how viable their aims were. Indeed, in psychoanalytic terms, they could have 'worked through' their conflicted wishes and realised the truth: that they couldn't have both affiliation *and* Lacan. Yet they didn't do this. In 1959, at the congress in Copenhagen, they tried for affiliation again.

The SFP President (Angelo Hesnard) made the formal request to affiliate. The IPA President, Pearl King, immediately asked for details of all SFP members and their practices. Information was specifically sought on whether analysts respected the international 50-minute hour/ four sessions a week rules. Another committee was formed. This time, it was explicitly one of investigation. The same SFP soldiers (particularly Granoff and Leclaire) stood up to do battle and/or negotiate.

The information requested was provided, but it was impossible to provide truthful information about Lacan that indicated that he conformed to the rules. He was analysing up to thirty analysands. If one session for each were to take an hour (including breaks between sessions) and if each analysand were to be attending four times a week, Lacan would have to be working one hundred and twenty hours a week in order to legitimately treat all his patients. Testimony indicates that he was *in fact* conducting sessions that lasted twenty minutes or less.

Still, negotiation and strategy continued. Leclaire availed the committee of the SFP archives, undertaking all the while to disclose the prestige and experience embodied by the society as a whole. Granoff tactfully reminded the IPA of the number of members that affiliation would bring them (at that time, the SFP had more than twice as many analysts in training as the SPP). Finally, the committee came to Paris to see things for themselves. They set themselves up in a hotel on the rue de la Paix. From there, they began interviewing analysts and trainees alike.

When asked about Lacan's short sessions, some of his peers pleaded ignorance. They said that they knew nothing of the detail of his practice.

Others were quite open about the short sessions and said that they knew they took place but defended them on technical and therapeutic grounds. Lacan, to his credit, took this line himself. For once, he didn't deny the varying length of his consultations, but rather sought to explain the reasons for what he did. Lacan's students were less consistent. They were frank about his practices and some criticised him. Their mood as a group had changed since 1954 and some had become dissatisfied. The unpredictability of the length of Lacan's sessions meant that none of his analysands could ever be entirely sure when they would see him, or, for that matter, when they would finish seeing him. His waiting room was full and no one knew how long they were going to have to spend there.

The investigation dragged on until 1961, when the committee's 'initial recommendations' were announced. They concerned all sorts of matters apart from technical ones, but the technical ones were decisive. The rules concerning session-length and frequency were insisted on. Such rules deemed the continuation of Lacan's current practice impossible. A stipulation was made that the society could only be affiliated if Lacan – and some of his sympathisers – discontinued their roles as teachers.

Still thinking that the situation was salvageable, the SFP negotiators sought to accept and implement the IPA recommendations, prevail upon Lacan to regularise his technique and convince the committee to rescind the prohibition they placed on his teaching. They succeeded in none of these aims. In the mean time the committee continued with their investigations. They conducted another round of interviews in 1963. After they completed these they wrote a final report.

This report, which included detailed and unambiguous stipulations for the affiliation of the SFP to the IPA, continued in the spirit of the 1961 recommendations but was even more hard-line. In short, it demanded that all of the said recommendations should be met unambiguously and in full and that Lacan should be excluded from teaching and training *entirely*. The report was a take-it-or-leave-it document. Unless all of its requirements were met, the SFP would not be affiliated to the IPA.

Excommunication

Lacan's supporters began to recognise the impossibility of their situation: they wished both to remain loyal to Lacan and to become members of the IPA. They quite quickly began to agree among themselves that the only thing to do in the situation was to proceed without him. Action was first taken informally, by asking Lacan to resign his position as a training analyst. Unsurprisingly, he refused. He also took the opportunity to angrily inform both his lieutenants and followers that they had betrayed him. Next there was a motion proposed at an Extraordinary SFP meeting that Lacan's teaching and supervisory duties be discontinued and that he cease to be either a training analyst of teacher at the SPP. The motion was passed. Lacan was both furious and bereft and the way was opened for the SPP to become affiliated to the IPA. (Roudinesco, 1990, 321–9)

Fixity

Lacan's integrity was completely compromised by the fact that he wanted – and acted as if he wanted – two contradictory and mutually exclusive things. On the one hand, he wanted to theorise and practice psychoanalysis in a way that challenged what was accepted. On the other he wanted to be a member (nay, a very influential member) of the group that sanctioned what was accepted and was the international orthodoxy: the IPA.

Lacan's defenders will often say that the IPA used the rules around session-length against him in an arbitrary and instrumental fashion. Such action, according to Lacanians, was not based on a fair assessment of Lacanian theory and was therefore unjust. Besides, they say, Lacan's theories were *right*. Yet whatever merits they did have, Lacan's theories didn't just eschew technical rules, they also *didn't* match the IPA understanding of Freud. By Lacan's own admission, the main thrust of his theories was *against* the IPA concentration on the ego (rather than the unconscious). This concentration wasn't just *wrong*, it was significantly based on a *particular* interpretation of Freud. It *had* gained purchase, largely due to the fact that it had been pioneered and sanctioned by Freud's daughter Anna. It's understandable that Lacan thought that the Anna Freudian/ ego-psychological interpretation of Freud was incorrect, and also that he challenged it. Yet what was delusional on his part was the belief that he could actively, stridently and even violently oppose the IPA view in both his theory and his practice and still be accepted, even promoted, in their ranks. When Lacanians say that Lacan's treatment by the IPA was unjust, what they're not saying (but what is true) is that *his* attitude towards them was utterly unrealistic and hubristic. He patronised them, defied them, didn't tell them the truth, told them that they had misunderstood Freud and psychoanalysis in almost every important way and expected them to embrace and even praise him.

Properly symbolising this last state of affairs is what allows Lacan's situation in the early 1963 to be *realised*. In truth (or one might say, in reality) Lacan *didn't* act consistently. He wasn't being honest and he wasn't being realistic. He was very far from acting with integrity. In fact, once again, he was *split*. He wanted to be inside and outside the group, a rebel but a law-maker, a cult leader but an international leader, a Freudian who was utterly unlike all other Freudians and a dissident but a member of the establishment. He hadn't matured enough to choose his own fate: to conform or to follow his own path.

Contrarianism

Lacan's contrarianism was obviously an aspect of his splitting. As explained in earlier chapters, this splitting served the purpose of avoiding or disavowing actual or potential loss. Lacan fought othodoxies, institutions and people in order to mark his difference from them. Yet at the same time he didn't want to *give them up*. Opposing them allowed him to both maintain a relationship with them *and* attack them at the same time.

If Lacan was genuinely unimpressed by the IPA, shouldn't he have just ignored them and joined a non-affiliated group or set up one of his own? Of course, this is what he eventually did, but this didn't happen until he was over sixty years old. It took Lacan most of his life to mature enough to realise that if he couldn't work on the terms of the authority in his field, he was going to have to work on his own.

Language

It's also a testament to Lacan's contrarianism that between 1953 and 1964, *while* his international fate was being decided, he embarked on *another* theoretical journey. He (once again) claimed that this was a Freudian one, but it was (once again) undertaken in a form that the IPA wouldn't recognise *as* Freudian.

Lacan's venture – and adventure – involved re-thinking Freud's discoveries on a linguistic model. Two things are worth noting about this. Firstly, what Lacan was attempting *was* plausible – it *is* possible to re-think Freud in this way. Secondly, it nevertheless *does* involve *revision* and is therefore not 'purely' Freudian. Freud did take account of language, but he *didn't* make it his model for psychic functioning. For him, the *psyche* was the model of psychic functioning. Admittedly, the psyche contains thoughts and these are not unconnected to language. Yet they are not reducible to or a subset of language either.

Saussure

Lacan's linguistic re-thinking of Freud was – once again – a reinterpretation of Freudian ideas in terms of the work of *someone else*. The person concerned was Ferdinand de Saussure, a turn-of-the century Professor of Linguistics at the University of Geneva. Saussure led a low-profile life and his work didn't really become influential until after his death. Then, during the 1950s, it became extremely popular and much applied by French intellectuals and academics.

Many of the French thinkers who took up Saussure's ideas were not linguists, but rather *employed* Saussure's concepts and models in other fields and disciplines. Key among them was the anthropologist Claude Levi-Strauss, who explicitly used Saussurian tools and methods in his analyses. Levi-Strauss was one of Lacan's good friends. It wasn't long before Lacan understood the usefulness and applicability of Saussure's discoveries for psychoanalysis too. It's thus worth looking at Saussure's discoveries and methods at source, in order to be able to see what Lacan was (or was at least claiming to be) accessing.

Between 1907 and 1911, Saussure delivered a series of lectures outlining a general theory of language. These were posthumously re-assembled from his students' notes as the 'Course in General Linguistics'. (Saussure, [1915] 1966) The text is often represented as having made a decisive break with the linguistics that preceded it. Lacan called Saussure 'the founder of modern linguistics' and he was not alone in this view. (EC, p. 344) By the 1950s, when Saussure's ideas were popular in France, they were being used not only to revise linguistics, anthropology and psychoanalysis, but also philosophy, psychology and the study of culture.[2] Lacan credited Saussure with not only having 'paved the way' for 'modern linguistics' but also with having built certain linguistic concepts into 'the foundations of the human sciences'.[3]

In 1911 Saussure was indeed ahead of his time. Yet his break with the past was not as total as it has since been represented. Rather, he identified a particular tendency in linguistics and attempted to accentuate and crystallise it so that the whole of the discipline could conform to it and be revised and re-devised with reference to it. More specifically, he revitalised a movement in linguistics to make it a *science*.

There had been previous and various attempts to render linguistics scientific, with mixed results. Different 'scientific' formulations had conceived language differently and ended up concluding different things about it. This had led to sub-disciplinarity. It was linguists' taste for scientificity that had produced phonetics (the science of speech sounds) *and* phonology (the study of relations between such sounds) *and* etymology (the history of language) *and* grammatology (the science of language considered as writing). All of these forms of study claimed to be scientific, yet all had distinct objects and approached their objects in different ways. Phonetics, for instance, worked with phonic substance and did so aurally, while phonology dealt with phonic form and did so logically. For Saussure, this all made for ontological and epistemological inconsistencies, which in turn compromised the scientificity of the field. He tackled the problem as follows.

Scope

Saussure declared that the 'scope' of linguistics 'should be…(a) to describe and trace all observable languages (b) to determine the forces that are … at work in all languages and (c) to limit and define [language]'. (Saussure, p. 6) He arguably did achieve this. Yet before he could do so, he had to establish what exactly the 'scope' contained. This involved identifying its 'essence', that is, is the essence of language.

In searching for language's essence Saussure was only doing what he took it to be necessary for science to do. Every science has an object that contains its essence. The object of physics is the physical world (whose components are time, space, matter and energy). Chemistry's objects are chemical elements and processes (which amount to the contents and possible combinations of the periodic table). In each case a science identifies its object and what is essential to that object, but also essential to the study of that object (which is hence its 'object of study'). It does this so that it can clearly and consistently know what it is looking *at* (which it turn dictates *how* it can be looked at). Saussure wanted to achieve the sort of clarity achieved in individual hard sciences in linguistics. He wanted to separate language's essence out from its extensions or involvements. He then wanted either to study the essence of language in itself or to study it in its applications.

Thus the scientific need to define essence was what led Saussure to ask a fundamental question. 'What is both the integral and concrete object of linguistics?' (Saussure, p. 9)

Essence

In order to identify linguistic essence Saussure did an apparently odd thing. Rather than asking what it was, he asked what it wasn't. This approach is only *apparently* odd, because it does in fact conform to scientific procedure as soon as we acknowledge that such procedure involves *reduction*. In effect, regarding language, Saussure was 'boiling it down' to its 'bare bones', removing what was inessential in order to discover what was left, what *was* essential to it. In doing so, he noted that *what is inessential to language is that it refers to things*.

This can be put another way. There is no necessary or essential relationship between any given word and any given thing. What the word 'door' refers to in English is referred to in French by the word 'porte'. The same thing can be named by two different words. These words themselves are not fixed, or eternal. If a group of people were to agree to do so, they might even call the thing that English people call 'door' something entirely new, like 'min' or 'gribble'. Whatever the essence of language is, it isn't to be found in any fundamental connection or relation between it and any material object.

Of course, this is counterintuitive. One might presume (and people often do presume) that words *belong* to objects, that they are *in* them or *come out* of them, or that they have been *given* to them in some fundamental way, by man or by God. Yet Saussure's point holds and is proved by the fact of its also working *the other way round*. Certain words – or sets of speech sounds – can apply to different objects in different languages. Thus 'face', in English, can refer to what is on the front of a person's head, whereas in French it can mean the side of something, for example the side of a piece of paper.

Thus in language there is no necessary relation between any given word and any given thing just as in the world there is no necessary relation between any given object and any particular set of speech sounds. Saussure held this principle to be true of *any* element of language or reality.

Terminology

In order to take this argument further, Saussure needed to employ some new terminology. He adopted a term for the basic integral element of language. This element is often a word, but is *not always* a word (it might, for instance, be an image or pictograph) so he couldn't call it one. Thus Saussure called the basic element of language *the sign*. It follows that what he concluded about the sign is that it is essentially unrelated to the world, just as the world is essentially unrelated to it. He thought this so important that he decided to establish it as a principle of linguistics and he referred to this principle as 'the arbitrary nature of the sign'. (Saussure, p. 67)

Although, according to Saussure, the sign is the basic integral element of language, it is not the only or the smallest element of it. In general, it unites two other elements. A word, for example, 'unites not a thing and a name, but a concept and a sound-image'. Put simply, each word includes a sound (or set of sounds, or image) and also a concept (or idea). Thus the word 'man' combines the sound or image associated with it in speech and the idea of a male human (this is obviously also true of a pictograph: ⚥). Saussure gave a technical name to the 'sound image': 'signifier'. He referred to the idea as 'signified'. He said that 'the two elements are intimately united and each recalls the other. Thus the sign can be represented as shown in Figure 1.

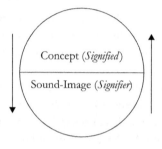

Figure 1

Arbitrariness

Figure 1 is Saussure's graphic representation of the sign, although it does not, in itself, represent the arbitrary nature of the sign as it has so far been described. In order to do that one would have to note that Saussure also has a technical name for the thing (as opposed to the word or sign), which is 'the referent'. Figure 2 gives a graphic representation of the arbitrary nature of the sign.

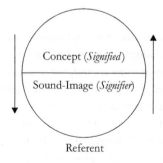

Figure 2

In this case the arbitrariness of the relation between the sign and the referent is represented by the *space* between them. (Saussure, pp. 65–70)

The arbitrariness of the sign also holds at another level than the one between the sign and the referent. It holds between the signifier and the signified. The idea behind the word 'man' might be represented by different speech sounds (for example, in French, 'homme'), just as 'man' might represent different things (for example mankind and the male). Thus the sign is arbitrary 'in itself' as well as in its relation to the referent.

Value

This is all very well, one might say, but it doesn't *in itself* provide what was initially promised. Saussure's theory of the sign doesn't answer the question concerning what is *essential* to language, or at least doesn't answer it adequately. The sign doesn't *constitute* language, in totality or as such. What's more, in describing it, Saussure didn't so much designate what is linguistically essential, as what isn't. His method was negative and reductive and sought to identify and rid language of what *isn't* essential. Yet why did it do this? The answer is to identify what *is*.

In seeking the essence of language, Saussure didn't so much identify the matter as the *mechanism* of it. In other words he showed *how it works*. Specifically, he explained how language contains or produces *meaning*. For this reason it's tempting to say that meaning is what Saussure designated as being essential to language. This wouldn't be wrong, but doesn't quite accord with what he said. Instead, he attributed the functioning of language to a *quality* of it. He called this quality 'value'. Value – like 'arbitrariness' – is an *essential* principle of linguistic functioning.

Saussure established that signs are not made meaningful by virtue of their relationship with reality but *by virtue of their relationships with other signs*. *This* is linguistic value. One does not understand the meaning of a sign in terms of its relation to reality. Neither does one understand it 'in itself'. One understands it in relation to *other signs*. For example, what is anger? One cannot touch it and one cannot point at it. Neither can one 'show' it (for example by acting it out) without ambiguity (it might get mistaken for something else, like frustration, or fear). However, one *can* describe it with reference to *other* signs. Thus one can say, for example, that anger is a stronger form of irritation or a weaker form of rage. As soon as one has done so, one has intimated a set of relations that 'anger' exists in and that could be represented as in Figure 3.

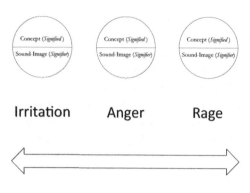

Irritation   Anger   Rage

Figure 3

One can describe these relations positively *or* negatively. One can either
say that anger is related to irritation in being a stronger form of it, or that
it is different from rage in being a weaker form of it. One could also note
that such relations hold at sub-atomic as well as atomic levels. Signifiers
are related to (and/or different from) each other (this is what phonology
shows when it pinpoints the phonic differences between words) just as
signifieds are related to (and/or different from) each other (this is what
etymology shows when it demonstrates how the meanings of words
change). Signifiers are also related to signifiers (which relation inheres in
what words *mean*) and different from them in being of a different order to
them (in being *ephonic* rather than *conceptual*). In any case *at all levels* signs
are made meaningful by virtue of their relations with other signs. Each
sign is thus made up of multiple relations. As a consequence, all signs are
placed in the *structure* that is *formed* by such relations (Figure 4).

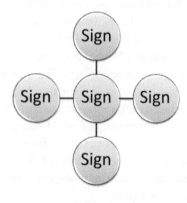

Figure 4

The totality of linguistic relations – which is a structure – makes up a language. All of the signs and the relations between them that constitute this language can be imagined as a structure that is similar to a molecular model (Figure 5).

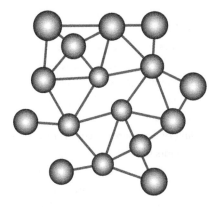

Figure 5

Structuralism

Explained thus, Saussure's principles provide the possibility of describing or imaging language as a *structure*. It's thus also obvious why Saussure's approach to the study of language was (and is) referred to as structuralism. (Saussure, pp. 111–22)

Unsurprisingly, there were philosophical engagements with Saussure's ideas in general and with his structural linguistics in particular. It's worth considering some of the key points that can be made about structuralism from a philosophical point of view.

The philosophical points in the next few sections are made in order to identify and also engage with the apparent limitations – more exactly the apparent ambiguities and inconsistencies – of Saussure's theory. These ambiguities and inconsistencies become both apparent and understandable when the theory they are manifest in is submitted to deconstruction, as it is here. Deconstruction of Saussure's theory not only shows how it doesn't work (or completely make sense) but also how it does work (and can make sense). This is generally what is achieved in the analysis of Saussure's theory by Jacques Derrida, to whom the following argument is indebted. (Derrida, [1967a] 1984 pp. 27–73; [1972b] 1981 pp. 15–36)

Reality

It's sometimes argued – from both a philosophical and a linguistic point of view – that Saussure's theory of language amounts to a sort of extreme nominalism. What this representation of Saussurianism is getting at is the way in which the notion of 'arbitrariness' seems to cast language as something that is detached both from the world and from meaning. Saussure effectively argues that there is no necessary relationship between words and things and that the same is true regarding the (non-) relation between sounds and meanings. Does this mean that there is no relationship between language and reality? Alternatively (or additionally) does it mean that language has no meaning?

This sort of reading of Saussure's theory is based on a misconception that 'arbitrariness' amounts to total detachment. It presumes that Saussure was saying that utterances are entirely unconnected with ideas or things. He wasn't saying this and his theory doesn't imply it either. The signifier cannot be entirely separated from the signified. They are, as Saussure said, like 'two sides of a piece of paper'. He improved on this imperfect and rather static analogy by explaining that the 'role of language...is...to serve as a link between thought and sound, under conditions that of necessity bring about the reciprocal delimitation of units.' (Saussure, pp. 112–13) Signifiers and signifieds have no given individual relations with each other, but each are always connected to the other, because signifiers imply signifieds and depend on them for their existence. The reverse is also true. All of this is perhaps most apparent at the meta-linguistic level. One cannot meaningfully say 'the signifier is completely unconnected to the signified' without knowing what the signifier is. Yet this means presuming that it *has* a signified, which means it cannot be completely unconnected to it. The same is also true at the level of the sign and with regard to the question of reference. If one says 'language bears no relation to reality' then one has to know what reality is for this claim to make sense. Yet if one does know what reality is the fact that one knows this implies that one at least has a concept of it and even empirical knowledge of it. Because concepts and knowledge are bound to language, it can't be true that language has no relation to reality.

Thus it is not the case that Saussure's theory is entirely nominalist (or idealist, or non-realist). Of course this does not mean that the idea of arbitrariness has no effect: Saussure's theory is obviously not a 'realist' one either. Thus if one thinks about linguistic structuralism with any sort of philosophical rigour, one arrives at a middle position. Language does and doesn't relate to reality and it does and doesn't make sense.

Infinity

This philosophical intervention could be seen as a *defence* of Saussure's theory against a misrepresentation of it as either anti-realist or realist. Yet a philosophical consideration of Saussure's theory can also show up its limitations as well as its consistencies and strengths. It's worth being aware of these limitations, because they're relevant to Lacan as well as to Saussure. Shortly, it will be shown that the former not only didn't fully understand the latter's ideas, but also that he misapplied them. He neither understood the force of Saussure's theory nor its shortcomings.

Linguisitc relations, for Saussure, form a *structure*. This structure is global and constitutes the totality of a language in which all signs are mutually related and mutually reinforcing. Saussure called this structure 'la langue'. It is constituted by the sum of all the relations contained in it and it situates and hence allows for the identification of every sign that is defined by those relations. On this basis Saussure sought to show that *all* signs could be scientifically identified. Yet is a total linguistic structure identifiable? If not, are all linguistic elements unidentifiable too? These questions can be thought through as follows.

How does one define a sign? Saussure claimed that each sign is made meaningful in relation to another sign. Yet of course, this other sign is also made meaningful in relation to a *further* sign, which is made meaningful in relation to *another* one (and so on). Because linguistic elements and even linguistic structures are always *to be defined,* there is never any second or third or final element on the basis of which any first one can ever be fully established and on the basis of which all others can be secured. The definition of individual signs and the structure of language as a whole can only ever be identified incompletely and at best *provisionally.* This doesn't make Saussure's theories invalid, but it does mean that they can never attain the positivistic and scientistic aims that he wished for them. Signs and structures can never be fully and positively identified (this means, among other things, that linguistics can never be entirely scientific).

Layering

It's now time to consider Lacan's engagement with structural linguistics in general and Saussurian linguistics in particular. This engagement was impressive but far from flawless. Lacan *did* tease out some of the most intriguing aspects of Saussure's theory and he did employ it in a novel and suggestive way. Yet what he *didn't* do was read Saussure carefully, interpret his ideas logically and apply them faithfully. As ever, he was *not* rigorous – even though he often claimed to be so.[4]

Lacan's appropriation of Saussure's theory was based on that theory but was also unlike it in significant ways. It refered directly to, but also radically altered – some might say perverted – it. Thus Lacan recounted Saussurian principles but held that they applied to quite different linguistic phenomena (most obviously the linguistic *subject* rather than the linguistic *object*); he operated a model of psycho-linguistic functioning, but one that was radically different to the one that was operated by Saussure (and that was constitutionally unconscious rather than cognitive and conscious); he commented on Saussure's work but described it inaccurately (attributing aspects to it that it did not have, or overlooking key features that it did have); he thoroughly mixed up Saussure's ideas with Freud's (when neither Saussure's work nor Freud's really sanctioned this) and he drew on the work of other structural linguists but whose perspectives and interests were different to Saussure's (Roman Jakobson's work is exemplary here and will be referred to below). Finally, Lacan constructed a discourse that combined linguistics, psychoanalysis, logic, mathematics and dialectics to produce equations and a meta-theory that bore no transparent relation to any of ideas that had given rise to them.

This list of what Lacan did and didn't do with Saussure's theory *already* suggests that his appropriation did and didn't work. Yet for these very reasons, it does provide a sort of template for understanding Lacan's Saussurianism. It would therefore make sense to proceed by dealing with all of the achievements/problems mentioned above in more detail. They can in fact be grouped together under three headings: the subject, Jakobson and theory. What follows will deal with each of these groupings in turn.

Subject

From the early fifties onwards, Lacan began to use a term used by linguisitcs quite frequently: 'subject'. What's more, he began to use it in a particular context: a linguistic one. It shouldn't be a shock to learn this, given his predilection for linguistic analyses and his focus on individual experience. Lacan had begun to think that 'man' was immersed in a sort of 'bath' that was not filled with water but with 'language'. (Lacan, [1966] 1967, p. 7) He thought that something was maintained of man's individuality nevertheless, just as the human body, although immersed in water, is not dispersed by it. Given this, his interest in the 'linguistic subject' is no great surprise.

Yet there was *another* reason why Lacan liked the word 'subject', which had to do with his previous as well as his current interests. 'Subject' was a word that had been used by Descartes and that had also been used by many of his French philosophical successors. Importantly, it had been used by phenomenologists. As Chapter Five showed, Lacan was a sort of inverted Cartesian (whether he liked it or not). He was also (and liked thinking of himself as) a phenomenologist. Hence from 1953 or so, and for phenomenological as well as linguistic reasons, Lacan used the word 'subject' to designate distinct human being.

Of course the phenomenological use of the term 'subject' and the linguistic use of it are different. This is already a problem for Lacan's readers, if not for him. It is an issue that will have to be returned to in a moment. Right now, it's best to try to clarify the nature of the specifically 'linguistic subject' that Lacan so keenly referred to from about 1953.

In structural linguistics the subject is primarily understood in terms of the linguistic rather than, say, the human or psychological context in which it appears. This can be put more exactly and by way of an example. A sentence will usually contain a subject, an object and a verb. In the sentence 'I like Björk', 'I' is the subject of the sentence, 'like' is the verb and 'Björk' is the object. The subject is that which relates to the object and that to which the verb pertains. It is what 'likes Björk', no more and no less and is defined purely in relation to the other signs in a sentence. A structural linguist would not be particularly interested in who or what the subject *refers to*, that is who *says* what is attributed to the subject. This (person) is extrinsic to the sentence in so far as the sentence is understood from a strictly linguistic point of view.

This subject operating on a primarily linguistic level interested Lacan greatly in the 1950s – and indeed in the 1960s and beyond. It's not hard to see how its formulation derives from the theories of Saussure. 'I' in the sentence – and the analysis – above is only attributed to a living being' in an 'arbitrary' or 'secondary' way. What's not important, for the linguist, is who this 'I' personally or materially is. What is important is that 'I' is a *sign* and that this sign is defined in terms of its linguistic relations. Lacan had begun to think that the 'I' that is spoken in psychoanalysis is similar. It isn't primarily meaningful in its relation to the *person* who speaks it, or for that matter their intentions. Instead, its meaning has to do with *other* signs that attend the psychoanalysis, ones that are both spoken and not and are hence both conscious and unconscious. It's not hard to see how *this* understanding of 'the subject' draws on the work of Freud as well as that of Saussure. After all, the psychoanalytic patient is drawn back to the significance of his words through their *associations* with other words. All of these other words are related to each other and eventually and ideally lead back to an unconscious symbolisation that explains the whole *trail* or *network* of words and symbols that constitute the symptom that brings the patient into the consulting room in the first place.

What is arguably unique about what Lacan claimed to be uncovering with this approach is a type of subject that is, in significant respects, unlike any other that had been described before *at least as a subject*. This is because it isn't just the linguistic subject or the phenomenological subject. It is also 'the subject of the unconscious'.[5]

Problems

Once again there are problems with this subject – or more exactly with the formulation of it – that should be mentioned, at least in passing. 'The subject of the unconscious' is identified by Lacan as having been the same one that was sought by Freud. Yet Freud never used this full term and only rarely used the atomic term 'subject'. Furthermore, the Lacanian subject is one that is supposed to disclose psychoanalytic 'subjectivity'. In the practice of Lacanian psychoanalysis, this quality is essential. Lacan was keen for his profession to identify those unconscious qualities that are *particular* to a patients and that begin to reveal his 'individual' truth (which is what Lacan *called* subjectivity). This has already been shown, as has Lacan's opposition to a psychoanalysis of consciousness, of the ego and of the re-modelling of that ego on the ego of the analyst. Yet these latter strategies can be seen as psychoanalytic and Freudian too (this has also been established). The 'truth of the subject' was a Lacanian pursuit, but this didn't make it the *only* psychoanalytic strategy, or even the key Freudian aim.

Another 'subjective' problem relates to one of the tradition of thinking that Lacan drew on that *did* use the term subject, but which wasn't Freudian, namely phenomenology. Lacan clearly *wanted* to evoke this. He wanted the term to (once again) bear something of phenomenology's interest in the 'individual' whose mind is 'directed towards' mental phenomena and who mental objects are 'for'. In other words he wanted to say that psychoanalysis significantly involves the uncovering of *subjective meaning* just as, in a sense, phenomenology does. Yet of course phenomenology largely does this with a presumption that phenomena and what witnesses it – the subject – are *conscious*. Lacan, didn't believe this. Yet he went on using a phenomenological term (subject) with phenomenological associations while completely contradicting a phenomenological premise (consciousness).

Finally (but not really finally because this problem will return) Lacan's use of the term 'subject' often contradicted the key context in which he used it. It should be clear, both from the description of Saussurian linguistics *and* from the account of 'the subject' in structural linguistics that followed it, that the said subject is not really 'subjective' in the sense that common language employs the term. Rather it is an 'object' of linguistic analysis, whose meaning is set in relation to other objects, *namely signs*. This sort of perspective is entirely in line with the Saussurian scientific ethos. Language is an *object* (or a collection of *objects*) for study. This includes 'the subject', which is a linguistic object like any other. How could Lacan coherently employ the term subject in the linguistic sense while uncovering subjectivity in a phenomenological or psychoanalytic one?

The answer to this question, of course is that Lacan *couldn't*, at least not without contradiction. In fact contradiction is inherent in all of the uses that Lacan made of the term 'subject' and is so because each of them contradicts and is contradicted by the others.

Jakobson

At this point it makes sense to refer to an area of theoretical work that Lacan operated in that was first established by a colleague and friend of his: Roman Jakobson. The latter was a linguist who had an interest in fields other than pure linguistics, including literature and psychology. He thought of himself as a structural linguist and hence, at least broadly, as Saussurian. Lacan was intrigued and motivated by Jakobson's identification of some key links between linguistic and psychical functioning. He thought that this dual functioning, when revealed, exposed the mechanisms of the unconscious. Seeing how Lacan extended and deployed Jakobson's theory allows one to understand one of Lacan's well known, influential and absolutely crucial claims, namely that 'the unconscious is structured like a language'.[6]

Sense

It's well worth summing up and explaining Lacan's extension of Jakobson's theory, which was generated by him in a paper entitled: 'Two Aspects of

Language and Two Types of Aphasic Disturbance'. (Jakobson and Halle, pp. 55–87) By and large, the following summing up will seek to explain Lacan's theory as he might have wished to have it understood, that is in so far as he would have wished it to make sense. Lacan's theory not only draws on Jakobson, but also on Freud and Saussure.

Jakobson noted that many instances of language, including sentences, have two important dimensions, which can be referred to as syntagmatic and paradigmatic. These notions are derived, indirectly, from Saussurian ones. The syntagmatic dimension of a sentence is that dimension in which it unfolds, in other words that dimension which is temporal and successive. It is the aspect of language which has to do with the way in which words relate to each other by following each other. The paradigmatic dimension of a sentence pertains to the sense in which parts of it, for example individual words, *might* be replaced by other parts, for example other words. It is the 'substitutive' aspect of language. (Jakobson and Halle, p. 59)

Here's an example of a how a sentence might have both syntagmatic and paradigmatic dimensions. It's a sentence that might be uttered by a bored businessman:

> I don't want to be a suit, I want to be a celebrity
> star

As just suggested, the syntagmatic dimension of this sentence has to do with the way in which its signs are related to each other successively and in a comprehensible order. They make successive sense where others might not. The sentence would also be nonsense if it read: 'don't I to want a be I suit to want a be celebrity'. The signs in it are related to each other in a meaningful syntactic order.

The paradigmatic dimension of the sentence is the one that allows it to be changed by substitution and still remain meaningful. Thus paradigmatic relations are ones that allow elements in a sentence to be exchanged with other elements that are external to it without that sentence becoming meaningless. There is a paradigmatic relation between 'celebrity' and 'star' in the above example because if the latter is substituted for the former the sentence still has meaning.

Jakobson had words for the functions that are at work in either of these (syntagmatic and paradigmatic) dimensions of language. Functions operative in the syntagmatic dimension are ones of combination while functions operative in the paradigmatic dimension are ones of substitution. Jakobson cited Saussure as the source for this sort of distinction and

Lacan cited Jakobson as the person who had properly identified and refined the 'opposition' concerned, namely 'between on the one hand the relations of similarity, or substitution, or choice and also of selection and concurrence...and on the other hand the relations of contiguity, alignment, signifying articulation, syntactic coordination'.[7]

Jakobson said that syntagmatic and paradigmatic, or combinative and substitutive, dimensions of language might be operating at any given time. Yet they are different functions that operate in different dimensions (of, for example, the sentence). Because they are opposite but also interact, Lacan described them as linguistic *poles* or *polarities*. As such they can be represented on the two axes of a graph (Figure 6).

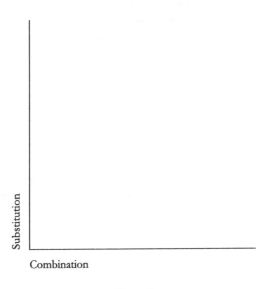

Figure 6

Now Jakobson went on to extend these different and related functions and to find others that are like them. He first of all did this by trying to discern the respective characteristics of substitution and combination. Lacan picked up his argument and elaborated on it a little too.

Substitution, Jakobson noted, involves the replacement of one thing by another on the basis of their being similar. It thus involves relations of *similarity*. So, for example, the word 'star' can be substituted for the word 'celebrity' because, like the word celebrity, it designates something 'high up' (in the sky, or on a pedestal) or 'shining' (because it is on fire or because it is attractive). Jakobson then noted that this substitution of one thing for another on the basis of a similarity is exactly what happens in metaphor (examples: 'the king is a lion', 'you're a prince') and 'star' is indeed a metaphor for 'celebrity'. 'Metaphor', as Lacan put it 'presupposes similarity'. (Jakobson and Halle, pp. 60–1; Lacan, [1955–6] 1993, p. 219) It is therefore a type of substitution. He added that it is one in which 'the poetic spark is produced'. (EC, p. 508)

Jakobson then went on to note that combination involves what he calls 'contiguity'. Contiguity strictly speaking, is the quality of being close to, or next to something. Jakobson extended this meaning to include being part of something. Contiguity pertains to syntagmatic elements which are both close to each other and part of a sentence. Such elements have what Lacan called a 'word-to-word' relation. Now contiguity holds in another linguistic function, namely metonymy. As Lacan defines it, metonymy is the linguistic 'part taken for the whole'. It involves, for example calling a ship a 'sail', or a car 'wheels'. Thus combinatory and metonymic elements function in a very similar way: through *contiguity* or *proximity*. (Jakobson and Halle, pp. 59–61; EC, p. 421)

The example sentence given above already has a metonym in it and furthermore one that functions by way of combination or contiguity namely 'suit'. Given all of this, it's possible to extend our graphic representation of linguistic functions (Figure 7).

Jakobson had plenty more to say about these linguistic poles. For example, he describes how people who suffer from a disorder known

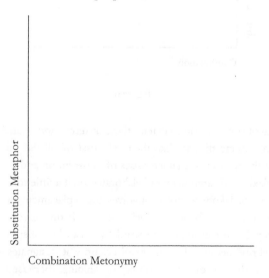

Combination Metonymy

Figure 7

as aphasia will only tend to be able to activate one or another of these poles. What's of most interest here, however, is how Lacan both extended and generalised Jakobson's argument to reveal something about linguistic functioning *per se* in both its normal and its psychopathologial modes. It was in the context of this larger application of Jakobson's discoveries that Lacan explained how language – and particularly speech – is motivated by unconscious factors that are built in to both its structure and the structure of 'the subject'. All of this amounted to revealing precisely how 'the unconscious is structured like a language'.

Dreams

Lacan likened the functions on the respective poles of Figure 7 to other functions described by Freud. First of all, he likened metaphor and metonymy, respectively, to two of the functions that Freud identified in *The Interpretation of Dreams*, namely condensation and displacement.

Freud said that dreams show (or say) something but hide (and mean) something else. What exactly they do conceal can usually be identified – after investigation and analysis – as a 'wish', or as Lacan would have it, a 'desire'. Freud discovered that there are two main mechanisms by means of which latent dream content (which figures desire) is hidden in, but indirectly communicated by, manifest dream content (the dream 'itself'). These mechanisms are 'condensation' and 'displacement'. (Freud, [1900] 1976, pp. 247–8, 380–2, 414)

Freud found that dreams are reminiscent of many other things. He demonstrated this with one of his own dreams. He dreamed that he was reading a botanical monograph. The elements of this dream had all sorts of associations for him, which appeared in different trains. For example, the monograph reminded him of something that he had written on cocaine, which in turn reminded him of a conversation with a medical colleague who had collaborated with him in his research on the drug, which conversation was to do with payment for medical treatment. Another train of associations derived from the botanical dimension of the monograph. It reminded Freud of a colleague named Gärtner (literally 'Gardener'), of the 'blooming' looks of Gärtner's wife and of a patient named Flora (the Latin name for 'flowers'). The cocaine-related chain of associations had to do with his ambivalence about having researched a drug for good medical reasons (he did work on its anesthetic qualities) when it also had deleterious (addictive) side-effects. The other, 'botanical' chain of associations in Freud's dream clearly had a sexual content. In any case and in general, the manifest elements of dreams represent a number of latent trains of association. There are very many more latent associations than there are manifest elements in a dream. Nevertheless, the manifest dream elements *imply* the latent ones *by association*. This means that associations are compressed into the elements that represent them and that they have thus been subject to a *condensation*. A simple way of summing this up is to say that latent content in dreams is condensed into manifest content.

Displacement is the mechanism whereby one or more elements of the latent content of the dream (or the meaning of the dream) is apparent (rather than invisible) in the manifest content of the dream which thus alludes in a 'literal' but minimal way to the latent content that the element is derived from. For example, one of Freud's patients has a dream in which there is a representation of climbing up and down stairs. Freud says that the patient's associations included a phantasy of having sex with someone from a lower class. There can be movements up and down between classes and movements up and down in sex. The characteristic of a latent element in the dream – movement up and down – had been dis-placed, that is moved into the manifest content. It was disguised by the context it appeared in but was literally apparent in it nevertheless and could be traced back to its latent context as a consequence. (Freud, [1900] 1976, pp. 381–419)

Metaphor

Referring directly to Freud, Lacan likened condensation and displacement to metaphor and metonymy respectively. He noted that metaphor implies something else. A 'star', for example, is first of all a dead sun that hangs in the sky, but it becomes a metaphor when it signifies celebrity. The latter sense of the term *substitutes for* the former in metaphoric usage. Yet one doesn't necessarily *think* this when one uses the term; one is not necessarily *conscious* of both its original and its metaphoric usages. In that sense metaphor can be seen as having something not immediately apparent – or something *unconscious* – in it. Because it is thus and is (at least) two things in one, it can be seen as *condensed*. Thus if one says when one is tired that one is slaughtered, this might not only mean that one is tired, but also that one feels like someone is trying to kill one, or that one is so frustrated that one might feel like killing someone oneself. This other meaning implied by metaphor is often not a consciously or socially acceptable one, which is precisely why it has to become manifest indirectly – through metaphor – by which mechanism it is subject to repression.

Displacement

Just as condensation is equivalent to metaphor, metonymy is comparable to displacement. Because metonyms work by way of contiguity, they involve the possibility of one symbolic element being taken for something else. The suit, for example, can be taken for the businessman because it is close to, or a part of, him. This sort of functioning closely resembles that of oneiric displacement, in which part of one one thing is sometimes put in or on another for reasons of contiguity proximity (to be close to it, of because of what it was formerly close to). If in a dream one finds oneself trying on glasses this may be because there is someone one desires who wears glasses and that one wishes to get close to them by getting close to something that *is* close to them, or is a displaced part of them. Now this displacement of one object onto another is a movement of desire. It allows an (imaginary) object to be passed from one being to another. It thus facilitates a passage of desire through psychical objects or part-objects that have a *close* relation with each other.

Once the relation between substitution and metaphor had been established on the one hand and the link between combination and metonymy had been established on the other, Lacan was able to add that 'what Freud calls condensation is what in rhetoric one calls metaphor, what he calls displacement is metonymy'. (Lacan, [1955–6] 1993, p. 221) He then pointed out that it was possible to 'read' the symptom metaphorically and that displacement tracked the (metonymic) movement of desire. When *all* of the relations between Freudian and Jakobsonian concepts and terminology have been established (by Lacan) it's possible to extend Figure 7 to look like Figure 8.

To the extent that it *works* Figure 8 depicts the possibility that 'the unconscious is structured like a language' and that it has an effect, linguistically, on a subject who is therefore 'the subject of the unconscious' as well as 'the linguistic subject'.

This subject would be 'subject' (precisely) to a larger psycho-linguistic mechanism that his words would be being produced in. At the level of the sentence and the level of intent he would be speaking and (mostly) producing words that made sense to him and that he was *conscious* of. Yet many other linguistic associations and implications would also be informing his words and these would be mostly or entirely *unconscious* to him, although maybe not to his analyst or to any of his interlocutors who might have a psychoanalytic bent. These would lead interpretation back, away from any self conscious subject or ego, to the 'intentions' of quite

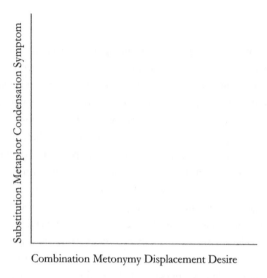

Combination Metonymy Displacement Desire

Figure 8

a different subject, one with quite different motivations and constitution, namely 'the subject of the unconscious'.

As indicated, the section above hopefully contains an accurate representation of what is so often referred to by Lacanians as 'The Lacanian Subject'. (Fink, 1996) Yet it's been shown that this subject, like Lacan, both did and didn't make sense. Having shown the former about the Lacanian subject and the way in which Lacan imagined it, it's time to reveal the latter. This can best be done from two sides: the side of the 'object' and the side of the 'subject'.

Signifier

Given that he claimed to be drawing on Saussure's fundamental insights and given that he also represented himself as employing Saussurian methodology, it's odd that Lacan chose to focus on a different linguistic element than Saussure. The central (and relatively indivisible) element of language for Saussure was the sign. Yet Saussure, the (largely) positivistic scientist, ultimately wanted to think of both words and languages as *unified* and the sign was the basic *unit* of this endeavour. Lacan sometimes claimed to be doing something scientific too. Yet for him the preponderant element of language was *the signifier*. For him, it was *signifiers* that were exchanged and displaced in metaphors and metonyms, that deceived the subject in consciousness, that indirectly represented his desire, that were repressed, that caught him in their 'defiles', that were his love objects and that surrounded and immersed him in life and in the psychoanalytic session. Why was this so and what did it mean?

Just as much as he spoke about 'the subject of language' or 'the subject of speech' Lacan spoke about 'the subject of the signifier'. He did this because he thought that 'the signifier' represented something significant about both language and its interaction with 'the subject'.

The Saussurian graphic that represents the sign does so as a circumscription of both the signifier and the signified, in which the latter is placed *above* the former. The signified is put *over* the signifier, as if meaning is at least as, or more important than, its representation. Lacan grasped this implication, but in his own 'equation', chose to reverse it (Figure 9).

$$\frac{S}{s}$$

Figure 9

In this representation, the signifier is shown as being *'over'* the signified and *unbound* by the sign. Lacan chose this representation in order to suggest that the signifier predominates over the signified, that language is generated and functions before or independently *of* signification and that it both precedes and exceeds meaning. Language gets ahead of any meaning that might be intended by the subject. This idea of the preponderance of the signifier over the signified, of the signifier over the subject and of relatively autonomous linguistic production, recalls the *automatism* that so transfixed Lacan in his youth. That excess of psychosis and modern art, in which language escapes any sense or intent the subject might want for it, was still being identified by Lacan towards the end of his life and career as not only the model for understanding psychoanalytic patients, but also as the nature of human being in general.

Other elements of Lacan's 'equation' are equally idiosyncratic. The 'bar' between signifier and signified does not (as it does for Saussure) represent a concomitant division and attachment of the two elements, but stands as a sort of 'resistance' between them, such that the signification (or meaning) of the sign is hardly or ever attained. To Lacan, the bar is quite literally a 'bar to meaning'. It's arguable of course that such a resistance to meaning, is exactly the effect of the unconscious. It is unconscious meaning that is *precisely* difficult to access, in language or otherwise. Yet Lacan, by using linguistic terminology to show 'unconscious resistance', can't help but indicate that it is characteristic of language as a whole. In doing so he overplays his hand and makes a sort of transcendental claim where he should be making a local, or contextualised, or contained one. It is obviously not true that language in general *is* highly resistant to meaning (or interpretation or understanding); if it were, common speech would be incomprehensible. (EC, pp. 414–5, 428–9)

It should be fairly obvious from all of this that it's not just the extent of the implications of Lacan's linguistics that is questionable, but also the thinking behind them. For Lacan the 'equation' $\frac{S}{s}$ indicated that the human being in language (that is human being per se) was subject to what Jacques Alain Miller liked to call 'the logic of the signifier'. (Miller, 1977 How this phenomenon looks or sounds is not in doubt (it looks and sounds like madness). What *is* in doubt is its logic (the *logic* of the 'logic of the signifier). As stated earlier, Lacan said that signifier does not answer to 'any signification whatsoever'? This was shown to be illogical in Chapter 3 when the claim was first noted. It was shown to be so again earlier in *this* chapter, when it was demonstrated that arbitrariness *can't* be total and that the signifier *can't* be completely unconnected to the signified (or for that matter the sign, or all reference). For sure, Lacan's insistence on the autonomy of the signifier could be said to be *rhetorical* rather than logical. Yet he often claimed to be being scientific *and* logical. Thus the general and basic problem of Lacan's linguistics is that they *don't make sense*.

Singularity

Apart from language, the other element that is active between the metaphoric and metonymic polarities of Lacan's 'language-graph' and that also doesn't make sense, is the subject or more precisely *the Lacanian subject*. That *this* subject – or rather the formulation of it – lacks sense has recently been shown independently of any reference to the graph and by way of identifying the multiple and contradictory registration (linguistic, phenomenological, psychoanalytic) that Lacan makes it bear.

Dazzle

This chapter has not attempted to provide a comprehensive or exhaustive account of Lacan's work after 1950, but it is hopefully a fairly good and accurate account and assessment of some of its critical components, arguments and conclusions. Like his institutional life and adventures, Lacan's best known theoretical ventures were complex, fascinating and dazzling. Many people *were* dazzled by him and his theories and were in awe of the heroic aura that surrounded him. Yet they were also blinded to the compromised and divided being and ideas that lay beneath both the theories and the man.

8

Ending and Beginning

Symbolic

By showing how the unconscious could be got at through an engagement
with *language*, Lacan was promoting a particular sort of psychoanalysis,
one that took representation in general as its field of study and words in
particular as the material and means of its truth. For Lacan, imaginary
phenomena – and the Imaginary in general – were of the order of representation, but not really of the order of meaning. As shown in Chapter
Five, images, phantasies and delusions are generally what populate the
Imaginary and are generally the products of the ego. The analysis of these
ephemera *in language* and psychoanalytically is what might lead to the truth
of representation in general, that is to the unconscious material that lies
beneath ie that might allow the analysand to understand his own dreams
and behaviour and to make sense of himself. This process involves a *symbolisation* of unconscious material and this is why Lacan located analytic
truth in *The Symbolic*. This, he said, is where the analysed patient should
end up.

Truth

Lacan has a reputation as a renegade and a dissident, as someone who
provided alternative thinking, or at least thinking that is different to
conventional or orthodox thinking. Thus what some people might
find surprising about the sort of description of Lacanian psychoanalysis provided above is that it is quite standard. It is not just a description
of Lacanian psychoanalysis but also a description of psychoanalysis in
general *except that it is given in Lacanian terms*. Many psychoanalytic theories
(including and notably those of Melanie Klein) speak of the importance
of patients symbolising their conflicts. They also, as Lacan does, employ
notions of unconscious *truth*.[1] In some respects Lacanian theory is just

psychoanalytic theory articulated in a different way. This sort of representation of Lacan corresponds with some of the things that he said
about himself, specifically that he was returning to Freud. From a certain
point of view Lacan can, rather surprisingly, seem like a traditional
Freudian analyst.

Whole

Yet even if this is the truth, it's not the whole truth because, as Lacan
intimated in the epigraph for this book, it's impossible to convey all of
this all the time. Lacan employed so many theories by others and occupied
so many theoretical positions and made so many polemical claims and
opposed so many vested interests and played so many roles that it was
impossible for his theory to *be* consistent all the time. He could never be
the Freudian he claimed that he was. Yet neither could he be the rebel
leader he wanted to be. He couldn't be both of these *at the same time*.

It should now be quite obvious that Lacan's mode of address didn't
always help him win friends, influence people or allow him to develop
and convey a consistent theory that could be used to establish, enhance or
sustain a practice or a school. At least he wasn't able to do this within the
global body of analysts or during his lifetime. Some people were (and are)
entranced by Lacan's 'style' and others were (and are) alienated by it. Yet a
more fundamental question than whether one 'likes' Lacan remains. Why
did he think that apparent arrogance, a combative manner and extreme
theoretical opacity and obscurity would get a majority of psychoanalysts,
psychoanalytic sympathisers and the psychoanalytic establishment *on his
side?* The answer to this question is one that has been mooted from the
beginning of this text. Lacan was split and was split in multiple ways. The
splits were in him, but extended to his ideas, his personal and intellectual
loyalties, his institutional involvements and his legacies. They didn't mean
that he didn't do some brilliant things, possibly even some great things.
However, they did mean that he didn't do these things in a way that could
ever, after analysis, be consistent.

This arguably also means that what Lacan did can never be seen as
entirely truthful. From a philosophical point of view, one might argue that
this might not matter. Of course the truth is a complex – even perhaps
ultimately impossible – thing. Yet how can one conduct an analysis, or
more importantly *psychoanalysis*, without it? Lacan and Lacanians might
have (indeed actually do have) an answer to this question. They say that
Lacan didn't just promote a 'truth', he also showed the impossibility of

the truth. He *did* do this and he did it increasingly as he got older. Yet how should one continue to do psychoanalysis when one thinks, or has come to think, that the truth is impossible? If psychoanalysis requires such truth and it is impossible, then what is psychoanalysis for? It's partly the contention of this book that Lacan and the Lacanians have never adequately answered *this* question.

Ending

After 1960, Lacan went on assimilating, producing and developing new ideas. He also established two new psychoanalytic schools which (also) split apart and dissipated. Being an introduction, and being near its end, this book will not be able to consider these ideas or historical developments. It has, however, attempted to relay and assess the bulk of the important events, theories and political actions of Lacan's life, many of which, it could be argued, took place *before* 1960. All of these phenomena have now been described and explained in terms of Lacan having been *split* and all of his personal, intellectual and institutional involvement having been split too.

The book has also hopefully broken down an opposition that was mentioned at its beginning and that suffuses a great deal of commentary and scholarship *on* Lacan, namely the opposition between genius and fraudulence. It was said early on that Lacan's critics tend to either cast him as a genius or a fraud. One of the main aims of this book has been to show that he was neither.

Beginning

Whether or not this is a useful conclusion to have come to isn't to be judged here. For some, the debate about Lacan is settled and over; for others, it is undecided and just beginning.

Notes

Chapter 1

1. In so far as it implies other things, the first thing said in psychoanalysis resembles a *metaphor*. Lacan was well aware of this and even stressed it. See, for example, Lacan [1955–6] (1993) pp. 218–21 and EC pp. 421–4.

Chapter 2

1. Spirit vinegar is cheaper to produce than wine vinegar.
2. EC pp. 51–7.
3. Lacan most literally explores the effect of individual history on 'personality' in Lacan [1932] (1975).
4. The examination of authority – most obviously in relation to symbolic paternity – suffuses Lacan's work. Examples of seminars in which authority and paternity are explicitly engaged with include Lacan [1955–6] (1993) and [1962] (1990).
5. Apart from anything else, telling Lacan's story will help undo the paradoxes of his character, which is part-explained by *actual* relations between *apparently opposite* aspects of it (for example it's capacity for resentment and love or achievement and failure). These actual relations become apparent *as* Lacan's story is told.
6. Lacan's young admirers not only included Julia Kristeva (the psychoanalyst and intellectual) but also Jacques-Alain Miller (Lacan's institutional heir). Lacan's bemused peers included the celebrated anthropologist Claude Levi-Strauss, who was nevertheless Lacan's friend. *His* friend, the influential philosopher Maurice Merleau-Ponty was as confused by Lacan's ideas as Levi-Strauss was and confessed as much to him. See Roudinesco (1997) p. 211, 280, and 342.
7. To see this, one need only look at secondary Lacanian literature, particularly in so far as it is written by 'Lacanians'. Instances of the too-complex sort of treatment abound. Here, for example, is Ellie Ragland apparently seeking to explain 'the drives':

> And the drives emanate from what Lacan, in 1960, described as the first eight objects-cause-of-desire, which are both constitutive of an Ur-lining of the subject and without specularity or alterity. In *Le sinthome: un mixte de symptôme et fantasme,* Miller describes the barred subject as a void: One

goes from the hole made by the perception of the sexual difference, the imaginary -ɸ, to the subject emptied of enjoyment (S); that is, one goes from the hole made by the loss of the object *a* to the lack of enjoyment (from Ø to S), insofar as its absence reflects traits of a positivized identity, but without representation. In his Seminars on James Joyce, Lacan maintained that Joyce sought to fill the void by making the real voice suture all the crevices in being and body: Ø/a.

The only thing that is clear about Ragland's exposition is that it is not clear. It is full of unexplained jargon, misused algebraic symbols and unfamiliar names.

There are also the *too-simple* cases. Sean Homer's book on Lacan is an example. Lacan's oeuvre is large, cross-disciplinary, ambitious and technical. Its aspiration is metaphysical and its style is obscure. Homer tries to deal with all this by bringing it down to earth. His aim is to explain Lacan simply, to provide an 'accessible overview' of his work. This is like trying to simplify Hegel by bypassing the question of contradiction: it means leaving out what's essential. See Ragland (2004) pp. x, 9; Homer, pp. 9, 20; EC, pp. 79–80.

8. There are indeed numerous and significant ways in which Lacan, in his written and spoken addresses, both drew attention to and joked about his own authority and authority in general. For example, the title of his twenty-first seminar (of 1973–4): *Les Non-Dupes Errent* is a pun on the name of one of the very significant figures in his theoretical universe: 'Le nom du père'. The latter term (introduced in an earlier seminar: Lacan [1955–6]) is (among other things) the symbolic manifestation of the authority of the father (whose 'nom' or name resonates with 'non' or 'no'). 'Les Non-Dupes Errent' could be translated as; 'those who think they are not duped are more duped than they think'. The homonym (nom du père/non-dupes errent)' implies an implacable and self assured authority on the one hand and an equivalent state of credulity – even idiocy – on the other.

9. Lacanians' claim that Lacan is 'self-conscious' about his authority is true but this self-consciousness is also a defense against the recognition that this authority is authoritarian. The self-consciousness thus takes the form of a sort of splitting. Ironically, but appropriately, this is exactly the sort of argument Lacan *does* make about self-consciousness in his *Mirror Phase* paper and elsewhere. See EC, pp. 75–81.

10. A couple of examples of Lacanian abnegation of responsibility, blame of others and projection of authoritarianism are worth mentioning here. Lacan referred to his expulsion from the IPA in his fairly well-known and often cited introduction to his 11th seminar, in which he cast his expulsion as an 'excommunication'. He did not treat this as a consequence of any of his own actions or misdemeanours or even refer to any of these. Instead, he complained that he was the 'object of a deal' between the IPA and his own local psychoana-

lytic institution. Lacan's conviction that his exit from and non-readmission to the IPA had little or nothing to do with him is shared by most Lacanians and has led them to despise and calumniate the IPA evermore. Thus accusations of 'political' bias on the part of the IPA are literally *written into* the principles of the World Association of Psychoanalysis (WAP) an umbrella body which seeks to unite like-thinking Lacanian associations worldwide. These principles denounce 'the existing supervision regulations in the Institutes of the IPA [because they] depend on political, bureaucratic and prejudicial factors [which is] a reason in itself for the violation of the constituted rule'. The WAP articles suggests that IPA rules and practices are authoritarian, corrupt and self-violating. This is an extraordinary refusal, renunciation and return of a charge made by the IPA against Lacan. The latter was 'expelled' from the IPA precisely because he had broken – and had not told the truth about breaking – key IPA 'rules' See Lacan [1964] (1987) pp. 2–6; WAP (2007); Roudinesco (197) pp. 244–59.

11. See Graves pp. 371–4 and *Oedipus the King* in Sophocles.
12. The original Freudian aspects of the Oedipus Complex as described above are detailed in Freud [1915a] (1984) pp. 144–54.
13. See, for example, Vanier, p. 12.
14. Georg Brandes originally represented Nietzsche and his philosophy in this way in a letter written to him in November 1887. See Hayman, p. 314.
15. Maurras was an influential French Chauvinist, pro-Catholic, pro-monarchist anti-Semitic and anti-republican writer and critic of the early Twentieth Century. He was the lead ideologist of *Action Française,* which advocated the violent overthrow of the parliamentary Third Republic (1870–1940). *Action Française* was not a fascist group *as such,* but it did mostly support the Vichy regime in France during the Second World War.
16. In the first Surrealist Manifesto of 1924, Breton claimed that he conducted the first experiments in automatic writing in 1919. See Nadeau, p. 87.
17. See, for example, EC p. 42 (on the strengths and weaknesses of surrealism) p. 204 (on the modern distortion, adaption, and enculturation of psychoanalysis in the US) pp. 79–80 (on existentialism) and Lacan [1972–3] (1998) pp. 82–3 (on God).
18. Lacanians cast Lacan as someone whose knowledge encompassed all fields of intellectual activity and whose genius allowed him reformulate all in an entirely new way. For Henry W. Sullivan, Lacan 'stands as the founding theoretician of a post-Modern Age, much as Augustine laid out the City of God blueprint for the Middle Ages, or as Descartes mapped out the preoccupations of the Modern Age' (Lacan's own comparison of himself with Spinoza is in keeping with this sort of view). Critics of Lacan, unsurprisingly, adopt an opposite view. Raymond Tallis represents Lacan's intellectual engagements as 'incoherent and mangled versions of others' ideas'. It has to be said that there is an increasing amount of evidence on the anti-Lacanian

side of this argument. Quite a number of experts in fields Lacan operated in – particularly scientific ones – have demonstrated quite clearly that his knowledge and understanding *was* deficient in those fields. See Sullivan, p. 36; Lacan [1964] (1987), Tallis p. 153 and Sokal and Bricmont.

19. For Sartre, a free choice involves the nihilation of the reality of a foregone choice and of the self that might have made that choice. It therefore always involves a loss. See Sartre [1943] (1996) pp. 433–556. Jean Genet makes a similar point more prosaically: 'You have to pay for everything'. See Genet.

20. Lacan's formulations – indeed *formalisations* – of psychoanalytic terms are more stressed and concentrated on from the mid-1960s onwards, for example in the title and content of seminars such as *The Four Fundamental Concepts of Psychoanalysis* [1964] (1987). By 1970, Lacan was coming up with 'scientific' accounts of psychoanalytic knowledge (which were meant to confirm the nature, status and means of transmission of such knowledge and hence its *scientificity*). These were developed in the areas of topology, mathematics and formal logic. They made recourse, among other things, to algebra. This rarified, multidisciplinary and formal approach led to some strange and abstruse theorisation. It led, for example, to the Baroque and largely un-comprehended prognostications on psychoanalytic knowledge contained in Seminars XIX and XXIII, which liken it to the 'Borromean knot' and the 'Matheme'. Similar inventions and vagaries are apparent in the reduction of sexual identities and identifications – or 'sexuations' – to algebraic equations in Seminar XX. See Lacan [1970–2] (2002); [1972–3] (1999) and [1975–6].

21. François Roustang, an ex-Lacanian, claims that by 1968 Lacanians had come to believe, as their master did, that Lacanianism had 'become the discipline of disciplines – indeed, the science of sciences...Whence the conviction, still held by many, that, in order to master the analytic object and remain at the pinnacle of humanity. it is enough just to read Lacan and never to leave the confines of his writings. What good is it to go on asking questions that he has already answered for us, given that we don't have the time to devote ourselves to philosophy, mathematics, ethology and Chinese in order to make sure that the whole thing actually holds together?' See Roustang, p. 7.

22. Louis Althusser, an influential intellectual contemporary of Lacan's claimed that 'if you go to his seminar you'll see all sorts of people prostrating themselves before a discourse that to them is quite unintelligible. These are the methods of intellectual terrorism'. See Roudinesco (1997) p. 211, 280, 304 and 342. Althusser, like Merleau-Ponty and Levi-Strauss before him, also declared himself confused by many of Lacan's ideas.

Chapter 3

1. Lacan's flirtations with politics were mentioned in the last chapter. His early religious aspirations led him to make late theological pronouncements. Lacan's

philosophical interests were profound and longstanding and obviously and directly influenced his psychoanalytic theories. The fact that he didn't become a professional philosopher was a matter of some regret for him. On Lacan's philosophical aspirations see Roudinesco (1997) p. 89 and elsewhere; on his political view see Roudinesco (1977) pp. 187–8 and elsewhere; on his view of 'God' see Lacan [192–3] (1998) pp. 98–9 and elsewhere.

2. See Roudinesco (1997) p. 170 and Stassinopoulos-Huffington p. 300.

3. Biographical accounts of Lacan frequently describe him as having been 'seductive', not only in his dealings with women (in which he was 'by nature polygamous') but also in his teaching methods and his treatment of colleagues and patients. Of course it wasn't just sex, or love, that Lacan wanted from others, but also recognition and admiration. He was both skilled at getting these things and 'impatient as always to capture the object of his desire'. See Roudinesco, 1990, p. 135; 1997, pp. 21–5, 79, 81, 254; Roustang, pp. 3–4 and Schneiderman pp. 12–14.

4. 'What makes the human world a world covered with objects [is] the fact that the object of human interest is the object of the desire of the other' where this object is an 'object of rivalry and competition'. Rivalry presumes (real or imaginary) conflict, even though this can be resolved through 'agreement'. This quotation lays out a number of general Lacanian principles. It holds that 'the world' is made up of objects that are the subject of conflict and negotiation and that these objects assume the shape that they do as a consequence of this. The *medium* of this conflict, negotiation and shaping is 'speech'. The world and its objects are thus dictated by arguments and agreements about them. [1955–6] (1993) p. 39.

5. The circumstances of the effective and then formal exclusion of Lacan and the Lacanians' from the IPA will be set out in full later. Suffice to say that the IPA and WAP (their Lacanian equivalent) do not recognise each other – and each others' analysts – as legitimate. Discord *between* Lacanian societies is rife too. It has mostly been documented in descriptions or histories of them or in Lacanian biography. See for WAP 2007 and 2008, Roudinesco 1990, pp. 633–677 and Menard and Massumi, 1982.

6. See Saussure pp. 114–20; EC pp. 414–16.

7. One might also claim the converse, that if the statement is true, it doesn't make sense.

8. Some would say that Saussure didn't say what Lacan said he said *at all.* See Tallis and Descombes 179–80.

9. Once again, opinion is divided as to whether Lacan's ideas are original or not. Henry W. Sullivan, for example, declares that Lacan 'stands as founding theoretician of a post-Modern Age, much as Augustine laid out the city of God blueprint for the Middle Ages, or as Descartes mapped out the preoccupations of the Modern Age' (Sullivan, p. 36). Lacan was by no means so original. The title of 'post-modfather' might just as legitimately go to Jencks

or Baudrillard as Lacan, as he certainly didn't contribute to 'postmodern' thought any more than they did. Yet non-Lacanian assessment of Lacan's ideas can be *equally* assertive. Mikkel Borch-Jacobsen *stresses* Lacan's derivativeness and accuse him of plagiarism, while also conceding that Lacan had a theoretical defence of his use of others' ideas. Lacan *did* concede that his ideas came from elsewhere, but said that this was to do with the general condition of language in which they were conveyed, in which the words that convey them derive from other words and ideas (this argument is itself a Saussurian one). Borch-Jacobsen takes Lacan's concession as his attempt to get himself off the hook of plagiarism, to show that he can't be a copyist when everything is copied. Thus Lacan 'was still no plagiarist', but 'never really had a thought of his own'. He was 'deliberately, openly *honestly* a plagiarist', but this amounted to little more than being 'incredibly agile at appropriating others' ideas' (Borch-Jacobsen, p. 2).

Chapter 4

1. Elisabeth Roudinesco compares Lacan with Balzac's Rastignac, (a character who appears in Balzac's *Comédie Humaine* novels, notably *Père Goriot*). Stuart Schneidermann likens him to Proust's Duchess of Guermantes and then to Shakespeare's King Lear. It has not been uncommon for authors to draw comparisons between Lacan's life and major works of literature. See Roudinesco (1990) p. 104 and Schneiderman (1983) pp. 16–17.

2. The Société psychanalytique de Paris (SPP) was founded in the same year that Lacan began his medical training: 1926 (although Lacan did not join the society until a few years later). Coincidentally, Freud wrote an influential paper arguing that psychoanalysts need not necessarily be medics during the same year. See Freud [1926] (1986) pp. 277–363.

3. Film and video artists who have practiced or drawn on surrealism include Alfred Hitchcock, Tim Burton and David Lynch. Less well-known and more 'authentic' surrealist filmmakers have included Luis Buñuel, Jan Švankmajer and Roy Andersson.

4. Examples of popular surrealism include album cover designs by 'Hipgnosis' videos by David Bowie and marketing projects like the renowned 1970s Benson and Hedges cigarette advertisements.

5. Many of the painters, like Dalí and Magritte, who would popularise surrealism did not join the movement for nearly a decade after its inception. Magritte properly became a surrealist when he moved from Brussels to Paris in 1927. Dalí only became an 'official' member of the group in 1929 when a film he co-directed with Luis Buñuel (*Un Chien Andalou*) was accepted by André Breton as an authentically surrealist product. This is not say that there weren't a few, like painters, like Hans Arp, who were associated with surrealism from the outset. See Nadeau pp. 168; 325 and Brandon, p. 325.

6. Some surrealists, like Max Ernst, had applied automatic means to other media as early as 1924. Ernst devised a method of making a 'rubbing' of a textured surface that could then be left or elaborated on by drawing on it. He called this artistic method 'frottage'.

7. Lacan [1931] quoted in Roudinesco, p. 26.

8. Lacan, 1975 [1931b] pp. 377–80 my translations.

9. For example: '...we take speech as the central feature of our perspective...' Sem.1., p. 11.

10. See, for example, ES p. 35, E p. 117.

11. See, for example, Lacan's challenge to and 'correction' of the psychoanalytic conception of the ego elaborated by the 'ego psychologists' Hartmann, Loewenstein and Kris, whose 'writings swarm with improprieties of method'. Also see his expansion on and extension of Jones' account of female homosexuality, which he says 'stop(s) short' of a full and proper explanation of it. Lacan [1953–4] (1988); [1964b] (1982).

12. As Richard Wollheim puts it, Freud's research into and theorisation of the mind is valuable for 'the precious evidence it provided for the deeper workings of the mind in normality and abnormality alike'. Wollheim p. 66.

13. Freud and Breuer [1893] in Freud and Breuer [1895] (1983).

14. Lacan [1953–4] and [1954–5] (1988).

15. It's worth noting that Freud and Breuer's speak of hysteria as having a 'cause'. There are good reasons why Lacan didn't use this term to describe the psychopathology of illness. He thought, like many 20th and 21st-century thinkers, that the notion of 'cause' is flawed, that it is paradoxical. This is apparent in Freud and Breuer's argument, which as shown includes the contention that hysteria is 'caused', that it has been effected by and can be traced back to a traumatic event. Yet this cause is also 'accidental': it has been visited on the subject from outside of the normal (specifically neurological) determinants of his or her being. See Lacan 1977 [1973] p. 21.

16. Long after Breuer finished treating her, Freud told Ernest Jones that her condition had not only been caused and sustained by traumatic memories, but also by her unanalysed 'transference' onto and 'desire for' Breuer. See Ibid. pp. 95–6 and Jones, E., pp. 203–4.

17. It is obviously possible for traumatic memories to be 'consciously repressed'. That is, it is possible that a subject might self-consciously try to forget a disturbing memory. Freud sometimes refers to this process as 'suppression' rather than repression. Of course, suppression and repression are not mutually exclusive and the latter can often supplement and then supersede the former. Freud and Breuer [1893] (1984) p. 16; Freud, [1914] (1984) p. 87; [1923] (1984) pp. 363–4; Freud, A., [1936] (1996) p. 117.

18. Thus strictly speaking, according to Freud, there are no 'unconscious feelings'. See Freud [1915b] (1984).

19. In 'The Question of Lay Analysis' Freud strong recommended that psycho-analysts be trained in non-medical as well as medical disciplines including philosophy, education, psychology, depth psychology, mythology, psychology of religion and literature. Elsewhere, he recommended the study of linguistics and anthropology. See Freud [1926] (1986) pp. 346–9.

20. 'Do I contradict myself? Very well, then I contradict myself, I am large, I contain multitudes.' Whitman, p. 53.

21. See Klein [1940] (1986) and Freud, A. esp. pp. 28–53.

22. See Baldwin, p. 323 and *Time* Magazine Monday, Apr. 08, 1957.

23. See Brandon, p. 303. A photograph of Péret insulting a priest was published in *La Révolution surrealiste* No 8, 1st December 1926, p. 13.

24. Breton [1924] (1972) p. 19; [1930] (1972) p. 163; [1935] (1972) pp. 225, 229, 230.

25. *Le Surréalisme au service de la révolution* 1 July 1930, p. 28.

26. This dispute was between Lacan and Gaëtan Gatian de Clérambault.

Chapter 5

1. Freud's earliest conception of the mind as an 'energy system' is articulated in Freud [1895] (2001).

2. Lacan explored and shared ideas with a friend and contemporary – Henri Ey – who became a leading light of the Dynamic Psychiatry movement in his own right.

3. Because Hegel was the 'originator' of the ideas in question, it's tempting to think of Lacan as a devotee of Hegel rather than of Kojève (Lacan tended to cite the former rather than the latter). Yet there are distinct aspects of Kojève's account of Hegel that are not strictly Hegelian, that offer a circum-scribed and particular version of Hegel's philosophy. Like Hegel's, Kojève's argument is dialectical. However, Hegel's dialectic leads (at least purportedly and by its own account) to resolution of all sorts (resolution of historical anomalies, of human conflict, of subjective and intersubjective division etc.). Kojève's dialectic (or rather his account of Hegel's dialectic) does not. One could sum up the difference by saying that Hegel's philosophy is synthetic, whereas Kojève's account of it is non-synthetic, or is a-thetic. Kojève's version of Hegel's philosophy carries over directly into Lacan's thought. This means that Lacan's Hegelianism is of a specific sort – one that owes as much in its premises and conclusions to Kojève's argument as it does to Hegel. One might say that Lacan was a Kojèvian Hegelian.

4. This quote was first attributed to Freud in Lehrman (1940) and then cited in Trilling (1940).

5. This meeting would set off a fascination with the Joyce's work that would be lifelong and that would lead to late literary-psychoanalytic musings about the embroilment of 'the symbolic' in 'the real'. See Lacan [1975–6].

6. Lacan [1933a] (1988).
7. In a letter to Medard Boss, Heidegger said of Lacan: 'It seems to me the psychiatrist needs a psychiatrist.' See Roudinesco (1990) pp. 298–300; (1997) pp. 228–31.
8. The formulation of the mind as 'The Ghost in the Machine' is often attributed to Descartes, but was first provided by Gilbert Ryle as a description of Descartes philosophy of mind. See Ryle pp. 1–13.
9. See, for example, Sartre [1946] (1980).
10. Lacan [1933] 1988. In general, Lacan tended to represent the human sciences as having been modelled on the natural sciences, but as also having gone wrong by not understanding the distinctiveness of the human animal (due to its access to language, for example). He even went so far as to say that the human sciences are only an *apparent* affirmation and extension of the experimental sciences and are in fact an *actual* symptom of their over-dominance and inadequacy. See Lacan [1966] (1977) p. 72.
11. This sort of charge can even sometimes be made of Freud, despite Lacan's championing of him.
12. The first 'Mirror Stage' paper wasn't published independently (although its 'delivery' at the 1936 conference was indexed in the International Journal of Psychoanalysis). Instead, Lacan interpolated a short written version of it into a 1938 encyclopaedia entry that he wrote on 'Family Complexes', in which it appeared as a section entitled 'The Mirror Stage'. See Lacan [1938] (1988); [1936] (1937).
13. For key work by Anna Freud see Freud, A., [1936] (1996); for Klein see Mitchell, J. (ed.) (1986). For reliable summaries of their respective ideas see Segal (1979) and Young-Bruehl (2008).
14. To put this in a specifically Lacanian way: impossibility persisted in *the real*.
15. See, for example, Bataille [1957] (1962).
16. Sartre was an influence on Lacan too – one of the unacknowledged ones.
17. See Bataille [1957] (1962) esp. pp. 252–64 and Lacan [1972–3] (1999) esp. pp. 61–77.
18. The phallus is not the penis, but might be described as what the penis symbolises (which might be something like power or authority). Indeed, Lacan even claimed that the penis *is* a phallic symbol and is thus *only* a symbol (of potency, or whatever) and is not significant in itself at all. If it has come to stand for something significant (notably power) this is only by accident and because it has been 'chosen as what stands out as most easily seized upon in the real of sexual copulation'. Lacan in Rose and Mitchell p. 82.
19. The term 'supplement' is used here in the exact sense given to it by Jacques Derrida, in which it represents an addition to something that is extra or unnecessary but that is also an essential need. See 'White Mythology' in Derrida [1972a] (1982).
20. Descartes [1637] (1977) Meditations I and II p. 79–94; Lacan, ES, p. 166.

21. Lacan's presumption here corresponds directly with one of Freud's. In [1923] (1984) Freud declared that the ego is not a fully conscious entity and that at least part of it is subsumed by the id.
22. See, esp. Lacan's Second Seminar [1954–5] (1998).
23. Freud's earlier theories of psychical functioning were famously derived from a 'self-analysis', most obviously conducted – or at least reported – in *The Interpretation of Dreams* [1900] (1976).

Chapter 6

1. Roudinesco, (1990) p. 236, (1997) pp. 87, 197; EC p. 93: Klein [1932] (1997).
2. There is a famous story told that on arriving in New York Harbour for the first time, Freud turned to Jung (who was accompanying him) and said 'They don't realise we're bringing them the plague'. Jacques Alain Miller has claimed that although this story isn't usually attributed to Lacan, it was he who first told it, or at least made it public in his lecture on 'The Freudian Thing' in 1955. Lacan did indeed tell this story in that lecture and even claimed to 'have it from Jung's own mouth'. EC p. 336.
3. See, for example, EC pp. 202–5; 335–6; 345–8 and Lacan, [1954–55] (1988)10–12; 324–6.
4. Ibid.
5. In short, Hegel demonstrates that thought is as much 'pure being' as matter is. Mind therefore cannot be entirely opposed to matter, or even 'separate' from it. Hegel shows this with specific reference to Descartes' philosophy. He comes up with an aphorism that might be set against, or that might supplement, the 'cogito': *thought is thinghood, or thinghood is thought*'. Hegel p. 352.
6. See, for example EC pp. 98, 100, 242, 341, 345, 410, 671, 685–6.
7. That Lacan would have been aware of the comparability of Kleinian object relations and Hegelian philosophy is evident in his description of 'the dialectic of fantasy objects promoted in practice by Melanie Klein'. EC p. 513.
8. Lacan [1938] (1988) pp. 14–16.
9. In a more purely Lacanian sense, the unconscious is sometimes not seen *even when it is visible*. This is why Lacan was so interested in 'scotomisation' that process by which something remains invisible even though it is in 'plain sight'. The letter in Poe's *The Purloined Letter* is the best-known Lacanian example of this. It is 'hidden' in a bookshelf, although it completely visible. See EC pp. 6–48 and Lacan [164a] (1987) pp. 85–9.

Chapter 7

1. In the early '50s, Lacan's trainees constituted more than a third of SFP juniors.

2. See, for example, Barthes [1953] (1967); (1977) pp. 79–124 and Levi-Strauss [1958] (1986) pp. 206–31.
3. Ibid. pp. 373 and 391.
4. See, for example, Lacan, [1953–4] (1988) p. 133 and EC pp. 198.
5. See, for example, Fink (1996) p. 46.
6. Lacan [1955–6] (1993); see also ES, p. 234 and elsewhere.
7. Ibid., p. 60 and Lacan [1955–6] (1993).

Chapter 8

1 See, for example, 'The Freudian Thing or the Meaning of the Return to Freud in Psychoanalysis'. The early sections of this paper contain a long disquisition on psychoanalytic truth within the context of Freudian theory. EC pp. 334–63.

Bibliography of Works by Lacan

Works are listed below in order of dates of original publication, which are provided in square parentheses and dates of referred-to publications, which are provided in conventional parentheses.

Many of the papers referred to are among those collected in Lacan's *Écrits*. I have most quoted from or referred one English translation of this: Fink's complete English edition, which is abbreviated below and in footnotes to EC. Very occasionally, I have referred to Forrester's selection of translations of the *Écrits*, abbreviated below and in footnotes to ES. I have also occasionally translated Lacan's texts myself. Where these are from *Écrits*, I have cited the French text, which is abbreviated below and in footnotes to E. The supplementary, mostly un-translated collection of Lacan's writing, entitled *Autres écrits* is abbreviated in footnotes to AE.

'Abasie chez une traumatisée de guerre' Revue neurologique vol. 1 no. 2 (1928) [with Maurice Trénel]

'Structure des psychoses paranoïaques' [1931a] *Ornicar?*, no. 44 (1988), originally published in *Semaine des hôpitaux de Paris*

'Écrits <<inspirés>>: Schizographie' [1931b] in Lacan (1975), originally published in *Annales medico-psychologiques* [1931]

De la psychose paranoïaque dans ses rapports avec la personalité [1932] (Paris: Éditions du Seuil, 1975)

'The Problem of Style and the Psychiatric Conception of Paranoiac Forms of Experience' [1933a] tr. Jon Anderson, *Critical Texts*, Vol. 5, Issue 3 (1988) originally published in *Le Minotaure* 1 (June 1933)

'Motives of Paranoiac Crime: The Crime of the Papin Sisters' [1933b] tr. Jon Anderson, *Critical Texts*, Vol. 5, Issue 3 (1988) originally published in *Le Minotaure* 3–4 (December 1933)

'Exposé général de nos travaux scientifiques' [1933c] in Lacan (1975)

Review of *Le Temps vécu: Etudes phenoménologiques et psychologiques* by Eugène Minkowski in *Recherches Philosophiques* (1935)

'The Looking Glass Phase' (index) [1936] *The International Journal of Psychoanalysis* 1 (1937)

'The Family Complexes' (edited version) [1938] trans. Carolyn Asp, *Critical Texts*, Vol. 5, Issue 3 (1988)

'The Mirror-Stage, Source of the I-Function, as Shown by Psycho-Analytic Experience (Author's Abstract) [1949] *The International Journal of Psychoanalysis* Vol. 30 (1959)

'The Mirror Stage as Formative of the *I* function as Revealed in Psychoanalytic Experience [1949] in EF

Seminar Book I: Freud's Papers on Technique [1953–4] trans. John Forrester (London: Norton, 1988).

Seminar Book II: The Ego in Freud's Theory and in the Technique of Psychoanalysis [1954–5] trans. Sylvana Tomaselli (London: Norton, 1988)

Seminar Book III: The Psychoses [1955–56] trans. Russell Grigg (London: Routledge, 1993)

Seminar Book XI: The Four Fundamental Concepts of Psychoanalysis [1964a] trans. Alan Sheridan] (Penguin: Harmondsworth, 1987)

Écrits: texte integral (two volumes) (E) [1966] (Paris: Éditions du Seuil, 1999)

Écrits, A Selection (ES) [1966] tr. Alan Sheridan (London: Tavistock, 1977)

Écrits, The First Complete Edition in English (EC) [1966] tr. Bruce Fink (New York: Norton, 2005)

Seminar Book XIX: Ou Pire (The Knowledge of the Psychoanalyst) [1970–2] t trans. Cormac Gallagher (Unofficial and Unedited, 2002)

Seminar Book XX: Encore [1972–3] trans. Bruce Fink (New York: Norton, 1999)

Seminar Book XXIII: Le Sinthome [1975–6] trans. Cormac Gallagher, lacaninireland. com

Television [1973] tr. Denis Hollier, Rosalind Krauss and Annette Michelson (New York: Norton, 1990)

Autres écrits (Paris: Éditions du Seuil, 2001) (AE).

'Le séminaire de Caracas', *L'Ane* 1 (1981)

General Bibliography

Allouch, J., 543 impromptus de Jacques Lacan (Paris: Mille et une Nuits: 2009)

Barthes, R., *Image Music, Text*, tr. Stephen Heath (London: Fontana, 1977)

Balakian, A., *Literary Origins of Surrealism* (London: University of London Press, 1947)

Bataille, G., *Eroticism* [1957] tr. Mary Dalwood (London: Calder: 1962)

Beck, J. S., *Cognitive Therapy: Basics and Beyond* (New York: Guilford Press, 1995)

Binswanger, L. *Grundformen und Erkenntnis menschlichen Daseins* [1942] (Munich: Ernst Reinhardt Verlag 1962)

Borch-Jacobsen, M., *Lacan, The Absolute Master* tr. Douglas Brick (California: Stanford University Press, 1991)

Brandon, R., *Surreal Lives: The Surrealists 1917–1945* (London: Macmillan, 2000)

Breton, A., *Manifestoes of Surrealism* tr. Richard Seaver and Helen Lane (Ann Arbor: University of Michigan, 1972)

Breton, A., Poems of André Breton ed. and tr. Jean-Pierre Cauvin and Mary Ann Caws (Boston, Black Widow Press, 2006)

Brentano, F., *Psychology from an Empirical Standpoint* [1874] tr. A.C. Rancurello, D.B. Terrell and L.L. McAllister (London, Routledge, 1995)

Burgoyne, B. and Sullivan, M. (eds.) *The Klein-Lacan Dialogues* (London: Karnac, 1996)

Dalí, S. 'L'âne pourri' in *Le Surréalisme au service de la révolution,* 1st July, 1930

—— 'Interprétation paranoïaque-critique de l'image obsédante: *L'angelus de Millet*' in *Le Minotaure* No. 1, 1933.

—— *The Secret Life of Salvador Dalí* (London: Vision Press, 1949)

Derrida, J., *Of Grammatology* [1967a] tr. Gayatri Chakravorty Spivak (Baltimore: Johns Hopkins University Press, 1984)

—— *Margins of Philosophy* [1972a] tr. Alan Bass (University of Chicago Press, 1982)

—— *Positions* [1972b] tr. Alan Bass (London: Athlone, 1981)

Descartes, R. *A Discourse on Method* [1637] (London: Dent, 1977)

Ellenberger, H.F. *The Discovery of the Unconscious: The History and Evolution of Dynamic Psychiatry* (New York: Basic Books, 1970)

Freud, A., *The Ego and the Mechanisms of Defence* [1936] (London: Karnac, 1996)

Freud, S. and Breuer J., *Studies on Hysteria* [1895] tr. James Strachey (Harmondsworth: Penguin, 1984)

Freud, S., 'Project for a Scientific Psychology' [1895] tr. James Strachey in *The Complete Psychological Works of Sigmund Freud, Vol. 1* (London: Vintage, 2001)

—— *The Interpretation of Dreams* [1900] tr. James Strachey (Harmondsworth: Penguin, 1976) PFL 4

—— 'Three Essays on the Theory of Sexuality' [1905a] tr. James Strachey in *On Sexuality* (Harmondsworth: Penguin, 1984) PFL 7

—— 'Psychoanalytic Notes on an Autobiographical Account of a Case of Paranoia (Dementia Paranoides)' [1911] tr. James Strachey in *Case Histories* II (Harmondsworth: Penguin, 1984) PFL 9

—— 'The Theme of the Three Caskets' [1913] tr. James Strachey in *Art and Literature* (Harmondsworth: Penguin, 1985) PFL 14

—— 'On Narcissism' [1914] tr. James Strachey in *On Metapsychology, The Theory of Psychoanalysis* (Harmondsworth: Penguin, 1984) PFL 11

—— 'Repression' [1915a] tr. James Strachey in *On Metapsychology, The Theory of Psychoanalysis* (Harmondsworth: Penguin, 1984) PFL 11

—— 'The Unconscious' [1915b] (1984) tr. James Strachey in *On Metapsychology, The Theory of Psychoanalysis* (Harmondsworth: Penguin, 1984) PFL 11

—— 'The Ego and the Id' [1923] tr. James Strachey in *On Metapsychology, the Theory of Psychoanalysis* (Harmondsworth: Penguin, 1984)

—— 'The Dissolution of the Oedipus Complex' [1924] tr. James Strachey in *On Sexuality* (Harmondsworth: Penguin, 1984) PFL 7

—— 'Some Psychical Consequences of the Anatomical Distinction Between The Sexes' [1925] tr. James Strachey in *On Sexuality* (Harmondsworth: Penguin, 1984) PFL 7

—— 'The Question of Lay Analysis' tr. James Strachey in *Historical and Expository Works on Psychoanalysis'* [1926] (1986) PFL 15

—— 'Fetishism' [1927]] tr. James Strachey in *On Sexuality* (Harmondsworth: Penguin, 1984) PFL 7

—— 'The Splitting of the Ego in the Process of Defence' [1940a] tr. James Strachey in *On Metapsychology* (Harmondsworth, Penguin, 1984) PFL 11

Genet, J., *The Maids* [1947] trans. Bernard Frechtman (London: Faber and Faber 2009)

—— 'Interview with Nigel Williams' in *The Declared Enemy: Texts and Interviews* (Palo Alto: Stanford University Press, 2004)

Hayman, R., *Nietzsche, A Critical Life* (London: Phoenix, 1995)

Hegel, *Phenomenology of Spirit* [1807] trans. J.N. Findlay (Oxford: Oxford Univerity Press, 1977)

Husserl, E., *Ideas. A General Introduction to Pure Phenomenology* tr. W.R. Boyce Gibson [1913] (London: Allen and Unwin, 1931)

Jones, E., *The Life and Work of Sigmund Freud* [1953–7] (Harmondsworth: Penguin, 1987)

Klein, M., 'The Importance of Symbol Formation in the Development of the Ego' [1930] in *The Selected Melanie Klein* ed. Juliet Mitchell (Harmondsworth: Penguin, 1986)

—— 'Notes on some Schizoid Mechanisms' [1940] in *The Selected Melanie Klein* ed. Juliet Mitchell (Harmondsworth: Penguin, 1986)

—— *The Psycho-Analysis of Children* [1932] trans. Alix Strachey (London: Vintage, 1997)

Kojève, A., *Introduction to the Reading of Hegel* [1969] ed. Allen Bloom, trans. James H. Nichols, Jr. (Ithaca: Cornell University Press, 1980)

Lévi-Strauss, C., *Structural Anthropology* [1958] (Harmondsworth: Penguin, 1986)

Marx, K. and Engels, F. *The German Ideology* [1846–7] trans. W. Lough, C. Dutt and C.P. McGill, ed. C.J. Arthur (London: Lawrence and Wishart, 1999)

Miller, J.A., '*Suture* (elements of the logic of the signifier)' in *Screen*, Winter 77/78, Vol.18, No. 4, pp. 24–34

Murray, M., 'Lacan and the Law' in *Angelaki*, Vol. 4, No. 1 (May 1999)

Nadeau, M., *The History of Surrealism,* tr. Richard Howard (Harmondsworth: Penguin, 1973)

Ragland, E., *The Logic of Sexuation: From Aristotle to Lacan.* (Albany: State University of New York Press, 2004)

Ragland-Sullivan, E. and Mark Bracher, M., (eds.) *Lacan and the Subject of Language* (London: Routledge, 1991)

Richter, H., *DADA: Art and Anti-Art* (London: Thames and Hudson, 1965)

Rose, J. and Mitchell, J., (eds.) *Feminine Sexuality: Jacques Lacan and the École Freudienne* (London: Macmillan, 1982)

Roudinesco, E., *Jacques Lacan & Co. A History of Psychoanalysis in France, 1925–1985,* tr. Jeffrey Mehlman (London: Free Association, 1990)

—— *Jacques Lacan,* tr. Barbara Bray (Cambridge: Polity, 1997)

Roustang, F. *The Lacanian Delusion* (Oxford: Oxford University Press, 1990)

Ryle, G., *The Concept of Mind* [1949] (Abingdon: Routledge, 2009)

Safouan, M., *Pleasure and Being* [1979] tr. Martin Thom (London: Macmillan, 1983)

Sartre, J.P., *Being and Nothingness: An Essay on Phenomenological Ontology* [1943] tr. Hazel Barnes (London: Routledge, 1996)

—— *Existentialism and Humanism* [1946] tr. Phillip Mairet (London Methuen, 1980)

Saussure, F. de, *Course in General Linguistics* [1915] eds. Charles Bally and Albert Sechehaye, trans. Wade Baskin (McGraw-Hill, 1966)

Schneiderman, S., *Jacques Lacan: the death of an intellectual hero* (Cambridge, Mass.: Harvard University Press, 1983)

Sokal, A. and Bricmont, J., *Intellectual Impostures: Postmodern philosophers' abuse of science* (London: Profile, 1998)

'School One', *The Principle Of Supervision In The School,* available at http://www.londonsociety-nls.org.uk/

Sophocles, *The Three Theban Plays,* trans. Robert Fagles [497–405BC] (London: Penguin, 1984)

Stassinopoulos-Huffington, A., *Picasso, Creator and Destroyer* (New York: Simon and Schuster, 1988)

Tallis, R., *Not Saussure: A Critique of Post-Saussurean Literary Theory* [1988] (London: Macmillan, 1995)

Vanier, A., *Lacan* (New York: Other Press, 2000)

Wallon, H., 'Comment se développe chez l'enfant la notion de corps propre' in *Journal de psychologie*, November-December 1931, pp. 705–48

WAP *Statutes of the World Association of Psychoanalysis* (Paris: AMP, 2008)

—— *The Principle of Supervision in the School* (2007) available at: www.londonsociety-nls.org.uk/

Whitman, W., *Song of Myself* (New York: Dover, 2012)

Wollheim, R., *Freud* (London: Fontana, 1885)

Index